DATA ETHICS
IN THE AGE OF AI

DATA ETHICS
IN THE AGE OF AI

Arshad Khan

MERCURY LEARNING AND INFORMATION
Boston, Massachusetts

MERCURY LEARNING AND INFORMATION
121 High Street, 3rd Floor
Boston, MA 02110
info@merclearning.com

A. Khan. *Data Ethics in the Age of AI.*
ISBN: 978-1-50152-411-0

Library of Congress Control Number: 2024952350

242526321   This book is printed on acid-free paper in the United States of America.

Our titles are available for adoption, license, or bulk purchase by institutions, corporations, etc.

All of our titles are available in digital format at various digital vendors.

CONTENTS

PREFACE

In today's increasingly digital world, the use of data has become a powerful force that shapes decisions, influences behavior, and drives innovation across every sector. From healthcare and finance to social media and retail, data is at the core of modern life. The vast opportunities presented by data, however, also come with profound ethical implications. The ability to collect, analyze, and utilize data brings about new responsibilities for individuals, organizations, and societies. As data use becomes more pervasive, the need for a comprehensive understanding of data ethics has never been greater.

This book, *Data Ethics in the Age of AI*, was conceived from the pressing need to examine the moral, legal, and social issues related to data in the digital age. It has been designed to provide readers with a thorough exploration of the principles, frameworks, and practices that guide ethical data management. By covering a range of topics—from privacy and security to fairness, bias, and transparency—this book seeks to provide both a broad overview of data ethics and a deep dive into specific ethical concerns.

The journey begins with an examination of the origins and evolution of data ethics, tracing its roots from early privacy concerns to the more complex ethical issues posed by artificial intelligence (AI) and big data analytics. It explores how traditional ethical frameworks have adapted to the rapidly changing technological landscape and introduces the concept of data dignity—a notion that underscores the importance of treating individuals with respect and fairness in all data-related activities.

As we move further into the book, we delve into the crucial role that data ethics plays in shaping public policy, influencing corporate practices, and impacting the lives of individuals. With growing concerns about data breaches, algorithmic bias, and the misuse of personal information, the need for ethical vigilance is more urgent than ever. This book aims to equip you with the knowledge and tools to navigate these challenges, emphasizing the importance of fostering a culture of ethical responsibility within organizations and society.

In addition to addressing key ethical principles such as consent, accountability, and data minimization, the book explores the broader societal implications of data practices. The chapters on data bias, transparency, and the future of ethical frameworks are particularly relevant as AI and machine learning systems play an increasingly prominent role in decision-making processes.

Ultimately, *Data Ethics in the Age of AI* is intended to serve as a guide for anyone interested in understanding and engaging with the ethical dimensions of data use. Whether you are a business leader, policymaker, researcher, or student, this book invites you to reflect on how ethical practices can help create a more just, equitable, and transparent data landscape. As we chart the path forward, it is essential that we remain committed to continuous dialogue, collaboration, and education in order to uphold the principles of ethical data use in a rapidly evolving technological world.

It is my hope that this book will not only inform but inspire you to contribute to building a future where data is harnessed responsibly and ethically, for the benefit of all.

Arshad Khan
January 2025

CHAPTER 1

INTRODUCTION TO DATA ETHICS

THE ORIGINS AND EVOLUTION OF DATA ETHICS

Early Foundations of Data Ethics

Data ethics, as a distinct concept, has evolved significantly alongside technological advancements and the increasing proliferation of data usage. Its origins can be traced back to early debates in the mid-20th century, a period marked by the rise of digital computing and the initiation of large-scale data collection initiatives. As governments and organizations gained unprecedented capabilities to collect, store, and analyze personal information, concerns about individual privacy rights began to emerge. These rapid advancements in technology outpaced existing legal and ethical frameworks, prompting critical discussions about how data should be used responsibly. Early conversations centered around the potential misuse of personal information, the consequences of surveillance, and the need for informed consent, laying the groundwork for the foundational principles of data ethics that we recognize today.

As society grappled with the profound implications of these technological changes, scholars, policymakers, and privacy advocates began to advocate for the protection of individual rights in the digital age. This period saw the emergence of pivotal movements aimed at safeguarding personal data, culminating in influential legislation such as the Privacy Act of 1974 and the establishment of ethical guidelines for data collection and usage. Over time, the discourse surrounding data ethics expanded to encompass broader themes, including algorithmic fairness, accountability, and the impact of data on marginalized communities. As the landscape of data usage continues to evolve with innovations such as AI and machine learning, the ethical considerations surrounding data remain at the forefront of public discourse. Today, data ethics encompasses a comprehensive framework that seeks to balance the benefits of data-driven advancements with the imperative to uphold individual rights, ensuring that technology serves the greater good while minimizing potential harm.

The Establishment of Fair Information Practice Principles

The initial concerns surrounding data ethics culminated in the establishment of the Fair Information Practice Principles (FIPPs) in the 1970s, which emerged as a response to growing anxiety about privacy and the ethical handling of personal data. These principles provided a foundational regulatory basis for protecting privacy in data management, addressing the increasing complexity brought about by technological advancement and large-scale data collection. The FIPPs articulated key tenets such as transparency, consent, and accountability, which became essential elements in guiding how organizations should approach the management of personal information. By emphasizing the need for clear communication about data practices and requiring organizations to obtain informed consent from individuals before data collection, the FIPPs established a framework that prioritized the rights and autonomy of individuals in the face of evolving data technologies.

As a cornerstone of the data ethics discourse, the FIPPs laid the groundwork for defining the responsibilities of data collectors and the rights of individuals, advocating for practices that respect and protect personal information. This regulatory framework marked a significant advancement in the ethical treatment of data, promoting a shift from a primarily technical perspective on data management to one that inherently incorporates ethical considerations. By formalizing standards for data-handling, the FIPPs encouraged organizations to adopt practices that not only complied with legal requirements but also reflected a commitment to ethical responsibility.

The establishment of the FIPPs set the stage for subsequent developments in the field of data ethics, fostering an environment where ethical considerations could be systematically integrated into data practices. This evolution has led to ongoing discussions about data governance, the ethical implications of emerging technologies, and the need for robust frameworks to protect individuals in an increasingly data-driven world.

Expanding Ethical Considerations Beyond Privacy

As technology continued to evolve, data ethics expanded beyond the narrow scope of privacy to encompass a broader array of issues, including consent, transparency, and the societal consequences of automated decision-making. The rapid rise of the Internet significantly amplified the scale and complexity of data collection, enabling the instant sharing of personal information across global networks. This transformation gave rise to new business models, particularly in targeted advertising, that rely on the accumulation and analysis of vast amounts of user data. While these advancements have allowed companies to tailor their services to individual preferences, they have also introduced unique ethical challenges, such as intrusive surveillance and the potential misuse of personal information. In this context, individuals often find themselves unaware of how their data is being collected and utilized, raising questions about the ethical implications of such practices.

One particularly troubling aspect of this new landscape is the manner in which users consent to data collection practices, typically through lengthy and complex terms of service agreements that are difficult to comprehend. Many individuals click "agree" without fully understanding the implications of their consent, which undermines the principle of informed decision-making. This phenomenon illustrates a significant disconnect between technological capabilities and ethical standards, as individuals may unknowingly relinquish control over their personal information. These developments highlighted the urgent need for a more comprehensive ethical framework to address complex issues in an interconnected world, prompting scholars, policymakers, and technologists to engage in critical discussions about the rights of individuals in the digital age. As data continues to play an increasingly central role in various aspects of life, the imperative to establish ethical guidelines that prioritize user rights and promote responsible data usage has never been more pressing.

The Impact of AI on Data Ethics

The development of AI and machine learning has dramatically transformed the landscape of data ethics, introducing new complexity that demands urgent attention. As these technologies gain traction, critical concerns regarding algorithmic bias, accountability, and fairness have emerged. Automated systems are increasingly being used for significant decision-making processes in various domains, including healthcare, employment, and criminal justice. This reliance on algorithms to determine outcomes raises profound ethical questions about account-ability: who is responsible when these systems produce biased or harm-ful results? For instance, if an AI system used for hiring inadvertently discriminates against a certain demographic due to biased training data, identifying accountability can be challenging. Are the developers who created the algorithm, the organizations that deployed it, or the data scientists who sourced the data accountable? Such questions under-score the urgent need for clarity in responsibility and governance as AI systems become more pervasive in decision-making.

Moreover, bias in data, whether it stems from historical inequality or flawed data collection processes, can lead to discriminatory outcomes that exacerbate existing societal disparities. As AI systems are often trained on historical datasets, they can inadvertently learn and perpetu-ate these biases, leading to outcomes that reflect and reinforce societal inequity. This reality has compelled ethicists and technologists to criti-cally examine how data is sourced, curated, and utilized in AI models, emphasizing the necessity of rigorous oversight and ethical considera-tions throughout the development process.

The ethical implications of these technologies extend beyond techni-cal performance; they necessitate a commitment to fairness and trans-parency to prevent the perpetuation of harmful stereotypes or inequities. By advocating for inclusive data practices and actively addressing bias in AI development, stakeholders can work toward creating systems that promote social justice and equitable treatment for all individuals, ensur-ing that the benefits of AI are shared broadly across society.

Flexibility in Ethical Frameworks

In this evolving landscape, the historical trajectory of data ethics under-scores the need for flexibility and adaptability in ethical frameworks. The rapid pace of technological advancement demands that ethical guidelines are not static but instead can evolve alongside emerging technologies. As new data practices emerge, historical precedents provide valuable lessons, revealing how rigid frameworks can fail to address the complexity of contemporary challenges. For instance, the evolution of data collection methods—from simple surveys to intricate algorithms that analyze massive datasets—highlights the necessity for ethical standards that can accommodate the nuances of these develop-ments. By being adaptable, ethical frameworks can respond to changes in technology and society, enabling organizations to navigate dilem-mas effectively and maintain the trust of individuals whose data they handle. This flexibility is particularly crucial as societies grapple with balancing technological capability against ethical responsibility, as the consequences of decisions made in the name of progress can significantly impact individual rights and freedoms.

As we confront the ethical issues surrounding emerging technologies such as deep learning and predictive analytics, it becomes evident that proactive measures must be taken to mitigate the risks associated with data misuse. Organizations and policymakers are increasingly faced with the responsibility to prioritize ethical considerations throughout the technology development lifecycle. This involves embedding ethical principles within data-driven innovations from the outset, rather than addressing ethical implications as an afterthought. For example, when developing predictive algorithms, it is essential to consider not only the technical accuracy but also the potential for bias and discrimination that may arise from the data used. By integrating ethical assessments into the design and implementation phases, organizations can proactively identify and address potential risks, ensuring that technology serves the greater good. This approach not only enhances the ethical integrity of technological solutions but also fosters public confidence in data practices, ultimately allowing societies to harness data for collective benefit while safeguarding individual rights and freedoms.

Toward Ethical Data Practices

Ultimately, a dynamic and forward-thinking approach to data ethics remains essential as data-driven innovations continue to permeate every aspect of daily life. The proliferation of data across various sectors—ranging from healthcare and finance to education and entertainment—has profound societal implications that extend beyond individual privacy concerns. Data usage influences the broader issues of equality, justice, and social responsibility, raising critical questions about who benefits from data-driven solutions and who might be left behind. For instance, as algorithms become integral to decision-making processes in areas such as lending or employment, the potential for bias and discrimination must be carefully examined to ensure equitable outcomes for all individuals. Failure to address these issues could result in the entrenchment of existing inequality, thereby undermining societal trust in both technology and institutions. As such, there is a pressing need for frameworks that not only promote ethical data use but also actively work toward enhancing social equity and justice.

As we move further into an era dominated by data, the importance of a well-defined ethical framework cannot be overstated. Such a framework must be robust yet flexible, able to adapt to the rapidly changing technological landscape and address both longstanding ethical concerns and emerging challenges in the field of data ethics. This includes reevaluating traditional concepts of consent and privacy in light of new data collection methods and technologies, such as the Internet of Things (IoT) and AI. Moreover, ethical guidelines should prioritize stakeholder engagement, ensuring that the voices of those affected by data practices—especially marginalized communities—are heard and considered in the decision-making process. By fostering a culture of ethical awareness and accountability, organizations can not only navigate the complexities of data ethics but also contribute to a more just and equitable society. This proactive stance is essential for fostering public trust and ensuring that data innovations genuinely enhance the human experience rather than diminish it.

Fostering a Culture of Ethical Awareness

By fostering a culture of ethical awareness and responsibility within organizations, it can be ensured that data practices serve the public good, promoting trust and accountability while respecting individual autonomy in the digital age. This cultural shift begins with leadership that prioritizes ethical considerations alongside business objectives, recognizing that ethical behavior is not just a regulatory requirement but a cornerstone of sustainable success. Organizations that actively promote ethical values can create an environment where employees feel empowered to voice concerns and contribute to ethical decision-making processes. This includes providing training on data ethics and the implications of data usage, ensuring that every team member understands their role in upholding ethical standards. By cultivating this sense of ethical duty, organizations can foster a workforce that is not only aware of legal compliance but also committed to enhancing societal welfare through responsible data practices.

Such an environment encourages organizations to not only comply with legal standards but also embrace ethical norms that prioritize the well-being of individuals and society as a whole. Ethical considerations should be woven into the fabric of organizational policies, influencing everything from data collection practices to the deployment of algorithms in decision-making processes. For instance, organizations can adopt frameworks that assess the potential societal impact of their data initiatives, helping to identify and mitigate risks before they materialize.

Moreover, by engaging with external stakeholders—such as communities, advocacy groups, and regulatory bodies—organizations can gain diverse perspectives that enhance their ethical approach. By cultivating this culture of ethical awareness and responsibility, organizations can be empowered to navigate the complex ethical landscape surrounding data usage effectively. In doing so, they can contribute positively to societal welfare, ensuring that technological advancements benefit everyone while safeguarding individual rights and freedoms.

Engaging Diverse Perspectives in Ethical Dialogue

As we look to the future, it is imperative to continue the dialogue around data ethics, inviting diverse perspectives and experiences into the conversation. Engaging a wide range of stakeholders—including technologists, ethicists, policymakers, civil society representatives, and those directly affected by data practices—enriches our understanding of the ethical implications of data use. Diverse voices bring unique insights that highlight the complexities of data ethics, ensuring that various social, cultural, and economic contexts are considered in the formulation of ethical guidelines. By facilitating inclusive discussions, we can identify potential bias, uncover blind spots, and foster a more holistic understanding of the implications of data practices. This collaborative approach is essential for developing comprehensive frameworks that not only respond to current challenges but also anticipate future developments in technology and society.

In doing so, we can work toward a future where data practices align with ethical principles, promoting a more just and equitable society in the face of rapid technological advancement. Such alignment requires a commitment to continuous learning and adaptation, recognizing that ethical standards must evolve alongside technology to remain relevant and effective. Organizations and policymakers should prioritize ongoing education about data ethics, fostering a culture of awareness and responsibility that permeates all levels of decision-making. By embedding ethical considerations into the core of data-driven innovations and establishing mechanisms for accountability and transparency, we can ensure that technological progress serves the broader interests of society. Ultimately, this proactive stance will not only safeguard individual rights and freedoms but also build public trust in data practices, creating a foundation for a future where technology enhances, rather than undermines, social equity and justice.

Charting the Path Forward

The historical evolution of data ethics demonstrates the necessity for continuous adaptation and thoughtful engagement with emerging technologies. The lessons learned from past experiences highlight the significance of remaining vigilant and proactive in addressing the ethical implications of data usage. As technology evolves rapidly, what was once considered ethical may quickly become obsolete or insufficient in the face of new challenges. By actively involving a variety of stakeholders— including ethicists, technologists, policymakers, and the communities impacted by data practices—we can create robust ethical frameworks that are informed by diverse perspectives. This collaboration is essential not only for identifying current challenges but also for anticipating potential future dilemmas, ensuring that ethical considerations are integrated into the fabric of technological innovation.

This proactive approach will ensure that as society becomes increasingly reliant on data, the ethical principles guiding its use will evolve in tandem, fostering a technological landscape that is not only innovative but also just and equitable. Emphasizing continuous dialogue and reflection within the data ethics community will help cultivate an adaptive mindset that prioritizes accountability, transparency, and social responsibility. By embracing a forward-thinking ethos, organizations can better navigate the complexities of data ethics and develop technologies that serve the public interest. Ultimately, this commitment to ethical evolution will help create a future where data practices not only drive progress but also contribute to the well-being of individuals and communities, paving the way for a more just and equitable society.

EVOLVING FRAMEWORKS IN MODERN DATA ETHICS

Defining Contemporary Data Ethics

Contemporary data ethics can be understood as a framework of moral principles that guide the responsible use, collection, storage, and sharing of data, particularly focusing on personal information. The rapid proliferation of data technologies in areas such as AI, machine learning, and big data analytics has transformed the way organizations operate and make decisions. With this transformation, ethical considerations have shifted from simple compliance with data protection regulations to more complex deliberations that address the ethical use of data in everyday interactions. Contemporary data ethics underscores the need for organizations to go beyond adherence to laws such as the General

Data Protection Regulation (GDPR), emphasizing a moral responsibility to handle data in ways that respect human dignity and autonomy. This approach encompasses not only preventing harm but also fostering transparency, accountability, and fairness in all data-related processes.

As the significance of data in society has increased, so has the need for ethical frameworks that reflect deeper concerns regarding human rights, privacy, and individual autonomy. At its core, contemporary data ethics aims to create a balance between safeguarding individual interests and harnessing the potential benefits of data-driven innovation. For instance, while data can be instrumental in advancing healthcare, improving public services, and fostering economic growth, these benefits must not come at the cost of individuals' rights or perpetuate inequality. This evolving landscape requires organizations and policymakers to recognize the broader societal implications of data usage, including the risks associated with surveillance, discrimination, and loss of privacy. By embedding ethical principles into data practices, contemporary data ethics seeks to promote a just society where the advantages of technology are accessible to all while mitigating the risks to individuals and communities.

The Concept of Data Dignity

One prevalent perspective within contemporary data ethics is the concept of *data dignity*, which posits that individuals should maintain control over their personal information. This approach marks a significant shift from traditional data collection models, which often treated data as a resource to be extracted without regard for the people behind it, to a more human-centric perspective that acknowledges the rights of individuals. Data dignity is based on the understanding that personal data is not a commodity to be exploited but is intrinsically linked to a person's identity, rights, and dignity. This perspective encourages viewing data subjects not as passive sources of information but as active participants with legitimate claims to ownership and control over their data. It advocates for recognizing individuals as the rightful owners of their personal information, thereby reshaping how organizations approach data collection, usage, and sharing.

Consequently, modern definitions of data ethics increasingly prioritize individual rights, autonomy, and the informed consent of data subjects. Data dignity emphasizes that individuals should be empowered to make decisions about how their information is used, ensuring that they have meaningful choices rather than being subjected to opaque data practices. This means going beyond merely obtaining consent through lengthy, complex terms of service agreements. Instead, it requires clear communication and genuine opportunities for individuals to understand and control their data. Ensuring that people have a meaningful say in how their data is used is crucial not only for respecting their autonomy but also for fostering trust in data-driven systems. This focus on data dignity promotes more ethical engagement with data by ensuring that individuals can exercise agency and are not disenfranchised in the digital age. Ultimately, embracing data dignity encourages organizations to be more transparent and responsible, fostering a more respectful and equitable relationship between data subjects and data controllers.

The Ongoing Evolution of Ethical Frameworks

The rapid pace of technological change has meant that new ethical dilemmas often arise more quickly than existing frameworks can adapt. This ongoing evolution necessitates continual dialogue among technologists, policymakers, and ethicists to navigate the complex terrain of data ethics effectively. As technologies such as AI, machine learning, and data analytics evolve, they introduce novel challenges that traditional ethical frameworks may not adequately address. For instance, the increasing use of biometric data—such as facial recognition, fingerprints, and retinal scans—raises critical ethical questions that require urgent attention. Biometric data is often considered more sensitive than other types of personal information because it is unique to individuals and can be used to identify them without their consent. As a result, ethical considerations surrounding consent, privacy, and the potential for surveillance must be rigorously examined to prevent misuse and protect individuals' rights. This demands a proactive approach, as reactive measures may be insufficient to address issues that are already embedded within rapidly advancing technologies.

Furthermore, questions about how biometric data is collected, stored, and used are paramount, demanding robust ethical standards to guide organizations in their practices. The manner in which biometric data is obtained can vary significantly, with some methods lacking transparency and proper consent protocols. For instance, individuals may unknowingly have their biometric data collected in public spaces through surveillance cameras or smart devices without being adequately informed. These practices not only infringe upon personal privacy but also raise concerns about the potential for discriminatory profiling and the misuse of such data by government or corporate entities.

Engaging diverse stakeholders in these discussions is critical to ensure that data ethics reflects a wide array of perspectives and values, fostering a collaborative approach to tackling ethical challenges in data management. By involving voices from various sectors—such as technology, law, civil rights, and academia—stakeholders can create a more comprehensive and inclusive framework for data ethics, which is essential for guiding the responsible use of technology in a rapidly changing world.

Adapting to Emerging Technologies

As technology continues to advance, the definitions and interpretations of data ethics must adapt to the new challenges and opportunities that arise. Emerging technologies such as AI, machine learning, and blockchain introduce unique ethical dilemmas that cannot be fully addressed by traditional data governance frameworks. AI and machine learning, for example, rely on vast datasets to make predictions and decisions, raising significant concerns about bias, fairness, and transparency. The complexity of these technologies means that ethical issues can often be hidden within algorithmic processes, necessitating continuous scrutiny and a willingness to reevaluate existing frameworks.

Blockchain, on the other hand, introduces questions related to data permanence, privacy, and decentralization—qualities that both provide benefits and entail ethical risks. The immutable nature of blockchain, while valuable for maintaining records, also creates challenges when individuals want to exercise their right to be forgotten. Thus, the ethical implications of emerging technologies must be thoroughly examined and incorporated into evolving data ethics standards to ensure responsible use that benefits society while mitigating harm.

Furthermore, the increasingly global nature of data flows presents additional challenges for data ethics, necessitating international cooperation and harmonization of standards. Data is no longer confined to local or national boundaries; it moves across jurisdictions and is processed by entities in multiple countries, each with its own regulations and cultural understandings of privacy and ethics. This complexity calls for a more unified approach to data ethics that goes beyond national policies and embraces international collaboration. Harmonizing data ethics standards can help ensure that ethical principles—such as fairness, transparency, and respect for individual rights—are upheld universally, regardless of where data is processed or by whom.

Such cooperation is essential for addressing cross-border challenges, such as differing privacy regulations or the use of surveillance technologies, which can have widespread implications for global human rights. By fostering international dialogue and collaboration, societies can work together to create ethical frameworks that are both flexible enough to accommodate local nuances and robust enough to provide consistent protection for individuals worldwide. This approach will help to build a digital future where technological advancements are aligned with shared human values and ethical principles.

Organizational Responsibilities in Data Ethics

Another significant perspective on data ethics emphasizes the responsibilities of organizations, particularly regarding the societal impacts of their data usage. Organizations are increasingly recognized as playing a crucial role in shaping the ethical landscape of data-driven technology, with obligations that extend well beyond mere legal compliance. It is not enough for companies to adhere to data protection regulations; they must also proactively consider the ethical implications of their actions, especially concerning how their data practices affect society at large.

Ethical obligations involve actively preventing harm, reducing bias in data and algorithms, and ensuring that data-driven decisions do not disproportionately impact marginalized or vulnerable communities. For example, if a predictive algorithm is used for hiring, loan approvals, or medical diagnoses, organizations must be vigilant about potential bias in their models that could lead to unfair treatment of certain groups. Organizations are also called upon to be transparent about how data is used and to seek ways to incorporate diverse perspectives in their design and development processes to prevent the perpetuation of inequality.

There is a growing expectation for organizations to demonstrate social responsibility by assessing the potential consequences of their data practices and actively working to mitigate any negative impacts. This requires an ongoing commitment to monitoring data usage and the effects of algorithmic systems on different populations. Ethical responsibilities also involve creating mechanisms for accountability, such as third-party audits, bias detection frameworks, and public reporting, to ensure that their data-driven systems operate fairly and transparently.

By considering the broader societal context of data use, organizations can recognize that the outcomes of their practices can either contribute to equity or, conversely, exacerbate existing inequality. Consequently, organizations are called upon to integrate ethical thinking into every stage of data management—from the initial stages of data collection, where data quality and consent are key, to the deployment of algorithmic systems, where fairness and accountability are paramount. Such integration ensures that ethical considerations are embedded into the core of organizational operations, helping to create a data-driven future that prioritizes not only innovation but also well-being and fairness for all members of society.

The Role of Governments and Regulatory Bodies

In addition to the roles of individuals and organizations, contemporary data ethics involves a shared responsibility that includes governments and regulatory bodies. Governments play a critical role in setting the boundaries and expectations for ethical data use by creating legal and regulatory frameworks that both protect individual rights and foster an environment conducive to innovation. These frameworks are necessary for ensuring that data is handled ethically and responsibly, particularly as technological advancement rapidly change the ways in which data is collected, processed, and shared.

Governments are responsible for establishing guidelines that uphold public trust in data-driven technologies, creating a foundation that balances innovation with the protection of personal freedoms. This includes developing and updating privacy laws that address contemporary challenges, such as the widespread collection of biometric data, AI-based decision-making, and the increasing use of personal data for targeted advertising. These laws must reflect the reality of modern technology while protecting individuals from misuse or exploitation of their data.

Moreover, governments must also implement effective enforcement mechanisms to hold organizations accountable for their data practices. Legal frameworks alone are insufficient without consistent enforcement that ensures companies adhere to the established ethical and privacy standards. Regulatory bodies must be empowered to monitor compliance, investigate breaches, and impose penalties for unethical or illegal behavior. This enforcement helps reinforce the notion that data ethics is not optional but an integral part of responsible digital governance. Beyond regulation, governments also have a role in promoting education and awareness about data ethics, helping individuals understand their rights and how their data is used.

This tripartite relationship between individuals, organizations, and governments fosters a balanced ecosystem where each party plays a role in promoting ethical data practices. Governments set the legal context, organizations operationalize these standards within their practices, and individuals are empowered to make informed decisions about their data. Together, this collaborative approach helps ensure that data ethics is not only a foundational principle but also a practical guide for responsible data use, ultimately reinforcing public trust in the evolving digital landscape.

The Role of Civil Society in Data Ethics

The involvement of civil society and advocacy groups is crucial in shaping the discourse around data ethics. These organizations often act as watchdogs, closely monitoring data practices and advocating for the rights of individuals in the face of powerful data-driven industries. Their efforts help bring attention to unethical or questionable practices that may otherwise go unnoticed, serving as a counterbalance to the interests of tech companies and ensuring that public welfare remains a priority.

Advocacy groups play a critical role in pushing for stronger regulations, ethical standards, and policies that protect citizens from potential abuse of power. They are instrumental in identifying gaps in existing legal frameworks and pushing governments to adopt more comprehensive and adaptive measures that reflect the evolving technological landscape. By elevating issues that affect privacy, security, and individual rights, civil society organizations ensure that data ethics remains a dynamic field that responds to the needs and concerns of the public.

Beyond advocacy and regulatory pressure, these organizations also play a pivotal role in raising public awareness about data privacy issues and giving a voice to marginalized communities that may be disproportionately affected by unethical data practices. Many vulnerable groups face heightened risks due to data misuse—such as targeted discrimination, biased decision-making, or surveillance—and civil society groups amplify these voices to ensure their concerns are heard. By fostering dialogue among stakeholders—including the tech industry, policymakers, and the general public—civil society organizations contribute to a more nuanced understanding of data ethics, which is necessary for developing effective solutions that promote fairness and accountability. Their involvement encourages transparency and ensures that ethical considerations are not just the domain of technologists and legislators but are also informed by the lived experiences of individuals affected by data-driven technologies.

This collaborative approach promotes public engagement and trust, both of which are essential for building a more ethical and inclusive data landscape, where data innovation serves not just technological progress but also the broader interests of society.

Holistic Approach to Data Ethics

Ultimately, contemporary definitions of data ethics represent a dynamic interplay between individual rights, organizational responsibilities, and governmental oversight. In this interconnected framework, individuals are recognized as active participants with the right to control their personal information and make informed decisions about how it is used. Organizations, on the other hand, carry the responsibility of ensuring that data practices are ethical, transparent, and fair, striving to minimize harm while maximizing the societal benefits of data-driven innovations. Governments and regulatory bodies play a crucial role in establishing and enforcing the guidelines that frame these interactions, ensuring that both individual rights are protected and organizations are held accountable.

This delicate balance requires the continuous evolution of ethical frameworks to keep pace with rapid technological advancements and emerging data practices. As new challenges arise—such as those related to AI-driven decision-making, data commodification, or global data sharing—these three pillars must adapt in a coordinated manner to uphold ethical standards.

By embracing a holistic approach to data ethics that prioritizes transparency, accountability, and fairness, society can navigate the complexities of the digital age while safeguarding individual autonomy. Transparency ensures that individuals are fully informed about how their data is being used, fostering trust and encouraging responsible data sharing. Accountability obligates organizations to take responsibility for the outcomes of their data practices, including the unintended consequences that may arise from bias or data misuse. Fairness demands that data practices do not discriminate against any group and work toward reducing inequality rather than exacerbating it.

Together, these principles help ensure that the benefits of data-driven innovations can be realized without compromising human dignity or individual freedoms. This balance is essential for building and sustaining public trust, which is a cornerstone of a data-driven society. A well-defined, adaptable ethical framework that respects individual rights, aligns organizational behavior with ethical principles, and is supported by effective governmental oversight is critical for fostering a more equitable and just society—one where data practices serve the common good rather than just private interests.

The Need for Continuous Dialogue

In this context, the evolution of data ethics serves as a reminder of the importance of continuous dialogue and collaboration among all stakeholders. As technology advances and reshapes our understanding of data, its collection, and its potential uses, the ethical considerations surrounding data use must also evolve to reflect these changes. A static approach to data ethics cannot adequately address the emerging complexities introduced by technologies such as AI, machine learning, and blockchain. Instead, ongoing dialogue is needed to address the unique ethical dilemmas presented by these innovations, which often lead to new risks and implications that cannot be fully anticipated during their development.

Engaging stakeholders across different sectors and disciplines ensures that ethical frameworks remain relevant and effective in addressing the real-world challenges associated with data use. This dialogue must be inclusive, inviting diverse voices—including technologists, policymakers, ethicists, and the broader public—to weigh in on the direction of data ethics to develop nuanced approaches that consider the varied needs and perspectives of society.

By embracing a collaborative approach that includes individuals, organizations, governments, and civil society, data ethics can transform from a rigid set of rules into a living framework capable of adapting to societal changes and technological progress. Each stakeholder has a unique role to play: individuals advocate for their rights and autonomy over personal data, organizations take responsibility for ethical data practices, governments provide regulatory oversight, and civil society serves as an advocate for transparency and accountability.

By fostering collaboration among these actors, a more comprehensive and flexible approach to data ethics can be developed—one that acknowledges the interconnectedness of technological progress and social values. This adaptability is crucial for ensuring that ethical principles keep pace with the fast-changing landscape of data use, helping to prevent potential harm while enabling innovation that benefits society as a whole. Ultimately, the inclusive development of data ethics frameworks will help create a more equitable digital future, where technological advancement is aligned with an ethical commitment to protect individual rights and promote social welfare.

Promoting Education and Awareness

As we move forward, it is crucial to prioritize education and awareness around data ethics at all levels of society. Data has become a significant force shaping everyday decisions—from personalized recommendations to credit assessments—making it essential for individuals to understand its ethical implications. By promoting education in data ethics, individuals can be empowered to make informed choices about how their data is used, become proactive in safeguarding their privacy, and demand greater accountability from organizations.

This awareness enables people to recognize the trade-offs involved in data-sharing agreements and better understand the rights they possess in relation to their personal information. Educational initiatives must therefore target a broad audience, including not only tech-savvy individuals but also vulnerable groups who may be disproportionately affected by unethical data practices. By bridging knowledge gaps, society can cultivate a more informed citizenry capable of engaging with the ethical challenges of the digital age.

Organizations, too, bear a significant responsibility in this regard. Embedding data ethics within corporate culture requires more than compliance with regulations—it necessitates fostering a mindset of responsibility across all levels of the organization. This involves investing in regular training sessions for employees that not only cover data protection laws but also explore ethical scenarios and encourage critical thinking about data practices. When employees are equipped with a deep understanding of the ethical dimensions of data use, they can identify potential risks and make decisions that reflect the organization's commitment to responsible data management.

This cultural shift can lead to practices that not only respect individual rights but also proactively seek to mitigate harm and promote societal good. Ultimately, by embedding ethical considerations into the very fabric of our interactions with data, we can contribute to a more responsible and equitable digital landscape. This approach aligns technological innovation with ethical commitments, ensuring that the potential of data is harnessed in ways that benefit society while respecting the rights of individuals.

CHAPTER 2

THE IMPORTANCE OF DATA ETHICS

THE ROLE OF ETHICS IN THE DIGITAL AGE

The Impact on Individuals and Society

Data ethics plays a critical role in shaping the relationship between individuals and digital technologies, influencing not only how people interact with digital services but also the quality of life, trust, and well-being within society. When data is handled ethically, individuals can engage with technology with a sense of security, knowing their personal information is being used responsibly, transparently, and in ways they have consented to. Ethical data practices ensure that privacy is protected, which is essential for people to feel comfortable sharing information and participating in digital spaces. This sense of safety stems from the assurance that organizations value user rights, prioritize informed consent, and maintain accountability in their data practices. In this context, data is seen as a tool that enhances individuals' lives rather than as a potential threat to their autonomy. The responsible use of data helps promote positive relationships between individuals and technology, fostering environments where innovation can thrive without compromising individual rights or freedoms.

Conversely, when organizations fail to adopt ethical data practices, it can lead to severe consequences for individuals and society as a whole. Unethical data-handling can result in privacy breaches, identity theft, discrimination, and intrusive surveillance—all of which undermine people's confidence in digital systems. For example, breaches that expose sensitive personal information not only cause immediate harm through the risk of identity theft but also have long-term effects on mental well-being, as individuals may experience anxiety or stress due to the lack of control over their data. Moreover, discriminatory outcomes from biased algorithms—such as those used in hiring, lending, or law enforcement—can perpetuate societal inequality, disproportionately affecting marginalized groups.

These negative experiences erode public trust in technology and create a digital divide where people become wary of using digital tools and services, fearing potential exploitation or misuse. This reluctance to engage fully with digital technologies ultimately hinders societal progress and innovation, as fewer individuals are willing to share their data or participate in digital initiatives that require trust in the ethical handling of their information. Addressing these challenges by embedding strong ethical principles in data practices is crucial for fostering a digital society where technology contributes to human progress rather than causing harm.

Creating a Just and Equitable Society

The impact of ethical data-handling extends beyond individual experiences; it plays a crucial role in fostering a just and equitable society. Organizations that adhere to ethical data guidelines take proactive measures to minimize the risks of biased decision-making that can unfairly profile or exclude certain groups. This is particularly critical in high-stakes sectors such as healthcare, finance, and law enforcement, where the use of biased algorithms can have far-reaching consequences for individuals and communities. For instance, in healthcare, biased data may lead to inadequate treatment recommendations for patients from marginalized backgrounds, exacerbating health disparities and undermining trust in medical institutions. Similarly, in finance, algorithmic bias can result in unjust credit denials, disproportionately affecting those with less access to financial resources. By addressing algorithmic bias through ethical practices, organizations can help ensure that decisions made by algorithms are based on equitable criteria, ultimately benefiting society as a whole.

Moreover, prioritizing fairness and transparency in data ethics cultivates an environment where technology is harnessed to create equitable opportunities rather than perpetuating historical inequality. When organizations commit to ethical data practices, they not only mitigate the risks of discrimination but also promote a culture of accountability and responsibility in data usage. This focus on ethical handling fosters a society in which all individuals are treated fairly and impartially, thereby enhancing social cohesion and stability.

Additionally, when marginalized communities see their interests represented and protected within technological systems, it fosters trust and encourages greater participation in digital initiatives. Ultimately, the ethical use of data contributes to the well-being of communities by promoting inclusivity, ensuring that technological advancement serves to uplift all members of society rather than exacerbate existing disparities. In this way, ethical data practices become fundamental to creating a more just, equitable, and harmonious society.

The Influence on Public Policy and Regulation

More broadly, the societal impact of data ethics is manifested prominently in public policy and regulation, where ethical standards play a crucial role in shaping responsible data governance. Governments, informed by the principles of data ethics, develop regulations designed to protect citizens' rights while establishing clear boundaries around data collection, usage, and sharing.

A prime example of this is the GDPR in Europe, which has become a benchmark for data protection legislation worldwide. The GDPR embodies ethical considerations by mandating transparency, consent, and accountability in data practices, thereby translating these principles into concrete legal protections for individuals. By establishing rigorous requirements for how organizations handle personal data, the GDPR empowers individuals with greater control over their information, fostering a sense of ownership and agency in an increasingly digital world.

Furthermore, regulatory frameworks such as the GDPR not only safeguard individual rights but also lay a robust foundation for societal trust in digital systems. By creating clear guidelines for data usage, these regulations enhance accountability among organizations and promote ethical responsibility throughout the data lifecycle. This encourages a culture of compliance, where organizations must prioritize ethical considerations in their operations, from data collection and processing to storage and analysis. As a result, all stakeholders—ranging from data collectors to end-users—are encouraged to adopt responsible practices that respect individual rights and societal values. This holistic approach to data governance enhances the overall integrity of the digital ecosystem, fostering an environment where individuals can engage with technology with confidence, knowing that their rights are protected and that their data is being handled ethically. Ultimately, this leads to a more informed and empowered citizenry capable of participating meaning-fully in the digital age.

Shaping the Social Narrative

Data ethics significantly shapes the social narrative surrounding tech-nology's role in everyday life by advocating for principles of transpar-ency, fairness, and accountability. In doing so, it cultivates a culture in which technological advancements are perceived as tools for enhancing human welfare rather than sources of exploitation or harm. This ethical framework encourages stakeholders—such as technologists, businesses, and policymakers—to prioritize societal benefits over profit-driven motives. As a result, innovations in areas such as AI, machine learning, and big data are more likely to be developed with a focus on inclusivity and equity. This shift from profit-centric to people-centered progress ensures that advancements are not only efficient and convenient but also contribute meaningfully to the broader social good.

When ethical considerations are deeply integrated into the techno-logical landscape, society reaps the benefits of innovations that respect and uphold human dignity and rights. This comprehensive approach to data ethics not only mitigates the risks associated with biased or harm-ful technologies but also fosters public trust in digital systems. As indi-viduals feel more secure about how their data is handled, they are more likely to engage with new technologies and services, ultimately lead-ing to a more robust and innovative digital economy. By promoting a harmonious relationship between technology and society, data ethics paves the way for both to flourish, allowing communities to harness the full potential of technological advancements while ensuring that ethi-cal principles guide their development and application. This synergistic interaction could lead to a future where technology enhances the qual-ity of life and empowers individuals, ultimately contributing to a more equitable and just society.

Promoting Education and Awareness

The impact of data ethics reaches deeply into education and awareness, highlighting the necessity of informed consent and digital literacy in today's data-driven society. As individuals become more cognizant of their rights and the implications of data usage, they are better posi-tioned to make informed decisions regarding their personal informa-tion. Educational initiatives focused on data ethics are essential in this regard, as they empower individuals with the knowledge needed to navigate complex digital landscapes. By understanding how their data is collected, used, and shared, individuals can engage with digital technologies more critically and assertively. This proactive engagement enables them to set boundaries regarding their personal information and recognize when their rights may be at risk, ultimately fostering a culture of respect for individual privacy and autonomy.

Moreover, heightened awareness of data ethics not only enhances personal agency but also generates demand for ethical practices among organizations, compelling them to prioritize responsible data management. When consumers are informed and vocal about their data rights, organizations are more likely to adopt transparent policies and ethical guidelines in their data practices. This dynamic creates a feedback loop where consumer advocacy drives corporate accountability, further reinforcing the importance of ethical considerations in data usage. By nurturing a culture of ethical awareness, society can develop a more robust and resilient digital environment that upholds individual autonomy while protecting against potential misuse. Such an environment not only promotes trust between individuals and organizations but also fosters a collective commitment to ethical data practices that can adapt to future challenges and innovations.

The Significance of Data Ethics Today

In the current digital landscape, the significance of data ethics cannot be overstated. It serves as a foundational pillar influencing individual experiences while shaping equitable societal structures, informing regulatory frameworks, and fostering a positive narrative around technological advancement. Ethical data practices enhance personal security and well-being, allowing individuals to engage with digital technologies with confidence, knowing their rights are protected. By prioritizing principles such as transparency, consent, and accountability, organizations can build trust with users, ensuring that data is handled responsibly and that individuals feel empowered in their interactions with technology. This ethical approach not only safeguards personal information but also promotes a culture of respect and integrity in data usage, which is essential for healthy relationships between consumers and digital service providers.

As society continues to navigate the complexities of the digital age, an unwavering commitment to data ethics will be essential in ensuring that technology acts as a force for good. This commitment involves recognizing the broader implications of data use, particularly in addressing issues of inequality and discrimination that can arise from biased algorithms and unjust data practices. By actively engaging with ethical considerations, stakeholders—including individuals, organizations, and governments—can work collaboratively to create an inclusive digital ecosystem that benefits all members of society while safeguarding their rights and dignity. In this way, data ethics not only enhances individual experiences but also lays the groundwork for a just and equitable future, where technological advancements contribute to societal progress rather than exacerbate existing disparity.

The Need for Collaboration

The intersection of data ethics and societal well-being highlights the critical need for collaboration among various stakeholders. Individuals, organizations, governments, and civil society must come together to establish and uphold ethical standards that reflect shared values and goals. This collaboration is essential for fostering a collective understanding of data ethics and addressing the multifaceted challenges posed by rapid technological advancements.

By pooling resources and expertise, stakeholders can engage in meaningful dialogue that informs the development of comprehensive guidelines tailored to navigate emerging ethical dilemmas. Such partnerships can lead to the establishment of robust frameworks that prioritize accountability and transparency, thereby enhancing public trust in digital systems. When the collective interests of society are prioritized over individual enrichment, the result is a more equitable digital landscape that fosters long-term sustainability and social cohesion.

This shared responsibility encourages proactive measures to address the ethical concerns associated with data usage, including privacy, security, and fairness. Through joint initiatives, stakeholders can develop educational programs aimed at raising awareness of ethical data practices and empowering individuals to understand their rights. Moreover, these collaborative efforts can result in the creation of regulatory policies that not only safeguard individual privacy but also promote ethical innovation within organizations.

By fostering a culture of accountability, organizations are more likely to embrace ethical data practices that consider the potential impacts on communities and the environment. Ultimately, by building a framework of shared responsibility, stakeholders can effectively navigate the ethical complexities of data usage, ensuring that technological advancements serve the broader principles of justice and equity while enhancing societal well-being.

Navigating Ethical Challenges in Emerging Technologies

The ongoing evolution of technology demands a proactive approach to data ethics, one that anticipates new challenges and adapts ethical frameworks accordingly. As emerging technologies, such as blockchain and quantum computing, become more integrated into everyday applications, they introduce unique ethical dilemmas that necessitate the continuous examination and refinement of existing principles. For instance, blockchain technology raises questions about data immutability and user anonymity, challenging traditional notions of consent and accountability. Similarly, quantum computing's potential to process vast amounts of data at unprecedented speeds, which may outpace existing regulatory frameworks, presents concerns regarding data security and privacy. By fostering a culture of adaptability and responsiveness, society can ensure that ethical considerations remain relevant and effective in the face of rapid technological advancements. This proactive stance enables stakeholders to stay ahead of potential issues, allowing for timely interventions and updates to ethical standards.

Moreover, a forward-thinking approach to data ethics not only safeguards individuals' rights but also promotes a data ecosystem that prioritizes ethical practices across all dimensions of data-handling. By continuously engaging with the complexities introduced by new technologies, organizations and policymakers can create a dynamic framework that encourages responsible data usage while mitigating the risks associated with data misuse. This involves ongoing education and training for individuals and organizations alike, ensuring that everyone involved understands the implications of their actions in an increasingly digital world. Furthermore, collaboration among technologists, ethicists, and regulators can yield innovative solutions to ethical challenges, fostering a culture of accountability and transparency. Ultimately, embracing adaptability in data ethics will help cultivate a landscape where technological advancement can be harnessed for the greater good, reinforcing the commitment to ethical practices that respect individual rights and promote societal well-being.

The Future of Data Ethics

The future of data ethics is inherently tied to our collective ability to maintain a delicate balance between technological progress and ethical responsibility. As we delve deeper into the digital age, the necessity to uphold data ethics as a fundamental principle guiding our interactions with technology becomes increasingly crucial. This involves not only recognizing the potential benefits of data-driven innovations but also acknowledging the ethical implications they carry. By prioritizing ethical considerations and fostering a culture of accountability, we can cultivate a digital landscape that not only respects individual rights but also promotes inclusivity and fairness within society. This commitment to data ethics serves as a safeguard against potential abuses and fosters trust among users, ensuring that technology serves humanity rather than undermines it.

The path forward will require ongoing dialogue, education, and collaboration among all stakeholders to ensure that data ethics evolves in tandem with technological advancements. Engaging diverse voices from various sectors—such as technology, academia, civil society, and government—will be essential in shaping comprehensive ethical frameworks that address the complexities of data usage in an interconnected world. Additionally, educational initiatives must be prioritized to raise awareness about data ethics, empowering individuals to become informed advocates for their rights and the rights of others. By cultivating a proactive and inclusive approach to data ethics, we can forge a future that serves the best interests of humanity as a whole, ensuring that technological advancements are harnessed responsibly to enhance the quality of life for all.

THE ROLE OF DATA ETHICS IN SHAPING MODERN TECHNOLOGIES

Data Ethics in Modern Technologies

Data ethics is increasingly recognized as a crucial component in the development and deployment of modern technologies, particularly AI and IoT. These technologies rely heavily on the collection and analysis of vast amounts of personal and contextual data, making ethical considerations paramount in their implementation. For instance, AI systems utilize large datasets to learn, make predictions, and automate decisions, which can lead to significant advancements across various sectors, including healthcare, finance, and transportation. In healthcare, AI can improve diagnostic accuracy and patient outcomes by analyzing patient histories and medical records. In finance, it can streamline processes and enhance fraud detection. The growing reliance on data-driven technologies, however, also brings ethical challenges that cannot be overlooked.

The absence of an ethical foundation raises numerous risks, such as biased algorithms, opaque decision-making processes, and unintended harm to individuals and communities. For example, if the data used to train AI systems reflects historical bias or inequality, the algorithms may perpetuate this bias, resulting in discriminatory outcomes. Similarly, IoT devices that collect personal data can raise significant privacy concerns if they are not managed ethically. Therefore, it is essential to establish a robust ethical framework that guides the responsible development and deployment of these transformative technologies. This framework should encompass principles such as transparency, accountability, and inclusivity, ensuring that all stakeholders, including individuals whose data is being used, have a voice in how their information is handled. By prioritizing data ethics, we can harness the full potential of AI and IoT while safeguarding individual rights and fostering trust in these innovative technologies.

Addressing Bias in AI

One of the pressing concerns in AI is the potential for bias in algorithms, which can have severe consequences for individuals and communities. Bias often arises from training data that reflects existing societal inequality, leading to discriminatory outcomes in critical areas such as recruitment, healthcare, and criminal justice. For instance, an AI model trained predominantly on data from one demographic may struggle to accurately assess conditions for individuals from underrepresented backgrounds, resulting in misdiagnoses in healthcare or unfairly biased hiring practices in recruitment. In criminal justice, biased algorithms could lead to disproportionately harsher sentencing for specific demographic groups, perpetuating cycles of inequality and injustice. These examples highlight the urgent need for ethical considerations in the development and deployment of AI technologies to ensure that all individuals are treated equitably and fairly.

By applying ethical principles to AI development, it becomes possible to create models that minimize bias and promote fairness across different sectors. This process involves not only diversifying training datasets to include a broader range of perspectives and experiences but also implementing rigorous testing protocols to identify and address potential bias before deployment. Furthermore, ensuring that decisions made by AI systems are transparent and justifiable enhances their reliability and builds trust among users who rely on these technologies for important aspects of their lives. Transparency can be achieved through clear documentation of how algorithms function and the data they utilize, allowing stakeholders to understand and challenge decisions made by these systems. Ultimately, a commitment to ethical AI practices fosters an environment where technology serves as a tool for empowerment and equality, rather than a mechanism that perpetuates existing disparity.

Ethical Implications in High-Stakes Contexts

The ethical implications of AI are especially urgent in contexts where the outcomes of AI-driven decisions have direct impacts on people's lives. In healthcare, for instance, AI can assist in diagnosing diseases or recommending treatments, significantly improving patient care and outcomes. Bias in the underlying data, however, can lead to harmful consequences for patients, particularly for those in underrepresented groups. An AI model that fails to accurately represent the diversity of the population may overlook critical symptoms or characteristics unique to certain demographics, leading to misdiagnoses or inappropriate treatment plans. Such oversights not only endanger the health of individuals but also exacerbate existing health disparity. Moreover, when marginalized communities receive inadequate care due to biased AI, it undermines trust in medical systems and can discourage individuals from seeking necessary treatment in the future.

Similarly, AI algorithms used in hiring processes may inadvertently exclude qualified individuals based on flawed assumptions or biased data. For instance, if an algorithm is trained on historical hiring data that reflects past discrimination, it may perpetuate those biases by favoring candidates from certain backgrounds while unfairly disadvantaging others. This not only limits opportunities for talented individuals but also stifles diversity within organizations. Data ethics provides a framework for identifying and mitigating these risks, promoting responsible AI that respects human rights and dignity. By ensuring accountability and transparency in AI decision-making, organizations can work toward achieving equitable outcomes that do not disproportionately disadvantage certain groups. Implementing ethical guidelines and regular audits of AI systems can help uncover bias and lead to more inclusive practices, ultimately contributing to a fairer society.

The Role of Data Ethics in IoT

For IoT, data ethics is equally critical as these devices become more integrated into daily life, continuously collecting data from homes, workplaces, and public spaces. IoT devices gather extensive information about user behavior, preferences, and even their physical environments, which raises significant concerns about privacy and control over personal data. The sheer volume and sensitivity of the data collected can lead to invasive monitoring practices, especially if adequate safeguards are not put in place. As these technologies become more pervasive, the potential for misuse of sensitive information increases, making the ethical management of this data essential. Users may unknowingly share their habits, locations, and other private details, creating opportunities for exploitation by malicious actors or even by the organizations that produce the devices themselves. This reality underscores the necessity for ethical frameworks that prioritize user privacy and data protection.

While smart home devices can significantly improve convenience and efficiency, they can also infringe privacy if their data policies are not transparent or if users have not given explicit consent. Ethical principles such as transparency, informed consent, and data minimization are vital for ensuring that individuals are fully aware of what data is being collected, how it is used, and who has access to it. Users must have clear, accessible information about the implications of their data sharing, empowering them to make informed decisions regarding their interactions with IoT technologies. By committing to ethical data practices, organizations can foster trust and accountability, leading to enhanced user engagement and satisfaction. This commitment not only protects individual privacy but also contributes to a more ethical digital ecosystem, where users feel a sense of control over their personal information, thus enabling a healthier relationship between people and technology.

Proactive Approach to Data Ethics

As AI and IoT technologies proliferate, there is a pressing need for a proactive approach to data ethics. This entails embedding ethical principles into the design and implementation of these technologies from the outset. Engaging various stakeholders—including developers, users, policymakers, and ethicists—in the ethical discourse surrounding these technologies is critical. Such collaboration can facilitate a deeper understanding of the potential societal impacts and ethical dilemmas posed by these innovations. By integrating data ethics into the development process, we can ensure that AI and IoT technologies align with societal values and contribute positively to human welfare. This proactive strategy might involve establishing ethical review boards to evaluate projects, conducting continuous impact assessments to monitor the effects of these technologies, and creating mechanisms for user feedback that shape their evolution. By doing so, developers can better understand users' concerns and expectations, allowing for adjustments that enhance the technology's ethical standing and public acceptance.

Prioritizing ethical considerations from the beginning not only helps to mitigate potential harm but also paves the way for innovations that enhance the quality of life for individuals and communities. This approach fosters a culture of accountability, encouraging organizations to take ownership of their ethical responsibilities in technology deployment. As trust in technology becomes increasingly essential, proactive data ethics can build confidence among users, reassuring them that their privacy and rights are protected. Furthermore, this commitment to ethics can spur the creation of technologies that are not only functional but also equitable and just. By championing ethical principles in AI and IoT, we can ensure that these powerful tools serve to uplift society rather than exacerbate existing inequality or create new ethical challenges.

Driving Innovation Through Data Ethics

Adopting a data ethics framework can drive innovation in responsible ways, enhancing business practices and fostering societal trust. Organizations that prioritize data ethics are more likely to gain a competitive advantage by cultivating consumer loyalty and safeguarding their reputations. In an era where public scrutiny of data practices is at an all-time high, companies that demonstrate a commitment to ethical standards are better positioned to resonate with consumers who value transparency and responsibility. By embedding ethical considerations into their operational strategies, organizations can create a strong alignment between their business objectives and the values of their customers, resulting in long-lasting relationships built on trust. Ethical practices in AI and IoT can also lead to improved user experiences, as people are more inclined to engage with technologies they trust. For instance, when users feel confident that their data is handled securely and ethically, they are more likely to adopt and advocate for these technologies, thereby fostering a positive feedback loop that benefits both users and organizations alike.

Moreover, organizations that commit to transparency and accountability can differentiate themselves in crowded markets, allowing them to capitalize on the growing demand for ethically developed products and services. This differentiation not only enhances their market position but also contributes to a broader cultural shift toward responsible consumption and production. By prioritizing ethical practices, businesses can address consumer concerns about data privacy and security, which are increasingly pivotal in purchasing decisions. In this way, the intersection of data ethics and innovation creates a win-win situation where businesses thrive while adhering to ethical standards that protect users' rights and foster social good. Ultimately, this synergy encourages a marketplace where ethical considerations are integrated into the core of business strategies, promoting sustainable growth and aligning profit motives with the welfare of society.

Ethical Considerations as a Core Principle

Ultimately, ethical considerations are not just a regulatory requirement but fundamental to ensuring that AI and IoT are used as tools for empowerment rather than instruments of control or inequality. As these technologies become increasingly woven into the fabric of daily life, their potential to influence individual freedoms and societal structures grows exponentially. When ethical principles guide the development and deployment of these technologies, they serve as safeguards against misuse, ensuring that the power dynamics inherent in data collection and analysis do not lead to oppression or discrimination.

A strong ethical framework encourages organizations and developers to prioritize the interests and rights of individuals, helping to create a technology landscape that respects diversity and promotes inclusion. This proactive approach not only mitigates risks but also enhances user confidence in adopting new technologies, reinforcing the belief that these innovations can be beneficial rather than harmful.

As technology continues to evolve at an unprecedented pace, a steadfast commitment to data ethics must remain in place, adapting to new challenges while reinforcing the core principles of respect, fairness, and accountability. Embracing ethical practices will enable society to harness the full potential of AI and IoT, transforming them into instruments that enhance human capabilities, promote social equity, and foster a sustainable future. By continuously engaging with ethical principles, we can ensure that the benefits of technological advancements are shared broadly, creating a digital landscape that prioritizes human rights and dignity in every facet of life. This commitment to data ethics is essential for building a just society where technology serves as a catalyst for positive change, empowering individuals and communities to thrive in an increasingly digital world. As we navigate the complexities of this new technological era, a focus on ethics will not only guide innovation but also illuminate the path toward a more equitable and humane society.

Education and Awareness Initiatives

The landscape of data ethics will evolve alongside technological advancements, necessitating ongoing education and awareness initiatives for both developers and users. As the intricacies of AI and IoT technologies deepen, individuals must be educated about their rights regarding data usage and the implications of these technologies on their lives. Understanding concepts such as informed consent, data ownership, and privacy rights is critical for individuals to navigate the complex digital landscape effectively.

Educational programs that emphasize data ethics can empower users to critically assess the technologies they use and advocate for their rights, equipping them with the knowledge to engage meaningfully in discussions about data practices. These programs should not only focus on the technical aspects of data-handling but also address ethical dilemmas and real-world case studies to illustrate the potential consequences of data misuse. By fostering a culture of ethical awareness, society can build a more resilient digital environment that supports individual autonomy while protecting against potential misuse.

In addition to educating users, it is equally important to incorporate ethical training into the development processes of AI and IoT technologies. Developers and organizations must understand the ethical implications of their work to create systems that prioritize user rights and societal well-being. This involves training that covers not only the technical skills needed for innovation but also the ethical considerations that should guide decision-making throughout the design and implementation phases. By integrating data ethics into the professional development of those who create these technologies, organizations can cultivate a workforce that is not only technically proficient but also socially responsible. Ultimately, this dual focus on user education and developer training can create a collaborative ecosystem where ethical considerations are embedded in every aspect of technology, ensuring that advancements contribute positively to society while safeguarding individual rights and dignity.

Looking to the Future with Data Ethics

The relevance of data ethics to modern technologies such as AI and IoT cannot be overstated. It serves as a critical framework that guides the responsible development and deployment of these technologies, ensuring they contribute positively to society while safeguarding individual rights. As technology continues to permeate every aspect of our lives, the need for ethical considerations becomes increasingly vital. A strong ethical foundation not only mitigates the risks associated with data misuse and discrimination but also fosters public trust in the technologies that shape our daily interactions. By prioritizing ethical principles such as transparency, accountability, and inclusivity, we can ensure that AI and IoT are developed with the best interests of society in mind.

As we continue to navigate the complexities of the digital age, our commitment to data ethics will be essential for creating a future where technology serves as a force for good, enhancing human experiences and promoting social equity. The road ahead will require collaboration among various stakeholders, including developers, policymakers, and civil society, to address emerging ethical dilemmas proactively. Continuous engagement with these issues will be crucial, as will the ability to adapt ethical frameworks to meet new challenges posed by rapid technological advancements. By ensuring that technological innovation aligns with the principles of justice, fairness, and respect for all individuals, we can build a digital landscape that empowers users, fosters inclusivity, and ultimately contributes to a more equitable society.

CHAPTER 3

CORE ETHICS IN DATA GOVERNANCE

OVERVIEW OF KEY CONCEPTS AND FRAMEWORKS

In the rapidly evolving digital landscape, the concepts of privacy, consent, and accountability serve as fundamental pillars of data ethics. Each concept plays a crucial role in shaping the ethical handling of personal information, ensuring that individuals' rights and freedoms are respected amid pervasive data collection and processing.

Privacy

Privacy, in essence, refers to an individual's right to control their personal data and maintain autonomy over how it is collected, used, and shared. This right is paramount, especially in an era where vast amounts of personal information can be harvested with relative ease. The ethical implications of privacy emphasize that individuals should have the final say over their data and that unauthorized access, misuse, or unwarranted exposure must be diligently avoided. This notion of control is not just about keeping personal information secret; it extends to how individuals perceive their relationship with technology and institutions. A robust understanding of privacy involves recognizing that data can significantly influence personal identity and decision-making, making it imperative for individuals to have agency over their information.

In the digital age, maintaining privacy has become increasingly challenging due to the vast scale at which data is collected. Individuals often find themselves navigating a complex landscape where their personal information is at risk of commercialization or exploitation. This vulnerability is exacerbated by the rapid advancements in technology, which enable more sophisticated methods of data gathering and analysis. Ethical data practices seek to combat this reality by advocating for data collection practices that are transparent and minimally invasive. Organizations are encouraged to gather only what is necessary for specific purposes, ensuring that the data collected is securely stored and used only for the purposes originally stated. By implementing these principles, organizations can not only protect individual privacy but also align their operations with ethical standards that prioritize respect for users.

By prioritizing privacy in this manner, organizations not only safeguard individual freedoms but also foster a climate of trust within digital systems. This trust is vital, as it enhances individuals' confidence in engaging with digital services, ultimately enriching their online experiences. When users feel secure that their data is being handled ethically, they are more likely to participate in digital interactions, whether through social media platforms, e-commerce sites, or other online services. Additionally, a strong commitment to privacy can serve as a competitive advantage for organizations, setting them apart in a crowded marketplace. As consumers become more aware of data ethics, they increasingly seek out companies that respect their privacy and demonstrate accountability in their data practices. In this way, the ethical imperative of privacy becomes not just a moral obligation but a strategic consideration for organizations aiming to thrive in an interconnected world.

Consent

Closely linked to the notion of privacy is the concept of consent, which serves as a cornerstone of ethical data management. Consent represents the agreement of individuals to the collection and use of their data, ideally accompanied by a comprehensive understanding of how that information will be handled. The significance of informed consent cannot be overstated; it is not merely a legal requirement but a fundamental ethical principle that respects individuals' autonomy. Informed consent requires that individuals receive clear, concise, and comprehensible information about data collection practices before deciding whether to participate. This ensures that individuals can make decisions based on an understanding of the potential implications of sharing their data, which is essential for building a respectful relationship between organizations and users.

Transparency is a crucial aspect of informed consent; it empowers individuals to make choices that align with their preferences and comfort levels regarding data sharing. For consent to be meaningful, organizations must clearly communicate the types of data they collect, the purposes for which it will be used, and any third parties with whom the data may be shared. This transparency enables individuals to weigh the benefits of participation against their privacy concerns, facilitating a more informed decision-making process. Furthermore, transparency in data practices can help demystify the often-complex algorithms and technologies that drive data collection, fostering a greater understanding of how personal information is utilized in the digital landscape. As individuals become more aware of their rights, they can make choices that reflect their values and expectations.

Ethical data management also emphasizes that consent must be revocable, allowing individuals to withdraw their consent at any time, thus maintaining their control over personal information. This principle underscores the dynamic nature of consent in the digital age, where individuals may change their minds about data sharing as their circumstances or preferences evolve. By promoting a culture of informed consent, organizations can cultivate stronger relationships with users, ultimately enhancing trust and engagement in the process. When individuals feel empowered to control their data and can easily revoke consent when desired, they are more likely to engage with digital services and share their information willingly. This reciprocity not only benefits individuals but also supports organizations in fostering long-term relationships grounded in respect, transparency, and ethical responsibility, ultimately leading to a healthier data ecosystem.

Accountability

Accountability is yet another critical element of data ethics, serving to ensure that individuals and organizations involved in data management are answerable for their practices. This accountability implies the establishment of clear standards and mechanisms to ensure compliance with ethical guidelines. By defining roles, responsibilities, and expectations for data-handling, organizations can foster an environment where ethical considerations are prioritized. This is particularly crucial in an era where data breaches and misuse can lead to significant harm, both to individuals and society as a whole. Those handling data must take responsibility for their actions, particularly when unethical practices result in harm. This responsibility extends beyond mere compliance with laws and regulations; it encompasses a commitment to ethical integrity and a proactive stance in addressing potential risks associated with data use.

To uphold accountability, organizations need to be transparent about their data practices, providing stakeholders with accessible information regarding how their data is used and what safeguards are in place. Transparency not only builds trust with users but also empowers them to hold organizations accountable for their data practices. For instance, organizations should clearly communicate their data collection methods, retention policies, and security measures. In instances of data breaches, organizations are expected to take responsibility not only for the immediate fallout but also to investigate the underlying causes and implement corrective measures to prevent future incidents. This level of openness is essential for demonstrating a genuine commitment to ethical data management and fostering a culture of accountability.

Thus, accountability acts as a safeguard against abuse and negligence, reinforcing the principle that data handlers must prioritize the best interests of data subjects and the public. By establishing a robust framework for accountability, organizations can mitigate risks associated with data management and demonstrate their commitment to ethical practices. This framework can include regular audits, assessments, and reporting mechanisms to ensure ongoing compliance with ethical standards. Additionally, cultivating a culture of accountability encourages employees and stakeholders to take ethical considerations seriously and report concerns without fear of retribution. In this way, accountability not only protects individuals' rights but also strengthens the integrity of data management as a whole, ultimately contributing to a more ethical and responsible digital ecosystem.

Interconnection: Privacy, Consent, and Accountability

Together, privacy, consent, and accountability form a cohesive framework that promotes ethical data practices and fosters trust in digital technologies. In a world where data collection is ubiquitous, these concepts serve as guiding principles, ensuring that individuals' rights are upheld and protected. Privacy grants individuals control over their personal information, allowing them to decide who can access their data and for what purposes. This control is crucial in maintaining autonomy in an increasingly interconnected world. Meanwhile, informed consent empowers individuals to make deliberate choices regarding data usage, ensuring they fully understand the implications of sharing their information. This informed decision-making process strengthens individuals' sense of agency and reinforces the idea that they have a stake in how their data is managed.

When organizations prioritize these principles, they signal to individuals that their rights are valued, creating an environment conducive to ethical data practices. By implementing robust privacy policies, facilitating clear consent processes, and embracing accountability measures, organizations can demonstrate their commitment to respecting individuals' data rights. This proactive stance fosters a culture of transparency, where individuals feel confident that their information is being handled ethically. Additionally, organizations that uphold these principles are more likely to build long-lasting relationships with their users, as trust is a fundamental component of any positive interaction in the digital landscape. When individuals feel assured that their data is safe and that their rights are being respected, they are more inclined to engage with technology and share their information.

This holistic approach fosters a culture of respect and dignity in data-handling, allowing individuals to engage more freely with technology without fear of exploitation or abuse. By embedding privacy, consent, and accountability into the core of data practices, organizations can create a sustainable framework that not only benefits individuals but also enhances their own reputations. As public awareness of data ethics grows, individuals increasingly seek out organizations that align with their values, making it essential for businesses to adopt these ethical practices. Ultimately, this integrated framework leads to a more ethical digital ecosystem, where both individuals and organizations can thrive in a manner that respects and upholds fundamental rights in an age dominated by data.

Societal Implications

Embedding privacy, consent, and accountability into data management practices has broader societal implications, contributing to a more just and respectful digital society. As awareness of personal rights and the potential risks of data misuse grows, individuals are becoming more vigilant about how their data is handled. Organizations that prioritize these ethical principles signal their commitment to safeguarding personal information and respecting users' autonomy. This proactive approach not only helps to protect individual rights but also plays a vital role in shaping societal norms around data ethics. By fostering a culture where privacy and consent are integral to data practices, society can advance toward a digital landscape characterized by mutual respect and dignity.

Organizations that embrace ethical data practices are likely to gain a competitive edge in today's marketplace. Public trust, cultivated through ethical data practices, can translate into brand loyalty and increased customer satisfaction. Consumers increasingly favor businesses that demonstrate accountability and transparency in their data-handling, making ethical considerations a key differentiator. This reinforces the idea that ethical practices are not merely regulatory obligations but also effective business strategies that can drive growth and innovation. By aligning their operations with the values of their customers, organizations can create stronger connections with their audience, fostering long-term relationships built on trust and shared principles.

Conversely, organizations that neglect these foundational pillars may face significant reputational damage and legal repercussions, highlighting the need to integrate ethical considerations into their operational frameworks. Data breaches and unethical practices can lead to public backlash, loss of customer trust, and potential legal actions, resulting in financial losses and long-term harm to an organization's reputation. In an environment where consumers are increasingly informed about their rights, failing to prioritize privacy, consent, and accountability can severely undermine a company's credibility. Therefore, embedding these principles into data management practices is not just a moral imperative; it is a crucial aspect of sustainable business strategy in a rapidly evolving digital landscape. By recognizing the importance of these ethical foundations, organizations can not only protect themselves but also contribute to a healthier, more equitable digital society.

BUILDING AN ETHICAL DIGITAL FUTURE

The Future of Ethical Data Practices

Ultimately, the integration of privacy, consent, and accountability into data ethics creates a robust framework that protects individuals while enhancing the overall quality of the digital ecosystem. This framework establishes clear guidelines that govern how personal information should be collected, used, and safeguarded, ensuring that individuals maintain control over their data. As technology continues to evolve and permeate various aspects of daily life—from social media to smart devices—these pillars will remain critical in guiding ethical practices. By adhering to the principles of privacy, consent, and accountability, organizations can foster an environment in which personal information is treated with the utmost respect and integrity, reinforcing public trust in digital technologies.

As the digital landscape expands, the importance of these ethical pillars becomes increasingly pronounced. Individuals are more connected than ever, and their data is often at risk of misuse or exploitation. By committing to privacy, informed consent, and accountability, organizations not only protect individuals but also contribute to the overall health of the digital ecosystem. This commitment enables individuals to navigate online spaces with confidence, knowing that their rights are respected and that they have a say in how their data is utilized. In doing so, organizations can help cultivate a future where individuals feel secure in their interactions with technology, empowered to make informed decisions about their data, and confident that their rights will be upheld in an increasingly data-driven world.

This vision of an ethical digital landscape is not merely desirable; it is essential for fostering a society that values human dignity and autonomy amid rapid technological change. As technological advancements continue to reshape how we communicate, work, and live, establishing a strong ethical foundation is vital for ensuring that the benefits of these innovations are realized without compromising individual rights. A society that prioritizes ethical data practices cultivates an environment where individuals are respected and valued, creating a sense of belonging and trust in the digital realm. By embedding privacy, consent, and accountability into the fabric of data management, we can strive toward a future that harmonizes technological progress with the principles of human dignity and respect, ensuring that the digital landscape serves as a space for empowerment and growth rather than exploitation.

Education and Awareness Initiatives

The ongoing discourse surrounding data ethics underscores the need for education and awareness initiatives that promote a better understanding of privacy, consent, and accountability. As technology becomes more integrated into everyday life, individuals must be informed about their rights regarding data usage and the implications of these technologies. The rapid proliferation of digital devices and platforms often outpaces the public's understanding of how their data is collected, stored, and utilized. This knowledge gap can leave individuals vulnerable to exploitation and misuse of their information. Therefore, fostering awareness about data ethics is essential for empowering individuals to make informed choices and actively participate in conversations about their rights in the digital age.

Educational programs that focus on data ethics can empower users to critically assess the technologies they engage with, advocating for their rights and fostering a culture of ethical awareness. By integrating data ethics into school curricula, community workshops, and corporate training, we can equip individuals with the knowledge necessary to navigate the complexities of digital environments. These programs should cover key concepts such as data ownership, the importance of informed consent, and the implications of data breaches. Such initiatives can enable individuals to not only understand their rights but also to recognize the power dynamics at play in the digital ecosystem, encouraging them to demand transparency and accountability from organizations that handle their data.

Ultimately, these education and awareness initiatives can help bridge the gap between technological advancements and public understanding, ensuring that individuals are equipped to navigate the complexities of the digital landscape. As users become more informed about data ethics, they can engage more meaningfully with technology, advocating for practices that prioritize their rights and dignity. Furthermore, a well-informed public can drive change by holding organizations accountable for their data practices, leading to a culture where ethical considerations are valued and upheld. In this way, investing in education about data ethics not only benefits individuals but also fosters a more responsible and ethical technological landscape that respects and protects personal rights in an increasingly data-driven world.

Toward a Trustworthy Digital Future

In conclusion, the foundational concepts of privacy, consent, and accountability are pivotal to the ethical management of data in today's digital environment. They create a framework that not only safeguards individual rights but also enhances the trust and quality of the overall digital ecosystem. As we continue to confront the ethical dilemmas posed by new technologies, it is imperative that organizations and individuals alike commit to these principles.

This commitment will pave the way for a future where technology serves as a tool for empowerment, fostering a digital landscape that prioritizes human rights, dignity, and ethical practices in every interaction. By nurturing a culture that values these principles, society can move toward a more equitable and just digital future for all.

BALANCING ETHICS IN DATA GOVERNANCE

Deontological ethics and consequentialism are two significant philosophical frameworks that provide essential guidance for ethical decision-making in data governance.

Deontological Ethics

Deontological ethics, often associated with the work of philosopher Immanuel Kant, emphasizes the importance of rules, duties, and principles when determining what is ethically right. This framework is centered around the belief that actions should be guided by moral rules that apply universally, regardless of their consequences. In the context of data governance, a deontological approach focuses on respecting individuals' rights, such as the right to privacy and the necessity for informed consent, irrespective of the potential outcomes. This perspective helps ensure that data is collected and processed according to a clear set of ethical guidelines, safeguarding individual rights as the primary concern.

Regulatory Implications of Deontological Ethics

The importance of deontological ethics in data governance becomes particularly pronounced when examining regulatory frameworks that prioritize user autonomy and data protection. Legislation such as the GDPR in the European Union (EU) exemplifies deontological principles by stating that individuals possess the right to be informed about and control how their personal data is used. This regulation enshrines the ethical imperative that organizations must treat individuals as ends in themselves, rather than merely as means to achieve their own objectives. By requiring transparency and consent in data practices, the GDPR emphasizes the intrinsic value of each person's rights and dignity. This focus on user autonomy not only empowers individuals but also reinforces the notion that ethical considerations should underpin all data-handling activities, ensuring that users are not exploited or subjected to invasive practices without their knowledge or consent.

Moreover, these regulations compel organizations to adhere to specific ethical standards regardless of the potential advantages of bypassing them, underscoring the duty to protect individuals' privacy. Deontological ethics establishes a framework that prioritizes moral duties and obligations, ensuring that ethical principles are upheld in data governance. By creating clear boundaries for acceptable behavior, deontological ethics significantly mitigates the risk of individuals' rights being compromised in favor of organizational or technological benefits. This proactive approach to ethics in data governance encourages organizations to cultivate a culture of responsibility, where adherence to ethical standards is viewed not just as compliance but as an integral part of their operational ethos. As data usage continues to evolve, the principles of deontological ethics will remain essential in fostering an environment where individual rights are safeguarded, ultimately leading to greater public trust in data-driven technologies.

Consequentialism in Data Governance

Conversely, consequentialism, particularly the utilitarian approach developed by philosophers Jeremy Bentham and John Stuart Mill, evaluates the ethics of actions based on their outcomes or consequences. In data governance, a consequentialist framework seeks to maximize the benefits and minimize the harms of data practices for the greatest number of people. This perspective encourages organizations to assess the overall impact of their data-related decisions, weighing the potential positive outcomes against the risks involved. For instance, an organization might justify extensive data collection practices if they lead to substantial societal benefits, such as enhancing healthcare outcomes through better diagnostics or improving public safety through intelligent city planning. By focusing on the overall welfare generated by these practices, organizations can make data-driven decisions that align with utilitarian principles, prioritizing actions that yield the highest net benefit for society.

While a consequentialist approach can stimulate innovation and foster initiatives that have far-reaching positive effects, it also raises ethical concerns about the potential for justifying harmful practices under the guise of the greater good.

The emphasis on outcomes can sometimes overshadow the need for individual rights and autonomy, leading to situations where the ends may justify the means, regardless of the potential for harm to specific individuals or marginalized groups. For example, if a data collection initiative is deemed beneficial overall but disproportionately affects a particular community, this could create ethical dilemmas that challenge the fundamental rights of those individuals. Therefore, while a consequentialist framework can drive organizations to harness data for societal advancements, it is essential to balance this perspective with a commitment to protecting individual rights and ensuring that ethical standards remain a priority in all data governance practices. This holistic approach ensures that data usage not only maximizes benefits but also upholds the dignity and autonomy of every individual involved.

Integrating Ethical Approaches for a Balanced Framework

While deontological and consequentialist approaches represent differing ethical perspectives, they both provide critical insights for creating an ethical framework in data governance. Deontological ethics emphasizes the importance of individual rights and duties, advocating for strict adherence to ethical standards regardless of outcomes. This perspective is essential in establishing fundamental principles such as informed consent and data protection, ensuring that individuals have the right to control their personal information. On the other hand, consequentialism focuses on the outcomes of data practices, encouraging organizations to consider the broader societal impacts of their actions. By integrating these two perspectives, organizations can develop a comprehensive understanding of ethical data governance that honors individual autonomy while also recognizing the need for data to serve societal goals.

In practice, this interplay is evident in various data governance initiatives, where organizations implement robust privacy policies and informed consent mechanisms, reflecting deontological ethics, while simultaneously promoting data-driven projects that aim to address societal challenges. For example, a healthcare organization may prioritize patient confidentiality and informed consent, ensuring that individuals are aware of how their data will be used. At the same time, the organization might leverage this data to develop predictive models that enhance patient outcomes or streamline operations. This dual approach allows a more holistic ethical framework that considers the complexities of modern data use, striking a balance between protecting individual rights and harnessing data for societal benefits. By fostering collaboration between deontological and consequentialist principles, organizations can navigate the ethical landscape of data governance more effectively, ultimately leading to practices that are both responsible and beneficial to society as a whole.

Concluding Thoughts on Ethical Data Governance

Ultimately, a comprehensive ethical framework for data governance integrates both deontological and consequentialist approaches, striving to create an environment where individual rights are upheld through clear rules and where data use serves the broader public good. This integrated approach encourages trust and transparency in digital technologies, paving the way for innovation that respects human dignity and contributes positively to society as a whole.

CHAPTER 4

ETHICAL PRINCIPLES IN DATA COLLECTION

INFORMED CONSENT

Definition of Informed Consent

Informed consent is a foundational ethical principle in data collection, aimed at ensuring individuals maintain control over their personal information. It refers to the process by which individuals are fully informed about how their data will be collected, used, shared, and retained, allowing them to make an educated decision about whether to provide their data. True informed consent requires individuals to understand the implications of data collection, including potential risks and benefits, and to provide their consent voluntarily, without any form of coercion or misleading information.

This principle is critical in today's data-driven world, where vast amounts of personal data are collected for various purposes, ranging from marketing and healthcare to research and public policy. Informed consent acts as a safeguard, ensuring that individuals are not merely passive participants in data transactions but active decision-makers regarding their personal information.

Protecting Individual Autonomy

The importance of informed consent lies in its ability to protect individuals' autonomy, ensuring they have the power to control what happens to their personal information. In an era where data collection is pervasive, providing transparent information about data practices is crucial. Informed consent empowers individuals to make decisions that align with their privacy preferences and ethical values. This respect for individual autonomy is a cornerstone of data ethics, recognizing that personal data should not be treated as a commodity without regard for the rights of the data subject. By allowing individuals to understand the implications of sharing their data and granting them the opportunity to decline participation, organizations can foster an environment where users feel safe and respected in their interactions with technology.

Moreover, informed consent promotes respect and fairness, particularly in contexts where the potential misuse of data can lead to serious consequences, such as discrimination or loss of privacy. When individuals are informed about how their data will be utilized, they are less vulnerable to exploitation and manipulation. This practice is especially critical in sectors such as healthcare, finance, and law enforcement, where data-driven decisions can significantly impact people's lives.

By prioritizing informed consent, organizations not only enhance their ethical standing but also build trust with their users. This trust is vital for fostering long-term relationships, as individuals are more likely to engage with services that prioritize their rights and well-being. Ultimately, informed consent is not just a legal obligation; it is a fundamental ethical principle that upholds dignity and ensures that data practices are conducted in a manner that is fair and just.

Building Trust and Credibility for Organizations

For businesses and organizations, obtaining informed consent is not only an ethical obligation but also a practical necessity that enhances transparency and trust. In an era marked by frequent data breaches and privacy violations, demonstrating a commitment to informed consent allows organizations to establish credibility with their customers. When individuals are made aware of how their data is collected and used, and when they are provided with the option to consent or decline, they are more likely to engage with digital services confidently. This trust is foundational for building long-term customer relationships, as consumers increasingly seek out companies that prioritize their privacy rights. In a landscape where privacy concerns are paramount, organizations that prioritize informed consent can distinguish themselves from competitors, creating a reputation for ethical data practices that resonates with consumers.

Moreover, organizations that embrace informed consent practices signal to consumers that they value their privacy, which can lead to stronger brand loyalty and advocacy. When customers feel secure in their interactions with a brand, they are more likely to become repeat users and recommend the organization to others, effectively serving as advocates for the brand. This positive feedback loop can translate into significant business advantages, including increased market share and enhanced customer satisfaction.

Furthermore, by fostering an organizational culture centered around ethical data practices, businesses not only comply with legal requirements but also position themselves as leaders in corporate responsibility. This proactive approach to informed consent can lead to innovative practices that respect user rights while also driving business growth, illustrating that ethical considerations can align with, and even enhance, corporate objectives.

Legal Requirements and Compliance

Informed consent is not merely a guideline; it is a legal requirement in many jurisdictions, underscoring the importance of compliance alongside ethical responsibility. Regulations such as the GDPR in the EU and the California Consumer Privacy Act (CCPA) in the United States emphasize the need for clear and informed consent when handling personal data. These laws mandate that organizations provide explicit information regarding their data practices and obtain unambiguous consent before processing personal information. Failure to comply with these regulations can lead to severe penalties, including hefty fines and reputational damage, making adherence to informed consent a crucial legal necessity. Therefore, organizations must remain vigilant in understanding and implementing these regulatory requirements, as noncompliance not only risks financial repercussions but can also erode public trust.

Consequently, organizations must implement robust mechanisms to ensure that informed consent is obtained in a manner that meets regulatory standards, highlighting the interplay between ethical considerations and legal obligations in data governance. This involves creating transparent consent processes, offering clear communication about data usage, and providing individuals with the opportunity to easily withdraw their consent at any time. By prioritizing informed consent as a foundational practice, organizations can build trust with their users while also fulfilling their legal responsibilities. Additionally, integrating informed consent into organizational culture fosters a deeper commitment to ethical data practices, aligning business objectives with user rights. This dual focus on ethical integrity and regulatory compliance not only protects individuals but also enhances the overall credibility and sustainability of the organization in the marketplace.

Protecting Individual Rights amid Technological Advances

Informed consent plays a vital role in bridging the gap between technological advances and individual rights, ensuring that the collection and use of personal data respect human dignity and uphold privacy standards. As data collection methods become increasingly sophisticated and pervasive, the potential for misuse also escalates, leading to heightened concerns regarding privacy violations and data breaches. In this context, informed consent serves as a protective measure, empowering individuals to navigate the complex landscape of data sharing with greater awareness and control. By ensuring that individuals are fully informed about how their data will be collected, used, and shared, informed consent fosters a sense of agency that is essential in today's digital age. This proactive approach to data ethics promotes transparency and encourages organizations to be accountable for their data practices, ultimately contributing to a more ethically sound digital environment.

Moreover, fostering a culture of respect for individual rights through informed consent helps mitigate the risks associated with data exploitation while encouraging responsible innovation. By prioritizing the ethical implications of data use, organizations can align their practices with societal values, ensuring that advancements in technology do not come at the expense of individual autonomy and privacy. This alignment not only enhances user trust but also encourages a more collaborative relationship between technology developers and users, as individuals feel more comfortable engaging with technologies that prioritize their rights. As a result, informed consent becomes a catalyst for ethical innovation, guiding organizations in developing solutions that not only meet business objectives but also contribute positively to the broader community. In this way, informed consent reinforces the notion that technological progress should advance hand in hand with a commitment to ethical principles, ultimately benefiting society as a whole.

Empowering Individuals and Enhancing Data Governance

Informed consent is an essential component of ethical data practices, serving to protect individual autonomy, foster trust between organizations and consumers, and ensure compliance with legal standards. It provides individuals with the knowledge and power to control how their personal information is used, allowing them to make informed decisions that align with their privacy preferences. As the digital landscape continues to evolve, marked by rapid technological advancement and increasing data collection, organizations must prioritize informed consent as a core element of their data governance strategies. This commitment not only upholds ethical principles but also enhances their reputation and credibility in a society that is increasingly concerned with privacy and data protection. By embedding informed consent into their practices, organizations demonstrate a proactive stance toward ethical data management, fostering an environment where individuals feel secure and valued.

Moreover, informed consent empowers individuals, reinforcing their rights and dignity in an era where personal information is a valuable commodity. It creates a more equitable and respectful digital ecosystem by ensuring that individuals are treated as active participants rather than passive subjects of data collection. When organizations prioritize informed consent, they contribute to a culture of accountability and transparency that benefits all stakeholders. This empowerment is crucial as individuals navigate a world where data-driven technologies shape everyday experiences. Ultimately, by championing informed consent, organizations not only comply with regulatory requirements but also position themselves as leaders in ethical data practices, fostering a sustainable relationship with consumers that can drive innovation while respecting human rights.

INFORMED CONSENT CHALLENGES: PRACTICAL ISSUES

Challenges in Informed Consent

Despite the fundamental importance of informed consent, achieving it in practice is fraught with significant challenges, particularly in the digital age. One of the most pressing obstacles is the complexity and opacity of data collection processes. Many organizations utilize intricate data collection methods that can be difficult for the average user to understand, leading to confusion about what they are consenting to. Often, lengthy terms and conditions, filled with legal jargon, obscure critical information that users need to make informed choices about their data. This lack of clarity can result in individuals unwittingly granting consent without fully comprehending the potential risks involved, thus undermining the very essence of informed consent. Furthermore, the rapid pace of technological change can outstrip regulatory frameworks, leaving gaps in the protections designed to uphold individuals' rights, which can further complicate the landscape of informed consent.

Another significant challenge lies in the inconsistent application of informed consent across different platforms and jurisdictions. Variations in regulatory standards and cultural attitudes toward privacy can create confusion for both organizations and consumers. For instance, what constitutes valid consent in one country may not meet the standards in another, leading to a patchwork of practices that complicate compliance efforts for multinational corporations.

Additionally, some digital platforms may exploit loopholes in the law, offering minimal options for users to opt out of data collection or presenting consent requests in a manner that nudges users toward acceptance rather than genuine choice. These challenges have profound implications, as they not only erode trust between consumers and organizations but also heighten the risk of data misuse, making it essential for stakeholders to collaborate in developing clearer guidelines and best practices for obtaining informed consent in the digital landscape.

Complexity of Communication

One of the primary difficulties lies in effectively communicating complex information to individuals in a way that is clear and easily understandable. Most privacy policies and terms of service are lengthy documents filled with technical or legal jargon, making it difficult for the average user to comprehend what they are agreeing to. Research has shown that many users simply scroll to the bottom of these documents and click "accept" without reading them, indicating that they may consent to data collection without fully understanding the implications, including how their data will be used, shared, or stored. This lack of genuine understanding raises ethical concerns, as consent given under such circumstances cannot be considered truly informed. Furthermore, users often face information overload, where they are bombarded with notifications and requests for consent across multiple platforms, leading to desensitization and fatigue. This can result in a culture where individuals feel overwhelmed by the choices they must make about their data, further complicating their ability to provide informed consent.

The challenge, therefore, is to simplify the language and presentation of consent mechanisms, employing plain language and visual aids to enhance comprehension so that individuals can make genuinely informed decisions. Organizations can adopt strategies such as using concise summaries of key points, infographics, and interactive elements that help clarify the purpose and scope of data collection. Additionally, implementing layered consent models can allow users to choose the level of detail they wish to engage with, empowering them to navigate the consent process more effectively.

By prioritizing clarity and user-friendliness in data practices, organizations can foster a greater sense of agency among individuals, enabling them to understand their rights and make choices that align with their values. Ultimately, this approach not only respects user autonomy but also enhances trust and credibility between organizations and consumers, paving the way for more ethical data governance in the digital landscape.

Implicit Consent and Dark Patterns

Another major challenge is the often implicit nature of consent in many digital interactions. Digital platforms frequently rely on default settings that opt users into data collection practices, effectively making consent a passive action. This approach, commonly referred to as *dark patterns*, involves designing user interfaces to manipulate users into making choices they might not otherwise make. For instance, users may find themselves automatically enrolled in data-sharing programs unless they actively opt out, which can create confusion and frustration.

The process to withdraw consent is often made deliberately inconvenient, further entrenching users in these data collection practices. As a result, individuals may unknowingly agree to terms that allow extensive monitoring and data usage, thereby diminishing their control over personal information. This type of implicit consent is ethically questionable because it undermines the notion of voluntary, informed decision-making, which is a cornerstone of ethical data practices.

Rather than empowering users to make conscious choices about their data, these practices essentially coerce consent by making it the easiest option available. This not only raises ethical concerns but also poses significant risks to user privacy and trust. Users may feel misled when they discover the extent of data collection practices they were automatically enrolled in, leading to a backlash against organizations perceived as exploitative.

To address this issue, organizations must prioritize explicit consent mechanisms that require active participation from users, clearly outlining what they are consenting to and providing straightforward options for opting out. Transparency in data practices and ensuring that users can easily understand their choices will foster a more ethical digital environment, where consent is genuinely informed and reflective of user intentions. By moving away from manipulative design practices and toward a more user-centric approach, organizations can rebuild trust and accountability in their data governance strategies.

Challenges with IoT Devices

The rapid rise of interconnected devices, such as those used in IoT, presents additional hurdles to achieving informed consent. With IoT, data collection becomes pervasive and often invisible; devices such as smart thermostats, home assistants, or even connected cars continuously collect data, often without explicit user input. Many users may not be fully aware of the extent to which these devices are gathering data or how that data is being used or shared with third parties. For example, a smart speaker may gather information about daily routines, preferences, and even sensitive conversations, but users may not understand how this data is stored, processed, or shared. This situation complicates the traditional model of obtaining informed consent, as users may be inundated with numerous devices and platforms that collect and process their data, leading to confusion and disengagement from the consent process.

Additionally, the interconnected nature of IoT devices amplifies the complexity of informed consent. With multiple devices often communicating with each other and sharing data with third-party applications, individuals may find it challenging to track where their data is going and how it is being used. This data ecosystem blurs the lines of responsibility and accountability, making it difficult for users to determine who has access to their information and under what circumstances.

Moreover, the lack of standardized practices across different manufacturers further complicates matters, as users may encounter varying consent requirements and privacy policies for each device. As a result, the existing frameworks for informed consent may become increasingly inadequate in the face of rapid technological advancements. To address these challenges, it is essential for organizations to adopt a more holistic approach to consent that considers the complexities of IoT and prioritizes transparency and user control, thereby ensuring that individuals are adequately informed and empowered in their interactions with connected devices.

Evolving Data Practices and Continuous Consent

The dynamic and fast-paced nature of technological development complicates the process of maintaining informed consent. As data practices evolve—often due to advances in analytics, AI, or new business models—organizations may begin using collected data in ways that were not initially disclosed to users. For example, data gathered for improving customer service could later be repurposed for targeted advertising or sold to third-party partners, extending beyond the original scope of consent. This shifting context means that consent, even if informed at the time of collection, may no longer be valid, as users may not be aware of these changes. Consequently, the ethical imperative to respect individual autonomy and decision-making becomes increasingly challenging. Organizations must navigate the fine line between leveraging data for business growth and maintaining user trust, necessitating a thoughtful approach to informed consent that adapts to technological advancements.

Maintaining informed consent in such cases requires a continuous process of re-engagement with users, regularly updating them about changes in data practices and obtaining renewed consent. This ongoing dialogue can be resource-intensive and may pose logistical challenges for organizations, particularly as they scale operations. Fostering a transparent communication channel, however, helps reinforce user trust and confidence in the organization's commitment to ethical data practices.

Employing proactive strategies, such as periodic notifications about data usage and clear explanations of any new purposes for data collection, can help ensure that users remain informed and empowered. By prioritizing this dynamic approach to informed consent, organizations not only uphold ethical standards but also cultivate a more trusting relationship with their users, which ultimately benefits both parties in the long run.

The Role of User Education and Regulatory Support

Another key consideration is the role of user education in achieving informed consent. Individuals must be equipped with the knowledge and skills to navigate the complexities of digital data practices and understand their rights regarding data privacy. This requires clearer communication from organizations and broader initiatives aimed at enhancing digital literacy among users. Educational programs focusing on data ethics, privacy rights, and the implications of data sharing can empower individuals to make informed choices about their personal information. By fostering a more informed user base, organizations can ensure that consumers engage with digital technologies more critically and thoughtfully. This not only enhances user autonomy but also helps create a culture of accountability where individuals feel empowered to advocate for their rights and demand transparency in how their data is handled.

Additionally, the challenge of achieving informed consent highlights the need for regulatory frameworks that prioritize individual rights while promoting ethical data practices. Policymakers must establish clear standards and guidelines for obtaining informed consent that account for the complexities of digital interactions and technological advancements. Such regulations should aim to simplify consent mechanisms, ensuring they are accessible and comprehensible to all users, regardless of their technical proficiency.

Moreover, continuous collaboration between organizations, educators, and regulatory bodies can help address emerging challenges in data governance. In summary, while achieving informed consent in the digital age is fraught with challenges, it is essential for safeguarding individual rights and fostering trust in digital ecosystems. A concerted effort toward user education and regulatory clarity can pave the way for more ethical data practices, ultimately benefiting both individuals and organizations alike.

DATA OWNERSHIP

Empowering Individuals Through Data Ownership

The concept of data ownership is central to the ethical handling of personal information, asserting that individuals should have control and ownership rights over the data that pertains to them. This principle asserts that personal data is not just a collection of information but an extension of a person's identity, deserving of the same respect and protection as any other personal property. Recognizing data ownership emphasizes the importance of viewing personal information through the lens of individual rights and autonomy. It calls for a paradigm shift where data is not merely exploited for commercial gain but treated as a valuable asset that reflects an individual's preferences, experiences, and beliefs. In this framework, individuals should be empowered to make decisions regarding who can access their data, how it is used, and whether it can be shared with third parties.

Implementing data ownership can lead to a more ethical and equitable digital landscape, fostering a sense of trust between individuals and organizations. When people feel that they have a genuine stake in their data, they are more likely to engage with digital services that respect their privacy and uphold their rights. This empowerment encourages transparency in data practices, as organizations must articulate how they handle personal information and justify their data usage.

Furthermore, embracing data ownership can inspire innovative business models that prioritize ethical data practices, shifting the focus from exploitation to collaboration. By enabling individuals to exercise their rights over their data, we can create an environment that not only respects personal autonomy but also promotes accountability and responsible stewardship of information in an increasingly data-driven world.

Empowerment Through Informed Decision-Making

One of the most important aspects of treating individuals as data owners is the idea of informed decision-making. When people own their data, they have the right to be informed about how their information is collected, processed, and utilized. This transparency allows individuals to make choices based on a comprehensive understanding of the implications of sharing their data, enabling them to give informed consent—or to opt out if they are uncomfortable with the terms. Ownership not only provides individuals with a voice in the management of their data but also fosters a more equitable relationship between users and organizations. This shift from being passive subjects in a data-driven economy to active participants empowers individuals to make decisions that align with their values and privacy preferences.

In an era where data is often used in ways that exceed individuals' initial expectations—such as for targeted advertising, behavioral profiling, and even surveillance—this sense of control becomes increasingly critical. As technological advancements continue to blur the lines between personal privacy and data utility, individuals must have the ability to delineate how their data is used, ensuring it aligns with their personal ethics and circumstances. This proactive stance allows for a more ethical approach to data practices, as individuals can withdraw consent at any point, thereby reinforcing their ownership and control over personal information. By prioritizing informed decision-making, society can create a framework that values individual autonomy and dignity, ultimately leading to more responsible and ethical data usage across industries.

Ethical Implications of Data Ownership

From an ethical perspective, recognizing individuals as data owners acknowledges their fundamental rights to privacy and dignity. This principle asserts that personal data is an extension of a person's identity, deserving of respect and protection similar to other forms of personal property. When organizations uphold these ownership rights, they shift the narrative away from treating personal data merely as a commodity that can be bought, sold, or exploited. Instead, this recognition fosters an environment where individuals can exercise agency over their information, ensuring that it is used in ways that align with their values and preferences. This ethical stance reinforces the idea that individuals are entitled to control how their data is collected, used, and shared, thereby affirming their rights to privacy and autonomy.

Moreover, respecting data ownership allows individuals to protect themselves from misuse, such as unauthorized sharing or discriminatory profiling. By placing control in the hands of individuals, this approach reduces the power imbalance between large, data-driven corporations and the individuals whose data fuels their business models. Organizations that embrace data ownership principles are more likely to engage in ethical data practices, prioritizing transparency and accountability. This not only helps mitigate risks associated with data exploitation but also fosters trust and loyalty among users. In a landscape where data breaches and privacy violations are increasingly prevalent, empowering individuals as data owners becomes crucial in creating a more equitable and respectful digital ecosystem that values the rights and dignity of every person.

Building Trust Through Data Ownership

Recognizing individuals as data owners fosters a greater level of trust between people and organizations. When data subjects have ownership over their information, they are more likely to engage with entities that demonstrate respect for their rights. This ownership paradigm allows individuals to make informed choices about how their data is used, reinforcing their sense of autonomy and agency in a data-driven world. Transparency, informed consent, and the ability to exercise rights over personal data become integral to establishing a trustworthy relationship between users and organizations. When individuals are aware of how their data is being collected, stored, and utilized, they are more inclined to share their information, knowing they retain control over it. This mutual understanding encourages open communication and fosters a collaborative atmosphere where trust can flourish.

Organizations that actively communicate their data practices and prioritize user control create an environment where individuals feel valued and respected. By implementing clear privacy policies, providing accessible consent mechanisms, and encouraging feedback from users, organizations demonstrate their commitment to ethical data governance. This proactive approach not only enhances user engagement but also leads to more meaningful interactions between companies and their customers. When users feel empowered and recognized as data owners, they are more likely to develop loyalty toward organizations that prioritize their rights and privacy. Ultimately, this trust is foundational for building long-term relationships in a digital landscape that increasingly relies on personal data, paving the way for sustainable business practices and customer satisfaction.

Strategic Advantage for Businesses

For businesses, respecting data ownership is not just about compliance; it is also a strategic advantage that can significantly enhance their competitive edge. In a world where consumers are increasingly concerned about privacy and data security, organizations that uphold data ownership rights are more likely to cultivate strong, long-term relationships with their customers. By prioritizing transparency and accountability in their data practices, businesses demonstrate a commitment to ethical standards that resonate with today's socially conscious consumers. This mutual trust and confidence create a favorable environment for customer engagement, as individuals are more willing to interact with companies that respect their privacy and allow them to retain control over their personal information.

Moreover, this trust is essential for fostering innovation and encouraging users to share data responsibly, ultimately benefiting both parties. When customers feel secure in how their data is handled, they are more likely to contribute information that can help organizations tailor products and services to meet their needs. By adopting practices that emphasize data ownership, organizations can differentiate themselves in the marketplace, positioning themselves as leaders in ethical data management. This differentiation not only attracts privacy-conscious consumers but also enhances brand reputation, paving the way for sustainable growth and customer loyalty. In this way, embracing data ownership rights transforms a regulatory obligation into a powerful business strategy that drives positive outcomes for both organizations and their customers.

Toward Ethical Data Governance

In conclusion, the recognition of individuals as data owners marks a fundamental shift toward a more ethical framework for data governance that prioritizes individual rights and autonomy. This principle underscores the importance of empowering individuals with ownership rights over their personal information, enabling them to make informed decisions about how their data is collected, used, and shared. By doing so, we can mitigate the risks associated with data misuse, such as unauthorized access, discriminatory practices, and breaches of privacy. In this more equitable digital landscape, ethical data practices are not just encouraged but are integral to maintaining trust and fostering positive relationships between individuals and organizations.

As the conversation around data ownership continues to evolve, it is crucial for organizations, regulators, and individuals to collaborate in upholding the rights of data owners. This partnership can foster a culture of transparency, trust, and respect in handling personal information, where individuals feel valued and secure in their digital interactions. By engaging in ongoing dialogue and developing robust regulatory frameworks that reflect the needs and rights of data owners, we can cultivate an ethical and responsible approach to data governance. Such collaborative efforts will ultimately benefit society as a whole, paving the way for a digital ecosystem where privacy is safeguarded, and ethical considerations guide the development and use of technology.

NAVIGATING OWNERSHIP AND BUSINESS USAGE ETHICS

Balancing Ownership and Business Needs

Balancing the concept of data ownership with business needs presents significant ethical and operational challenges, particularly as organizations increasingly rely on data to drive insights, personalize services, and enhance customer experiences. The immense value of data fuels everything from targeted advertising to predictive analytics and AI-driven innovations.

As companies strive to harness this wealth of information, they may inadvertently prioritize their objectives over the privacy and autonomy of individuals. For instance, aggressive data collection practices can lead to situations where consumers feel surveilled or manipulated, ultimately resulting in a negative perception of the brand. This tension between the desire for innovative data use and the respect for individual rights necessitates a careful reevaluation of how data practices are structured and implemented within organizations.

Furthermore, the pursuit of business objectives can sometimes conflict with individuals' rights to control their data, leading to privacy violations and exploitation. This dissonance can erode trust between consumers and businesses, as individuals may become wary of how their personal information is being utilized. As consumers grow more informed about their data rights and increasingly demand transparency, businesses must adopt ethical frameworks that prioritize both data ownership and their commercial goals. By doing so, organizations can not only enhance consumer trust and loyalty but also foster a sustainable business model that respects individual rights.

Establishing clear guidelines for ethical data practices—such as obtaining informed consent, minimizing data collection, and ensuring data security—can help reconcile the need for innovation with the imperative of protecting personal information, ultimately leading to a healthier relationship between consumers and businesses.

Transparent Data-Handling Practices

To ethically balance the needs of businesses with individuals' ownership rights, organizations must adopt transparent and fair data-handling practices. Implementing clear data-sharing policies is essential for informing users about how their information will be used, empowering them to make informed decisions regarding their data. This transparency not only helps in building trust but also aligns with the growing public demand for accountability in data practices.

Providing users with the ability to opt in or out of data collection activities is another critical component of ethical data management. By giving individuals control over their data, organizations can foster a sense of respect and agency, making users feel more secure in their interactions with digital platforms. Furthermore, adhering to the principle of data minimization—collecting only the information necessary for a specific purpose—can significantly reduce the risk of privacy violations and enhance the overall integrity of data practices.

In addition to transparency and data minimization, meaningful consent mechanisms play a vital role in balancing business needs with individual ownership rights. These mechanisms should ensure that users are fully informed about how their data will be used beyond its initial collection purpose. For instance, if data collected for a specific service is later used for targeted marketing or analytics, users should have the opportunity to consent to this additional use. Such practices not only reinforce the idea of data ownership but also empower individuals to maintain control over their personal information.

Moreover, organizations that prioritize ethical data management through clear policies and meaningful consent are likely to cultivate greater consumer loyalty and trust. This, in turn, creates a more sustainable business model that respects individual rights while achieving commercial objectives, leading to a mutually beneficial relationship between businesses and their customers.

Shift to Data Stewardship

Another critical aspect of balancing data ownership with business needs is the shift from data ownership to data stewardship. This change in perspective recognizes that personal data should not be seen merely as a corporate asset to be exploited for profit; instead, companies are increasingly called upon to act as responsible stewards of the information they collect.

Ethical data stewardship involves acknowledging that while organizations may process data for specific business purposes, the ultimate ownership of that data resides with the individual. This shift necessitates a fundamental change in how businesses approach data management, compelling them to treat personal information with respect and integrity. By prioritizing the privacy and interests of data subjects, companies can build a more ethical framework that aligns with societal expectations regarding data use.

Implementing privacy-by-design principles is vital to this stewardship model, as it integrates data protection and user control into products, services, and business processes from the outset. This proactive approach ensures that privacy considerations are embedded in the development lifecycle, rather than treated as an afterthought or merely a compliance requirement. By designing systems that prioritize user privacy and provide individuals with meaningful control over their data, organizations can foster greater trust and engagement from their customers.

Additionally, this framework encourages organizations to consider the ethical implications of their data practices continually, promoting a culture of accountability and responsibility. Ultimately, by embracing data stewardship, businesses can navigate the complexities of modern data governance while simultaneously meeting their operational needs and enhancing their reputations in an increasingly privacy-conscious market.

Transparency and Accountability

Transparency and accountability are essential components in effectively balancing data ownership with organizational needs. Companies must prioritize providing users with clear, concise, and accessible information regarding their data practices. This includes detailing what types of data are being collected, the rationale behind the collection, and the specific ways in which the data will be used.

By fostering transparency, organizations empower individuals to make informed choices about their data, ultimately creating a sense of security and trust regarding how their information is handled. When users feel confident that they understand the implications of their data sharing, they are more likely to engage willingly with organizations and their services.

Transparency alone is not enough, however; it must be paired with robust accountability frameworks that ensure organizations adhere to ethical data practices that go beyond mere legal compliance. Accountability means that companies must be prepared to justify their data usage practices and respond promptly to inquiries from consumers. This includes addressing any concerns related to privacy or the potential misuse of data, thereby reinforcing consumer trust. By establishing mechanisms for accountability, organizations can demonstrate their commitment to ethical standards and responsible data stewardship.

This proactive approach helps mitigate tensions that may arise between individual data ownership and corporate interests, allowing businesses to build lasting relationships with their customers based on mutual respect and understanding. Ultimately, prioritizing transparency and accountability not only benefits consumers but also enhances the long-term viability and reputation of organizations in a data-driven world.

The Role of Education in Ethical Data Management

Education plays a pivotal role in fostering an ethical data culture that respects individuals' ownership rights while simultaneously meeting business needs. Organizations should prioritize investment in educational initiatives aimed at both employees and consumers to enhance understanding of data practices, privacy rights, and the implications of data collection. By creating awareness around these topics, businesses empower individuals to make informed decisions regarding their personal information. This not only helps consumers navigate the complexities of data sharing but also encourages a sense of agency over their data, fostering a more trusting relationship with organizations.

Training employees on ethical data management is equally crucial, as those who handle data must fully understand and respect individual rights while recognizing the consequences of mismanaging personal information. This comprehensive approach ensures that employees are equipped with the necessary skills and knowledge to navigate ethical dilemmas in their work. Furthermore, providing resources for consumers to manage their data rights enhances transparency and enables individuals to take control of their information. Educational programs, workshops, and accessible online resources can demystify data practices, allowing users to comprehend their rights and how to exercise them effectively. This dual focus on employee training and consumer education contributes to a robust ethical data culture that benefits both individuals and organizations, promoting responsible data usage and reinforcing trust in the digital ecosystem.

Toward an Ethical Data Ecosystem

In conclusion, balancing data ownership with business needs is a complex endeavor that requires a multifaceted approach. Organizations must prioritize transparency, accountability, ethical stewardship, and education to effectively navigate the ethical challenges of data management. This includes being open about data practices, ensuring that individuals understand how their information is collected and used, and creating channels for them to voice concerns or withdraw consent. By fostering a culture of accountability, organizations can build trust with consumers, demonstrating that they are committed to respecting individual rights while achieving their business objectives. This proactive stance not only protects individuals' rights but also enhances businesses' reputations in an increasingly data-driven landscape.

As data continues to play a central role in the modern economy, developing frameworks that respect and empower individuals is crucial for ensuring that the benefits of data are shared equitably and ethically among all stakeholders. Organizations that successfully implement ethical data practices not only comply with regulatory standards but also position themselves as leaders in corporate responsibility. This alignment between ethical stewardship and business strategy creates a win-win scenario, where companies can innovate and thrive while consumers feel secure and respected. Ultimately, this balance between data ownership and business needs is vital for fostering a sustainable digital ecosystem that serves the interests of individuals, businesses, and society as a whole.

CHAPTER 5

PRIVACY IN DATA ETHICS

PRIVACY IN THE DIGITAL ERA

The Evolution of Privacy

Privacy in the digital age has transformed significantly, evolving from traditional notions of keeping personal information confidential to a complex and multifaceted concept. In today's digital landscape, privacy extends beyond mere physical boundaries, encompassing a vast range of considerations related to data collection, storage, and processing across multiple digital channels. This shift means that personal data is not only generated through direct interactions but also inferred through patterns of behavior, location tracking, and social interactions online. As a result, the scope of digital privacy now involves a more profound understanding of how individuals' data can be utilized, aggregated, and shared by various entities, often without their explicit consent. The implications of this transformation are far-reaching, as individuals find themselves navigating a landscape where their digital footprints are constantly monitored and analyzed.

Digital privacy grants individuals the right to control who has access to their personal data and the ability to make informed choices about data sharing. Achieving this level of control is increasingly challenging, though, due to the complexities of data ecosystems and the often-opaque nature of data practices employed by organizations. The rapid advancement of technology, including the rise of AI, big data analytics, and IoT, has further blurred the lines of personal privacy. Individuals frequently encounter intricate privacy policies that are laden with legal jargon, making it difficult for them to fully comprehend their rights and the implications of sharing their data.

As society becomes increasingly reliant on digital platforms for everyday activities—from shopping and banking to socializing and healthcare—promoting digital literacy and awareness becomes essential. Individuals must be equipped with the knowledge and tools to navigate their rights and responsibilities in this evolving digital landscape, ensuring that their privacy is respected and safeguarded.

Informational Self-Determination and Autonomy

The understanding of privacy has expanded to encompass not just the right to keep information confidential but also the necessity for individuals to actively engage with how their data is collected, used, and shared. In the digital age, privacy is increasingly viewed as a dynamic and interactive process, requiring individuals to be informed and proactive about their personal information. This shift emphasizes the importance of transparency in data practices, as individuals must be made aware of what data is being collected, the purposes for which it is used, and the potential consequences of sharing their information.

For organizations, this means moving beyond merely complying with legal requirements; they have a responsibility to communicate their data practices clearly and provide users with the tools to manage their privacy preferences effectively. This active engagement empowers individuals to assert their rights and ensures that privacy is not merely an afterthought but a fundamental aspect of their digital experience, fostering a more respectful relationship between users and technology.

The principle of informational self-determination is central to this modern concept of privacy, empowering individuals to decide how their personal information is utilized. This principle recognizes that individuals should have a say in their digital identities, ensuring they are not merely subjects of data collection but active participants in determining the fate of their information. By promoting this sense of ownership and responsibility, individuals are better positioned to navigate the complexities of the digital landscape, where personal information can be easily commodified and exploited. This empowerment is especially critical in a world where data-driven technologies influence various aspects of life, from targeted advertising to social interactions and even public policy. As individuals gain greater control over their data, they are more likely to engage critically with the technologies they use and advocate for their rights, thereby enhancing their agency in the digital space.

Encouraging individuals to take an active role in managing their data fosters a culture of privacy that values personal agency and autonomy, ultimately contributing to a more ethical and equitable digital ecosystem. By equipping individuals with the knowledge and tools necessary to understand their rights and responsibilities, society can create an environment where privacy is respected and upheld. This cultural shift not only benefits individuals but also incentivizes organizations to adopt ethical data practices that prioritize user consent and transparency.

As individuals increasingly recognize their power in the digital age, they can push back against exploitative practices and advocate for policies that protect their rights. In this way, the principle of informational self-determination not only enhances individual autonomy but also contributes to a collective movement toward a more just and respectful digital society, where privacy is recognized as a fundamental human right.

Managing the Digital Footprint

In the modern context, privacy encompasses the management of one's digital footprint, a task that has become increasingly challenging due to the proliferation of technologies such as social media, IoT, and big data analytics. These advancements have blurred the lines between private and public information, complicating how individuals perceive and maintain their privacy. Social media platforms, for instance, encourage users to share personal experiences, thoughts, and photographs with wide audiences, often leading to oversharing without a clear understanding of the potential long-term implications.

This culture of openness can inadvertently expose sensitive information, making it easier for others to access and misuse that data. In a world where everything from a casual post to a seemingly harmless photo can become part of an individual's digital identity, it is essential for users to understand the implications of their online activities. Meanwhile, IoT devices, which gather data from everyday activities—such as fitness trackers, smart home devices, and connected appliances—continuously contribute to a digital footprint that is often beyond the individual's immediate control.

The pervasive nature of this data collection can lead to individuals being constantly tracked and profiled, frequently without their knowledge or explicit consent. As users engage with various platforms and devices, they often leave behind traces of their preferences, behaviors, and interactions that are aggregated and analyzed for commercial gain. This results in a growing sense of vulnerability and loss of control over personal information, as individuals find themselves subjected to profiling and targeted marketing based on their digital behaviors.

The implications of this extensive data tracking extend beyond mere commercial interests; they can also affect personal privacy, security, and autonomy. This feeling of being under surveillance can have profound psychological effects, leading to anxiety and a diminished sense of personal freedom. The constant awareness of being monitored can hinder individuals from expressing themselves freely or exploring new ideas, further reinforcing the need for effective management of their digital footprints.

Moreover, the lack of transparency in how data is collected, stored, and utilized exacerbates these concerns, leaving individuals unsure about who holds their data and how it is being used. Many users are unaware of the extent to which their data is shared with third parties, often hidden behind lengthy privacy policies that few take the time to read. Consequently, the modern landscape of privacy necessitates a more proactive approach, where individuals are equipped with the knowledge and tools to manage their digital footprints effectively. This involves not only understanding the privacy settings of social media and IoT devices but also actively making choices that align with their privacy preferences.

Educational initiatives that promote digital literacy and awareness about data privacy can empower individuals to take control of their digital identities. By fostering a culture of informed decision-making and encouraging responsible sharing, we can ensure that individuals maintain control over their personal information in an increasingly interconnected world, ultimately enhancing their sense of security and autonomy.

Protecting Sensitive Data and Addressing Vulnerabilities

Privacy in the digital age is crucial for protecting sensitive data, including health records, financial information, and personally identifiable information (PII). The vulnerabilities associated with this type of data—especially in a landscape where cyber threats are increasingly sophisticated—underscore the necessity for robust privacy measures. As individuals share personal information online, often in exchange for services or convenience, the risk of unauthorized access and misuse grows exponentially.

Cybercriminals are constantly evolving their tactics, making it imperative for individuals and organizations to remain vigilant in their data protection efforts. Data breaches can have devastating consequences, leading not only to financial loss but also to identity theft, reputational damage, and emotional distress. Consequently, the imperative to ensure the confidentiality and security of sensitive information is more urgent than ever. Organizations must prioritize privacy by integrating advanced security protocols into their operations, recognizing that safeguarding personal data is not just a legal obligation but a critical aspect of maintaining consumer trust.

To effectively protect sensitive data, organizations must implement stringent data protection measures that encompass a variety of strategies, including encryption, access controls, and regular audits. Encryption acts as a protective barrier, ensuring that even if data is intercepted, it remains unreadable without the proper decryption keys. This is particularly important for sensitive information, as encrypted data provides a layer of security that can deter unauthorized access. Access controls limit who can view or manipulate sensitive information, ensuring that only authorized personnel have the ability to access specific datasets. By implementing role-based access controls, organizations can further minimize the risk of insider threats and unauthorized data exposure.

Regular audits are essential for identifying vulnerabilities and assessing compliance with data protection policies. This proactive approach not only helps prevent data leaks and unauthorized access but also fosters a culture of accountability within organizations. Such measures signal to stakeholders that an organization is committed to protecting sensitive data, reinforcing trust and confidence in their operations.

In this context, the dual role of privacy becomes evident: it emphasizes the need for informed individuals who understand their rights regarding data use and the importance of secure handling of their information. As users become more aware of their rights and the potential risks associated with data sharing, they can make better-informed decisions about what information they disclose and to whom.

Educational initiatives focused on data privacy and security can empower individuals to recognize the value of their personal data and the importance of safeguarding it. Together, these elements contribute to a more resilient and trustworthy digital environment, where individuals can confidently engage with digital services while their personal information remains protected. In an era where data is often viewed as a commodity, fostering a culture of respect for privacy not only enhances individual autonomy but also supports the broader goal of creating a secure and ethical digital landscape for all users.

Transparency and Consent in Data Practices

Privacy in the digital age necessitates a commitment to transparency and consent in data-handling practices. Individuals must be provided with clear, accessible information about how their data is being collected, processed, and shared across various platforms. This transparency fosters trust between individuals and organizations, allowing users to make informed decisions about their privacy. When organizations proactively communicate their data practices and make it easy for individuals to understand what they are consenting to, they empower users to take control of their information. This approach is vital in a time when data is often collected in complex ways that can easily be misunderstood or overlooked. By establishing a culture of openness, organizations can mitigate concerns about data misuse and enhance user engagement, ultimately creating a more ethical digital ecosystem where individuals feel respected and valued.

Moreover, consent should not be treated as a mere checkbox but as an ongoing dialogue between organizations and individuals. This means providing individuals with the ability to easily modify their preferences regarding data usage and ensuring that they are informed about any changes in data practices. By adopting a more dynamic approach to consent, organizations recognize that privacy is not a one-time agreement but a continuous process that evolves with changing circumstances and user needs.

This evolving understanding of privacy compels organizations to adopt ethical data practices that prioritize the rights and autonomy of individuals. For instance, organizations could implement mechanisms that allow users to periodically review and update their consent preferences, which ensures that users remain informed and in control of their data. By embedding principles of transparency and consent into their data governance frameworks, organizations can demonstrate their commitment to ethical standards, ultimately fostering stronger relationships with users built on trust and mutual respect.

This focus on transparency and consent not only strengthens user trust but also enhances the overall integrity of the digital landscape. When individuals feel confident that their data is being handled responsibly and ethically, they are more likely to engage with digital services and share their information without fear of misuse. This positive relationship between users and organizations can lead to increased customer loyalty and long-term engagement, benefiting both parties. Furthermore, by prioritizing transparency and consent, organizations can position themselves as leaders in ethical data practices, differentiating themselves in a competitive market. In an era where consumers are increasingly concerned about their privacy, organizations that embrace these principles will likely gain a significant advantage, establishing themselves as trusted partners in navigating the complexities of the digital age.

Collective Effort for Ethical Privacy

As privacy continues to be redefined in the digital age, a collective effort among stakeholders is necessary to establish frameworks that prioritize individual rights while enabling the benefits of data sharing and technology. This requires collaboration between governments, regulatory bodies, organizations, and individuals to create standards that go beyond mere compliance with existing laws. Organizations must actively participate in developing and adhering to ethical guidelines that foster a culture of respect and accountability in their data practices. By doing so, they not only protect consumer privacy but also enhance their reputation and credibility in a market increasingly concerned with ethical considerations. This proactive approach ensures that the technological advancements we embrace are grounded in the principles of respect and dignity for individuals.

By fostering transparency, consent, and responsible data-handling, we can empower individuals to take control of their personal data in an increasingly interconnected world. This empowerment is crucial for fostering a sense of security and trust, enabling users to engage more freely with digital services and technologies. As individuals become more aware of their rights and the implications of data sharing, they are better positioned to make informed choices that align with their values and privacy preferences. Ultimately, this collective commitment to ethical data practices leads to a more secure and trustworthy digital landscape, where the benefits of data sharing can be realized without compromising individual rights. By prioritizing the protection of personal data, we can ensure that technological progress serves the interests of all stakeholders, fostering a more equitable and ethical digital future.

CONSEQUENCES OF PRIVACY BREACHES

The Impact of Privacy Breaches on Individuals and Organizations

Privacy breaches can have serious and far-reaching consequences, impacting not only individuals but also organizations and the broader community. When personal information is compromised, individuals may face identity theft, financial loss, and emotional distress, which can undermine their trust in digital services. For organizations, the repercussions can be equally severe, including significant financial penalties, damage to reputation, and loss of customer loyalty, all of which can hinder long-term growth and stability. As technology continues to evolve, the potential for breaches increases, necessitating a deeper understanding of their implications and the urgent need for robust data protection measures to safeguard personal information effectively.

Consequences for Individuals

For individuals, the repercussions of a privacy breach can be profound and multifaceted. Compromised personal information—such as social security numbers, bank account details, or health records—can lead to identity theft and financial fraud. Victims may experience immediate financial losses due to unauthorized transactions or loans taken out in their names, resulting in a chaotic and stressful situation. This sense of violation is exacerbated by the fact that many individuals may not discover the breach until significant damage has been done, further complicating the recovery process.

The aftermath of a data breach often involves a long and arduous journey to restore one's financial reputation, which can include disputing fraudulent charges, contacting banks, and possibly engaging in legal action to rectify their credit reports. This lengthy ordeal not only drains time and resources but can also leave individuals feeling vulnerable and overwhelmed, as they grapple with the consequences of an invasion of their privacy.

Beyond the financial implications, privacy breaches can inflict significant emotional distress, leading to anxiety, embarrassment, and a pervasive fear of further violations of privacy. The psychological impact of such breaches is often underestimated; individuals may find themselves constantly on guard, second-guessing their digital interactions, and avoiding online platforms altogether. This heightened sense of vigilance can create a barrier to engaging with digital technology, limiting opportunities for personal and professional growth. The emotional toll of being a victim of privacy breaches can result in a diminished sense of safety and trust in the digital world, which is critical for modern life. Over time, this anxiety can escalate into chronic stress, negatively affecting overall mental health and well-being, leaving individuals struggling to reclaim a sense of normalcy in their lives.

As trust in digital services erodes, people may withdraw from opportunities that require the sharing of personal information, ultimately limiting their access to essential services and hindering their ability to fully participate in a technology-driven society. This withdrawal can manifest in various ways, such as opting out of beneficial online services, avoiding social media, or forgoing health technology that requires personal data sharing. In a world that increasingly relies on data for services, this aversion can lead to social isolation and a diminished quality of life. Furthermore, it can perpetuate a cycle of exclusion, where those who are most vulnerable to privacy breaches are also the ones who are least able to access the benefits of technology. Therefore, the consequences of privacy breaches extend far beyond immediate financial loss, shaping individuals' relationships with technology and impacting their broader engagement in society.

The Impact on Organizations

On the organizational side, privacy breaches carry substantial risks that can threaten both financial stability and brand reputation. Companies that fail to implement adequate data protection measures often face severe penalties under regulations such as the GDPR or the CCPA. Non-compliance can result in hefty fines that jeopardize an organization's financial health, particularly for smaller businesses that may not have the resources to absorb such losses. The costs associated with a breach extend beyond fines; organizations may incur additional expenses related to incident response, legal fees, and public relations efforts to mitigate the fallout from a breach. This financial strain can divert resources away from innovation and growth, hampering overall business performance and limiting the organization's ability to invest in future opportunities.

Beyond immediate financial implications, breaches erode consumer trust, making it challenging for companies to rebuild their reputation. As consumers become more aware of data privacy issues, they tend to gravitate toward businesses that prioritize the protection of their information. This shift in consumer behavior can have a lasting impact on a company's market position, as loyal customers may seek alternatives after a breach. The repercussions of lost trust can be far-reaching, affecting not only current customer relationships but also potential partnerships and collaborations.

Rebuilding trust often requires companies to invest heavily in new security measures, transparency initiatives, and community outreach, which can take significant time and effort to implement effectively. In a competitive landscape where data security is increasingly seen as a vital aspect of customer service, organizations that fail to address privacy concerns may find themselves at a significant disadvantage.

Furthermore, the impact of privacy breaches can also influence an organization's ability to attract and retain talent. Employees are increasingly concerned about the ethical implications of the companies they work for, and a history of privacy violations can deter potential candidates from applying. A tarnished reputation in data privacy can lead to high employee turnover rates, as current employees may seek out more secure and trustworthy work environments. This challenge not only affects staffing and operational continuity but can also diminish the overall morale of existing employees who may feel uneasy about their organization's commitment to ethical practices. As privacy becomes a cornerstone of corporate responsibility, organizations must recognize that their data-handling practices will not only affect their customer relationships but also shape their internal culture and overall success in the marketplace.

Legal and Financial Ramifications

The consequences of privacy breaches extend beyond immediate financial losses and reputational harm; they also expose organizations to legal risks that can have far-reaching implications. A high-profile data breach often invites litigation, resulting in lawsuits and potential class-action claims from affected individuals seeking redress for the mishandling of their personal information. The legal landscape surrounding data privacy is complex, with various laws and regulations dictating the obligations of organizations to protect consumer data.

Laws such as the GDPR in Europe and the CCPA in the United States impose strict requirements on organizations regarding data protection, consent, and breach notifications. As a result, companies can find themselves ensnared in lengthy legal battles, which not only drain financial resources but can also distract leadership from focusing on core business objectives and strategic initiatives. These legal challenges often come with significant financial penalties, which can compound the original costs of a breach.

Moreover, managing the legal aspects of a breach can divert organizational resources from critical areas such as product development or customer service. The financial burden of litigation, combined with the costs associated with incident response strategies and public relations efforts, can strain a company's budget. Organizations may also face increased scrutiny from regulators and stakeholders, leading to potential compliance audits or investigations that require further allocation of time and resources. For instance, a company found in violation of data protection laws might have to undertake extensive compliance measures, incurring additional expenses while diverting attention from strategic initiatives.

In the aftermath of a breach, businesses must invest significantly in improved cybersecurity measures to prevent future incidents, which can lead to an environment of uncertainty and apprehension among employees and customers alike. Consequently, the legal ramifications of a privacy breach can create a cycle of financial strain, operational disruption, and reputational damage that may take years to fully recover from.

Finally, the financial and legal repercussions of privacy breaches can have a broader impact on market dynamics and competition. Companies that suffer breaches may find it challenging to secure partnerships or attract investors, as stakeholders may view them as high-risk entities. This diminished investor confidence can limit growth opportunities and affect long-term sustainability. Additionally, competitors may seize the opportunity to capture market share by emphasizing their commitment to data protection and ethical practices.

In an environment where consumer awareness of data privacy is rising, organizations that fail to effectively manage their privacy obligations may find themselves at a competitive disadvantage, struggling to regain trust in a marketplace that increasingly prioritizes security and ethical data-handling. Ultimately, the legal and financial ramifications of privacy breaches can resonate throughout the organization, affecting not only immediate operations but also long-term viability and strategic positioning in the industry.

Broader Community and Regulatory Implications

The implications of privacy breaches extend far beyond the immediate impacts on affected individuals and organizations; they resonate throughout entire sectors and communities. As data breaches become more prevalent, there is a growing awareness among regulators and policymakers about the vulnerabilities inherent in data-handling practices.

This increased scrutiny often results in pressure on industries to adopt more rigorous data protection measures.

Consequently, public policy is likely to evolve, with governments implementing stricter regulations and standards that mandate heightened accountability for organizations that collect and process personal information. Such changes could include stricter penalties for non-compliance and more comprehensive reporting requirements, compelling organizations to reevaluate and enhance their data management practices. This ripple effect underscores the collective responsibility of the community to uphold data protection standards, as the actions of one organization can impact the perceptions and expectations of consumers regarding the entire industry.

In response to these regulatory shifts, organizations may find themselves needing to invest significantly in their cybersecurity infrastructure and employee training programs to comply with the new legal frameworks. This proactive approach not only helps to safeguard sensitive data but also demonstrates a commitment to consumer protection, which can foster public trust. By establishing strong data governance frameworks and transparent data-handling practices, organizations can position themselves as ethical leaders in their respective fields.

The necessity for robust privacy protection measures becomes increasingly evident as the landscape of data privacy continues to evolve, with technological advancements and changing consumer expectations driving the demand for greater accountability and transparency. Moreover, by engaging in ongoing dialogue with regulators and stakeholders, organizations can contribute to shaping the future of data privacy legislation, ensuring that regulations remain relevant and effective.

As industries adapt to the evolving regulatory environment, those that prioritize ethical data management and compliance will likely emerge as leaders in an increasingly competitive marketplace. The commitment to safeguarding personal information not only enhances consumer confidence and loyalty but also mitigates the risks associated with privacy breaches.

Additionally, organizations that are proactive in their approach to data protection may also gain a competitive advantage by differentiating themselves from those that are reactive or neglectful. This creates a positive feedback loop: as organizations strengthen their privacy practices, they not only protect their customers but also contribute to a broader culture of accountability and respect for personal data across the community. Ultimately, the collective effort to address privacy concerns can lead to a more secure and trustworthy digital ecosystem, benefiting both individuals and organizations while fostering a sustainable environment for innovation and growth.

Cultural and Societal Effects

The societal implications of privacy breaches are profound, significantly affecting public trust in both institutions and the technologies that shape everyday life. As more individuals become aware of the risks associated with sharing personal information, they may grow hesitant to engage with digital platforms, online services, and emerging technologies. This reluctance can stifle innovation, as data-driven solutions—ranging from personalized healthcare to smart city initiatives—rely heavily on public participation and the free flow of information. When people lose confidence in how their data is handled, they may opt out of digital ecosystems, reducing opportunities for advancements that depend on big data and widespread user engagement. As a result, the broader societal benefits that digital innovations promise—such as improved public services, enhanced convenience, and more personalized experiences—could be significantly curtailed, leaving communities without the improvements that such technologies can offer.

This growing mistrust can also lead to a backlash against technology companies, many of which are seen as prioritizing profit over privacy. High-profile breaches often trigger public outrage, prompting individuals to demand accountability and reform from organizations that mishandle personal data. In response, there is an increasing movement toward data protection and privacy advocacy, with both individuals and organizations calling for stronger safeguards to protect personal information. This shift in public sentiment emphasizes the need for companies to adopt a more consumer-centric approach, where ethical considerations are woven into the fabric of their operations. By proactively addressing privacy concerns, companies can work to regain public confidence, demonstrating that they prioritize user rights over mere profitability.

Addressing privacy breaches effectively requires more than just enhanced security measures; it demands a fundamental shift in the way data privacy is valued and treated by institutions. Companies must commit to fostering a culture of privacy awareness, embedding ethical data practices into their operations, and demonstrating respect for individuals' rights. This cultural transformation within organizations is crucial not only for rebuilding public trust but also for ensuring that technological advancements can continue to thrive in a way that aligns with societal values and expectations. As a result, organizations that prioritize privacy and ethics can create a more balanced and responsible digital future, where innovation flourishes alongside robust protections for individuals. This harmonious coexistence can ultimately lead to a more equitable society, where technology serves the public good without compromising personal rights.

Ensuring Ethical Responsibility in Data Privacy

In conclusion, the ramifications of privacy breaches are vast and complex, affecting individuals, organizations, and society as a whole. For individuals, the consequences can be deeply personal, leading to significant emotional and financial distress that can linger long after a breach occurs. Victims often grapple with identity theft, unauthorized transactions, and the long, arduous process of restoring their financial standing, all of which can severely impact their quality of life. Meanwhile, organizations face the dual threat of reputational damage and potential legal consequences, including hefty fines and litigation costs. The ramifications extend beyond immediate harm; as public trust diminishes, businesses may struggle to maintain customer loyalty and confidence in their brand.

Moreover, the broader community may experience shifts in public trust toward institutions and a heightened regulatory environment, prompting governments to impose stricter data protection laws. This reality underscores the necessity for organizations to adopt proactive data protection measures that go beyond mere compliance with legal requirements. In navigating this increasingly data-driven world, it is crucial to recognize the importance of privacy and the need for ethical data practices. By prioritizing ethical considerations and transparent practices, organizations can foster trust and ensure the responsible handling of personal information. This commitment not only contributes to a safer digital landscape but also paves the way for a sustainable digital future where the rights and dignity of individuals are respected.

CHAPTER 6

SECURITY IN DATA ETHICS

EFFECTIVE DATA SECURITY METHODS

The Importance of Data Security

To ensure the ethical handling of data and protect against unauthorized access or breaches, organizations must adopt best practices for data security. This involves implementing robust security measures such as encryption, firewalls, and multi-factor authentication (MFA) to protect sensitive information from potential cyber threats. Additionally, organizations should conduct regular security audits and vulnerability assessments to identify and address weaknesses in their data protection strategies. The evolving landscape of cyber threats necessitates a proactive approach to safeguard sensitive information and maintain consumer trust, ultimately fostering a culture of accountability and responsibility in data management.

Encryption: A Fundamental Security Measure

One of the most fundamental security measures is encryption, which involves converting sensitive information into an unreadable format that's accessible only to individuals with authorized decryption keys. This process serves as a robust defense against unauthorized access, ensuring that even if data is intercepted during transmission or storage, it remains unusable to malicious parties. For instance, encrypting personal information, such as Social Security numbers or financial details, can significantly prevent identity theft and financial fraud in the event of a data breach. By employing strong encryption protocols, organizations can create a formidable barrier that protects their most sensitive data, thereby bolstering consumer confidence in their data security practices.

Furthermore, encryption acts as a proactive strategy that enhances the overall security posture of an organization by establishing a baseline level of data confidentiality that must be maintained. This not only ensures compliance with various data protection regulations but also mitigates the risk of reputational damage resulting from data breaches. Additionally, encryption fosters a culture of accountability within organizations, as employees are trained to recognize the importance of protecting sensitive information through secure practices. As cyber threats continue to evolve, maintaining robust encryption practices will be vital for organizations looking to safeguard their data and retain the trust of their customers.

Strong Authentication Mechanisms

In addition to encryption, strong authentication mechanisms are essential for enhancing data security. MFA is particularly effective, requiring users to verify their identities through multiple means before accessing systems or sensitive data. This approach mitigates the risk of unauthorized access, even if login credentials have been compromised. For example, an organization could implement MFA by requiring users to enter a password followed by a verification code sent to their mobile device. This additional layer of security significantly reduces the likelihood of unauthorized access, making it much more difficult for attackers to exploit stolen credentials. Moreover, incorporating biometrics—such as fingerprint scanning or facial recognition—into the authentication process can further strengthen security, adding another barrier that potential intruders must overcome.

Combining MFA with user training on recognizing suspicious login attempts fortifies defenses against common attack vectors, such as credential stuffing or phishing attacks. Organizations should regularly conduct awareness programs to educate employees about the latest cybersecurity threats and the importance of maintaining secure authentication practices. This proactive approach not only empowers users to identify and report potential security issues but also fosters a culture of security mindfulness within the organization. By making employees active participants in the organization's data security strategy, organizations can enhance their overall resilience against cyber threats. Implementing strong authentication measures alongside comprehensive user training is vital for safeguarding sensitive data and maintaining consumer trust in today's increasingly digital landscape.

Principle of Least Privilege and Security Audits

Another best practice for data security is adhering to the principle of least privilege, which limits data access strictly to individuals whose job roles require it. This principle is critical in minimizing the risk of insider threats, as it prevents employees from accessing sensitive information that is not pertinent to their work. For example, an employee in the marketing department does not need access to confidential financial records, and restricting such access helps mitigate the risk of unintentional leaks or malicious misuse. By ensuring that employees only have access to the information necessary for their roles, organizations can reduce the potential attack surface available to external malicious actors. This strategic limitation not only enhances data protection but also encourages a culture of responsibility among employees regarding the handling of sensitive information.

Additionally, regular security audits and vulnerability assessments play a crucial role in identifying and addressing potential weaknesses in security systems before they can be exploited. By systematically evaluating security protocols and conducting thorough vulnerability scans, organizations can uncover gaps that may leave them susceptible to attacks. Implementing thorough logging and monitoring mechanisms further enhances security by helping to detect suspicious activities and respond to incidents promptly. These systems can track user behavior, alerting administrators to any anomalies that may indicate a breach or unauthorized access attempts. The combination of limited access, proactive auditing, and vigilant monitoring creates a robust security framework that safeguards sensitive data and maintains consumer trust in an organization's commitment to data protection.

Employee Training and Incident Response Planning

Employee training is an equally important component of data security, as human error remains one of the most significant vulnerabilities in data systems. Employees may inadvertently expose sensitive information through careless practices, such as using weak passwords or mishandling data. They may also fall victim to sophisticated phishing attacks, leading to unauthorized access to sensitive information. Regular training sessions can equip employees with the knowledge and skills needed to recognize phishing emails, securely handle data, and adhere to organizational security policies. By fostering a culture of security awareness, organizations can significantly reduce the likelihood of data breaches caused by human error, empowering employees to take proactive steps to protect sensitive information.

In addition to ongoing training, organizations should develop well-defined incident response plans that enable them to act quickly and effectively in the event of a data breach. A comprehensive incident response plan outlines the steps to be taken when a breach occurs, including immediate containment measures, communication protocols, and notification procedures for affected individuals. This preparation minimizes damage and ensures business continuity by allowing organizations to address incidents with efficiency and clarity.

Moreover, conducting regular drills and simulations can help employees become familiar with their roles during a crisis, ensuring a coordinated response that mitigates the impact of a breach. Ultimately, investing in employee training and robust incident response strategies is essential for creating a resilient security posture that protects both sensitive data and the organization's reputation.

Physical Security Measures

Effective data security extends beyond digital measures, encompassing the implementation of robust physical security protocols to safeguard data infrastructure. Access controls, such as keycards, biometric identification, and security personnel, play a critical role in limiting physical access to sensitive areas, such as data centers and server rooms. By ensuring that only authorized personnel can enter these locations, organizations can significantly reduce the risk of unauthorized access, theft, or sabotage of essential hardware.

In addition to access controls, surveillance systems and alarm systems can further enhance security by monitoring for unusual activity and alerting personnel to potential breaches in real time. This multi-layered approach to physical security establishes a strong foundation for protecting sensitive information from a variety of threats.

Data Backup

Another vital practice in effective data security is the implementation of backup solutions to ensure that data remains intact and accessible in the event of hardware failures or cyberattacks, such as ransomware incidents. Regularly backing up essential information and storing those backups in secure, offsite locations not only preserves data but also enhances organizational resilience during emergencies. In the face of a cyberattack, having reliable backups can mean the difference between recovery and catastrophic data loss.

Moreover, organizations should conduct periodic tests of their backup systems to verify data integrity and the effectiveness of their recovery processes. By integrating these physical measures with digital practices, organizations create a holistic approach to data security that emphasizes the protection of personal information and maintains operational continuity even in challenging circumstances.

Building an Ethical Data Security Framework

By adhering to these best practices, organizations can create a robust defense against potential threats, effectively protecting personal data while demonstrating a strong commitment to ethical data-handling and privacy protection. The integration of encryption, strong authentication mechanisms, least privilege access protocols, employee training initiatives, incident response planning, and comprehensive physical security measures forms a comprehensive security framework that addresses various aspects of data protection. Each of these elements plays a crucial role in creating multiple layers of defense, ensuring that sensitive information remains secure from unauthorized access and breaches. This proactive stance not only fortifies the organization's defenses but also instills confidence in consumers, reinforcing their trust in the organization's ability to protect their personal information.

As data breaches grow increasingly sophisticated and commonplace, organizations prioritizing these best practices are better positioned to safeguard their data and maintain consumer trust. The commitment to ethical data-handling goes beyond compliance; it fosters a culture of respect for privacy that resonates with both employees and customers. By actively promoting ethical data practices that align with organizational values and societal expectations, businesses can differentiate themselves in a crowded marketplace. Such an approach not only protects sensitive information but also enhances the organization's reputation, attracting customers who prioritize data security and privacy. In a world where personal data is both valuable and vulnerable, organizations that embrace a proactive and ethical approach to data security can pave the way for a more trustworthy and responsible digital landscape.

BALANCING SECURITY, ACCESS, AND TRANSPARENCY

Ethical Dilemmas in Data Security

While robust security measures are essential for protecting data, they also come with ethical considerations, particularly regarding the balance between protection and the rights of individuals. Organizations must navigate the fine line between implementing strong security protocols and respecting the privacy of the individuals whose data they collect and process. For instance, aggressive monitoring measures designed to detect potential breaches can inadvertently infringe personal privacy, creating an environment of surveillance that may lead to distrust among employees and consumers. This ethical dilemma raises critical questions about how much intrusion is justified in the name of security and what safeguards are in place to ensure that personal rights are not sacrificed for the sake of organizational safety.

Organizations face pressing ethical dilemmas in their pursuit of effective data security that respects personal privacy while maintaining a transparent environment. Striking the right balance requires organizations to engage in open dialogue with stakeholders, including customers and employees, to understand their concerns about privacy and data security. Transparency in data practices can help alleviate fears and build trust, ensuring that individuals feel informed about how their data is being used and protected. Furthermore, organizations should seek to incorporate ethical frameworks into their data security strategies, ensuring that policies and practices prioritize not only the security of data but also the dignity and rights of individuals. By fostering a culture of ethical data stewardship, organizations can enhance their security measures while respecting the fundamental rights of those whose data they handle.

Surveillance Technologies and Privacy Concerns

One of the most significant ethical dilemmas involves the use of surveillance technologies to ensure data security. Organizations often employ techniques such as monitoring employee activities, tracking digital footprints, and deploying behavioral analytics to detect potential threats and prevent data breaches. While these practices can enhance security, they can also infringe personal privacy, creating a sense of distrust within the workplace. Employees may feel that they are being constantly watched, which can lead to anxiety, reduced morale, and a culture of fear rather than one of collaboration and trust. Therefore, organizations face the pressing challenge of implementing these measures transparently, ensuring that employees understand their purpose, the extent of monitoring, and how the collected data will be used. Clear communication and employee involvement in discussions about surveillance policies can help alleviate concerns and promote a more positive perception of security measures.

The challenge lies in implementing these surveillance measures proportionately and ethically, ensuring that they are strictly aligned with the risks they are designed to address. Organizations must carefully assess the potential impact of monitoring practices on employee privacy and overall workplace culture. Striking a balance between protecting sensitive information and maintaining a respectful work environment is crucial for fostering a culture of trust and ethical data-handling.

By establishing clear policies that define the scope and limitations of surveillance, organizations can help ensure that employees feel valued and respected. Additionally, regular reviews of monitoring practices can help organizations adapt to changing privacy expectations and legal requirements, creating an environment where security and privacy coexist harmoniously. Ultimately, addressing this ethical dilemma requires a commitment to not only safeguard data but also to uphold the dignity and rights of individuals within the workplace.

Balancing Security Controls with User Access

Another ethical challenge in data security is the necessity of balancing stringent security controls with providing users access to critical information. Overly restrictive security measures can hamper productivity, limit legitimate access to information, and foster frustration among users. For instance, healthcare professionals require timely access to patient data to deliver quality care. Cumbersome security protocols, though, may result in delays that negatively impact patient outcomes, leading to ethical dilemmas regarding the right to timely treatment versus the imperative to protect sensitive information. Striking this balance is particularly crucial in sectors where prompt access to data can save lives, such as healthcare and emergency services. Therefore, organizations must recognize that an inflexible approach to security can inadvertently compromise the very objectives they aim to protect.

Ethical security practices must adopt a nuanced approach that safeguards data while addressing the practical needs of users. By implementing flexible security solutions that prioritize both protection and accessibility, organizations can ensure that security measures do not become barriers to effective service delivery. This might involve adopting role-based access control, which provides tailored access to information based on job responsibilities, ensuring that users can access the data they need without compromising security.

Additionally, organizations can invest in user-friendly technologies that streamline authentication processes without sacrificing security, such as biometric systems or single sign-on solutions. By focusing on creating a balanced security framework that values both data protection and user accessibility, organizations can enhance operational efficiency while maintaining ethical standards, ultimately fostering a more effective and secure environment.

Transparency in Data Protection Practices

Transparency is another crucial ethical consideration in data security. Users have a right to know how their data is being protected, what measures are in place, and how their privacy is maintained. This need for transparency helps to build trust between organizations and their users, empowering individuals to make informed decisions about their data; however, revealing too much about specific security protocols can inadvertently expose vulnerabilities that malicious actors might exploit. For instance, if organizations disclose intricate details about their encryption methods or access control systems, they may unintentionally provide a roadmap for potential attackers. This creates a delicate balance between providing transparency to build trust and maintaining confidentiality to safeguard security systems.

To navigate this challenge, organizations should communicate general information about their security practices while demonstrating a commitment to data protection. This approach includes sharing high-level insights into security measures without compromising specific operational details. For example, organizations can inform users about the implementation of encryption, MFA, and regular security audits while withholding information on the exact configurations or technologies used.

Additionally, organizations should provide users with clear and concise privacy policies that outline how data is collected, used, and secured. By assuring users that their information is handled ethically and securely, without disclosing sensitive details that could compromise their security posture, organizations foster trust while ensuring the integrity of security measures remains intact. This balanced approach not only enhances user confidence but also reinforces the organization's commitment to ethical data-handling.

The Social Impact of Security Measures

Ethical data security requires considering the social impact of security measures. For example, biometric security technologies, such as facial recognition and fingerprint scanning, offer a high level of security but raise concerns about potential misuse, such as surveillance or profiling.

The deployment of these technologies can lead to significant ethical dilemmas, particularly regarding consent. Many individuals may not fully understand how their biometric data will be used or the extent to which they are being monitored, leading to a lack of informed consent.

Additionally, there are concerns about bias in these systems; studies have shown that facial recognition technology (FRT) can be less accurate for certain demographic groups, potentially leading to discriminatory practices. Organizations must be aware of these societal implications and assess the fairness and transparency of biometric systems to avoid further entrenching existing inequality.

Furthermore, the issue of data permanence adds another layer of complexity to the ethical considerations surrounding biometric security. Unlike traditional passwords, which can be reset if compromised, biometric data is permanent and inherently tied to an individual's identity. If this sensitive information is hacked or misused, the implications can be severe and lasting, leaving individuals vulnerable to identity theft and unauthorized access.

Organizations must thoughtfully evaluate these implications and weigh the risks before implementing such technologies. This includes developing clear policies that address consent, data retention, and the protocols for handling breaches involving biometric data. Ultimately, security measures should respect individuals' dignity and rights while ensuring that they do not exacerbate existing social inequality or contribute to a culture of surveillance. By approaching biometric security thoughtfully and ethically, organizations can foster a more equitable environment that prioritizes the well-being of all individuals.

Engaging Stakeholders and Fostering Ethical Practices

Ultimately, ethical data security practices involve a careful balance between protecting sensitive information, respecting individual rights, maintaining transparency, and ensuring that security measures contribute positively to society. This balance is crucial in an era where data breaches are prevalent, and the ramifications of poor data-handling can have far-reaching consequences. Organizations need to engage in a continuous dialogue about ethical data practices, considering both the potential benefits and the implications of their security measures. This ongoing conversation helps organizations stay aligned with societal values and expectations, ensuring that their security protocols not only meet regulatory requirements but also reflect the ethical considerations of their stakeholders.

Soliciting feedback from various stakeholders—including employees, customers, and advocacy groups—is vital in fostering a culture of ethical data security. By actively seeking input from those affected by their data practices, organizations can better understand concerns and expectations regarding privacy and security. This inclusive approach not only enhances the legitimacy of the security measures implemented but also promotes a sense of shared responsibility among all parties involved. Ultimately, by prioritizing ethical considerations alongside robust security measures, organizations can build a culture of trust and accountability that strengthens their reputation and fosters long-term relationships with their stakeholders. This commitment to ethical data security not only protects individuals but also contributes to a more responsible and equitable digital landscape.

Building an Ethical Framework for Data Security

In conclusion, navigating the complexities of ethical data security demands a multifaceted approach that harmonizes the essential imperatives of data protection with the rights and privacy of individuals. Organizations must acknowledge that their security practices have significant implications for their stakeholders, including employees, customers, and the broader community. By prioritizing ethical considerations, implementing transparent practices, and fostering an environment of trust, organizations can create a security framework that effectively safeguards sensitive information while respecting individual rights. This commitment to ethical data security not only helps mitigate risks associated with data breaches but also reinforces the organization's reputation as a responsible steward of personal information.

Moreover, this holistic approach cultivates a culture of ethical responsibility that can yield long-term success and societal benefit. By embedding ethical principles into their security strategies, organizations position themselves as leaders in data protection, enhancing consumer trust and loyalty. Such an environment encourages open dialogue around privacy and security, allowing stakeholders to feel empowered and valued. As the digital landscape continues to evolve, organizations that embrace ethical data security will be better equipped to navigate emerging challenges, foster innovation, and ultimately contribute to a more equitable and secure digital future for all.

CHAPTER 7

ETHICAL DATA USAGE AND MINIMIZATION

GUIDING PRINCIPLES OF ETHICAL DATA USE

Upholding Trust: Ethics of Data Usage

In the context of data ethics, *data usage* encompasses the various ways collected data is analyzed, applied, and shared within organizations. Ethical data usage is fundamentally about ensuring that data is utilized solely for the purposes for which it was originally collected, in alignment with the expectations and consent of the individuals from whom the data originates. This principle is foundational to data ethics, as it underscores the importance of respecting the trust that individuals place in data handlers. When organizations uphold ethical data usage, they not only safeguard individual privacy but also mitigate the risk of misuse that can lead to significant harm, including identity theft and data breaches.

Central to ethical data usage are the principles of purpose limitation and transparency. Purpose limitation requires organizations to clearly articulate the reasons for data collection and ensures that the information is not repurposed for activities beyond the original intent without obtaining explicit consent from the data subjects. This proactive approach fosters trust and accountability, as individuals are more likely to feel secure when they understand how their data will be used. By adhering to these ethical standards, organizations can create a culture of integrity in their data practices, thereby enhancing their reputation and maintaining the public's trust. In a world that is increasingly reliant on data, prioritizing ethical data usage is not just a best practice; it is essential for sustainable and responsible growth.

Data Integrity Matters

In a digital age dominated by data-driven decision-making and advanced technologies such as AI and machine learning, the ethical use of data has become increasingly critical. Organizations are leveraging vast amounts of data to refine customer experiences, enhance operational efficiency, and gain deep insights into human behavior. While these capabilities can drive significant benefits, they also come with a substantial ethical responsibility to ensure that data is used in ways that do not harm individuals or society at large. For instance, the unauthorized use of health data to set discriminatory insurance premiums and the manipulation of personal data for political gain are egregious violations of ethical standards. Such practices not only jeopardize individual rights but also erode public trust in organizations, ultimately threatening the integrity of the broader data economy.

Upholding ethical standards in data usage is essential for maintaining the trust that underpins consumer relationships and societal progress. Organizations that prioritize ethical data practices are more likely to foster a culture of accountability and responsibility, reinforcing their commitment to protecting individual rights. This commitment is crucial not only for compliance with existing regulations but also for cultivating long-term relationships with stakeholders who are increasingly concerned about data privacy and ethical considerations. By establishing robust ethical frameworks for data usage, companies can ensure that their data-driven innovations serve the greater good, enhancing societal well-being while simultaneously driving business success. Ultimately, the responsible handling of data is not just a moral imperative; it is integral to sustaining trust and promoting a healthier, more equitable data landscape.

Preventing Exploitation of Data

The role of ethical data usage in data ethics is essential for preventing the exploitation of data for unforeseen purposes. As modern analytics evolve, the ability to repurpose data for secondary uses has become increasingly easy, raising ethical concerns about the intentions behind data collection. For example, data initially gathered for enhancing customer service might later be used to construct detailed consumer profiles. This could lead to invasive practices such as aggressive targeted advertising or discriminatory practices that unfairly disadvantage certain groups. Establishing clear ethical guidelines that limit data usage to its original, specified purpose is vital for promoting fairness and preventing misuse. These guidelines serve as a safeguard against the slippery slope of data repurposing that can erode the trust of individuals whose information is being utilized.

When companies commit to using data solely for the purposes they have explicitly stated, they not only align with legal regulations such as the GDPR but also meet the ethical expectations of transparency and trust that consumers have come to expect. This commitment reinforces the notion that data-handling should be guided by respect for individual privacy and autonomy, rather than merely serving organizational interests. By adhering to these ethical standards, organizations can cultivate positive relationships with consumers, enhancing their reputations and establishing a loyal customer base. Ultimately, fostering an environment of ethical data usage not only mitigates the risk of potential harm but also contributes to a more equitable and just digital landscape, where the rights of individuals are upheld and respected.

Implementing Robust Internal Policies

Ensuring ethical data usage necessitates the implementation of robust internal policies and systems that promote accountability within organizations. Companies must establish comprehensive data governance frameworks that clearly define how data is accessed, processed, and utilized across various departments. These frameworks should outline specific rules regarding data-sharing practices, delineate responsibilities for data stewardship, and provide mechanisms for regular audits to ensure compliance with ethical standards.

Furthermore, organizations should implement comprehensive employee training programs focused on data ethics to prevent accidental misuse and cultivate a culture of responsibility. By fostering an environment where all stakeholders understand the ethical limits of their work with data, companies can enhance their ability to handle information responsibly and ethically.

In addition to governance frameworks, organizations must ensure that consent mechanisms are transparent and straightforward, empowering individuals to easily understand and control how their data is utilized. Clear communication about data practices is essential for building trust with consumers, as it enables them to make informed decisions about sharing their information. Companies should adopt user-friendly interfaces that facilitate consent management, allowing individuals to modify their preferences easily as their circumstances change. By embedding these practices into their organizational culture, companies can reinforce their commitment to ethical data usage, ultimately contributing to a responsible and trustworthy digital ecosystem. This proactive approach not only protects individuals' rights but also enhances the overall integrity of data practices, fostering a positive relationship between organizations and their stakeholders.

Continuous Evaluation and Adaptation

Another critical aspect of ethical data usage is the need for the continuous evaluation and adaptation of data practices in response to emerging technologies and societal expectations. As new data analytics tools and techniques evolve, organizations must remain vigilant and proactive in assessing the implications of these innovations on ethical data usage. This includes regularly updating data governance frameworks to address new ethical challenges that may arise from advancements such as AI, machine learning, and big data analytics.

Additionally, ensuring that staff are well informed about changes in regulations, industry standards, and best practices is essential for maintaining compliance and fostering a culture of ethical responsibility. By prioritizing ongoing training and education, organizations can empower their employees to make informed decisions regarding data-handling, thereby reducing the risk of ethical lapses.

Engaging in ongoing dialogue with stakeholders—including consumers, advocacy groups, and industry peers—can provide valuable insights into public sentiment regarding data usage and help organizations align their practices with societal values. This engagement can take various forms, such as surveys, focus groups, or community forums, allowing organizations to gather diverse perspectives on how data should be handled ethically. By listening to and incorporating feedback from various stakeholders, companies can build trust and demonstrate their commitment to ethical data practices.

Furthermore, fostering a culture of continuous improvement and responsiveness enables organizations to adapt to the ever-changing digital landscape, addressing emerging ethical dilemmas proactively. This adaptability not only enhances their reputation but also contributes to a more ethical and responsible approach to data usage, ultimately benefiting both the organization and society as a whole.

The Cornerstone of Data Ethics

Ethical data usage is a cornerstone of data ethics that requires organizations to commit to using data responsibly and transparently. By adhering to principles such as purpose limitation and transparency, companies can not only respect individuals' rights but also foster public trust in their operations. This commitment is further enhanced through the implementation of robust governance frameworks that establish clear guidelines for data access, sharing, and usage. Additionally, fostering a culture of accountability within organizations helps ensure that all employees understand their responsibilities in handling data ethically. Such an environment empowers individuals to make conscientious decisions about data usage, reducing the likelihood of unethical practices and reinforcing the organization's dedication to ethical standards.

As the digital landscape continues to evolve, organizations must remain adaptable, continuously evaluating and refining their data practices to address emerging ethical challenges. This adaptability involves staying informed about advancements in technology, changes in public sentiment, and evolving regulatory requirements. By actively engaging with stakeholders—including customers, advocacy groups, and industry peers—organizations can gather insights that inform their practices and ensure they align with societal values. Prioritizing ethical data usage not only benefits organizations by enhancing their reputation but also contributes positively to society at large. By ensuring that data-driven innovations are harnessed for the common good while safeguarding the rights and privacy of individuals, organizations can play a pivotal role in shaping a more ethical and responsible digital future.

ETHICAL AND UNETHICAL DATA USAGE

Ethical Data Use

The distinction between ethical and unethical data use is often shaped by how well organizations respect the boundaries of transparency, consent, and purpose limitation when handling data. Ethical data usage exemplifies how data can create value for individuals and society without compromising privacy or autonomy. This includes clear communication about how data is collected and used, ensuring that individuals understand their rights and the implications of their consent. When organizations prioritize these ethical principles, they not only enhance trust and accountability but also foster an environment where data can be leveraged responsibly for innovation and societal benefit.

Examples of Ethical Data Usage

A notable example of ethical data use can be found in the healthcare sector, where patient data is utilized to improve medical outcomes through evidence-based treatments. Hospitals and research institutions leverage anonymized patient data to track the spread of diseases and develop effective treatments. By ensuring that data is anonymized and collected with explicit consent, these practices prioritize patient privacy while advancing medical knowledge for public benefit. This approach highlights the potential for data to serve the greater good when handled responsibly, ensuring that individuals benefit from innovations in healthcare without sacrificing their rights.

Another example of ethical data usage is evident in customer personalization initiatives. Companies such as Spotify and Netflix harness data collected from user behavior—such as viewing history or music preferences—to provide tailored content recommendations. These organizations are transparent about their data collection practices, informing users that their activity is monitored to enhance the user experience. This transparency and adherence to purpose limitation illustrate ethical data usage, as the data collected is strictly employed for personalization, with clear communication regarding its purpose and value to the consumer. By allowing individuals control over their data through opt-in and opt-out options, these platforms ensure that users feel comfortable with how their personal information is leveraged. This not only fosters a positive user experience but also builds trust, which is essential for the long-term success of data-driven business models.

Examples of Unethical Data Usage

In contrast, unethical data usage often involves scenarios where data is repurposed without proper consent, resulting in significant harm to individuals or society. A prominent instance of unethical data use is the Facebook-Cambridge Analytica scandal, in which personal data from millions of Facebook users was harvested without consent and exploited for political advertising. The data, initially collected through a seemingly harmless personality quiz, was used to influence voter behavior during major political events, such as the 2016 United States presidential election and the Brexit referendum.

This egregious misuse of data not only violated individuals' trust but also underscored how unauthorized data repurposing could have profound implications for democratic processes. The scandal highlighted the critical importance of purpose limitation and explicit consent in data-handling, as well as the pressing need for stringent regulations to prevent manipulative or deceptive data practices.

Another concerning example of unethical data usage involves racial profiling through predictive policing technologies. In cities such as Chicago, predictive policing programs utilize historical crime data to forecast potential criminal activity and allocate police resources accordingly. These systems have been criticized, though, for reinforcing bias embedded in the original data, leading to discriminatory outcomes, particularly against minority communities. The data used in these programs often reflects systemic inequality and bias, which can result in over-policing certain neighborhoods based on flawed or prejudiced information. This represents an unethical use of data because it amplifies existing societal biases rather than promoting fair and unbiased decision-making. Such instances reveal the critical need for fairness and bias mitigation strategies when using data to make decisions that directly affect people's lives, emphasizing the responsibility of organizations to ensure that their data practices contribute to justice and equity.

The Impact of Ethical vs. Unethical Data Use

These examples underscore the significant impact that ethical or unethical data use can have on individuals and society as a whole. Ethical data practices, which prioritize transparency and fairness, can lead to innovative solutions that enhance user experiences and drive social good. For instance, when organizations utilize data responsibly, they can develop personalized services that truly benefit consumers, such as tailored healthcare solutions or improved customer support. On the other hand, unethical data use, such as exploiting personal information for manipulation or discrimination, can create a climate of mistrust and fear, ultimately damaging relationships between organizations and their stakeholders.

Organizations must, therefore, not only comply with data protection regulations but also commit to ethical principles in their data usage, including transparency, fairness, and respect for individual rights. This commitment involves implementing comprehensive data governance frameworks that guide ethical decision-making and promote accountability at all levels of the organization. By actively engaging with stakeholders and encouraging open dialogue about data practices, organizations can better understand the societal implications of their actions. Such a proactive approach not only safeguards individual rights but also enhances the organization's reputation and fosters a culture of ethical responsibility that can contribute to a more equitable and trustworthy digital environment.

The Impact of Ethical Data Practices on Trust and Innovation

By learning from real-world successes and failures, organizations can better navigate the complexities of data ethics, ensuring that their data practices contribute positively to both business objectives and societal welfare. Case studies of companies that have implemented ethical data practices successfully illustrate how prioritizing transparency and accountability can enhance consumer trust and brand loyalty. Conversely, examining instances where unethical data usage has led to significant backlash, such as privacy breaches or discriminatory practices, highlights the potential risks associated with neglecting ethical considerations. By analyzing these examples, organizations can develop strategies that not only mitigate risks but also harness data responsibly to drive innovation and positive change within their industries.

Ultimately, the ethical considerations surrounding data usage are integral to building a sustainable and responsible data ecosystem. As society becomes increasingly reliant on data-driven technologies, organizations must recognize their role in shaping ethical standards that protect individual rights and promote fairness. This involves not only adhering to regulatory frameworks but also fostering a culture that values ethical behavior and continuous improvement. By embedding ethical principles into their core operations, organizations can ensure that their data practices align with societal expectations, thereby contributing to a more equitable and trustworthy digital landscape. Such commitment not only supports long-term business success but also reinforces the broader social responsibility that companies have toward the communities they serve.

Commitment to Ethical Data Practices

Organizations that prioritize ethical data practices can cultivate a culture of accountability and trust, significantly enhancing their reputation while promoting long-term success in an increasingly data-driven world. When organizations consistently demonstrate their commitment to ethical behavior in data-handling, they not only build consumer confidence but also strengthen their relationships with stakeholders, including employees, partners, and regulators. This proactive stance encourages transparency and open communication, creating an environment where ethical considerations are integrated into every aspect of data management. In turn, this culture of trust can lead to increased customer loyalty and a competitive edge in the market, as consumers are more likely to engage with companies that align with their values regarding privacy and ethical conduct.

As technology continues to evolve, the commitment to ethical data usage must remain a priority, ensuring that the benefits of data are realized without compromising the rights and dignity of individuals. Organizations are tasked with navigating the complexities of advanced analytics, AI, and machine learning, all of which hold the potential for both positive and negative impacts on society. By actively engaging in ethical data practices, organizations can lead the way toward a more equitable and responsible data landscape, fostering a future where data serves as a force for good in society. This involves not only adhering to existing regulations but also anticipating future challenges and proactively addressing them through innovative solutions. In doing so, organizations can play a pivotal role in shaping a data-driven future that respects individual rights while harnessing the power of data for collective benefit.

DATA MINIMIZATION

Data Minimization: The Key to Ethical Data Practices

Data minimization is a critical principle in data ethics that underscores the importance of collecting only the data that is essential for a specific purpose. In today's data-driven world, where organizations gather vast amounts of personal information, the ethical implications of excessive data collection cannot be overstated. By limiting data collection to what is strictly necessary, organizations can reduce the risk of exposing sensitive information to unauthorized access or misuse, thereby protecting individuals' privacy. This intentional approach encourages organizations to carefully consider their data practices, ensuring that they gather only the information needed to achieve their objectives without overreaching into individuals' private lives.

Embracing data minimization serves as a fundamental strategy to mitigate ethical risks, enhance individual privacy, and build trust between organizations and consumers. When individuals see that organizations are committed to collecting only the minimum required data, they are more likely to feel secure and confident in sharing their information. This trust is crucial in today's digital landscape, where consumers are increasingly concerned about their privacy and how their data is used. By adhering to the principle of data minimization, organizations not only comply with regulatory requirements but also foster a more responsible and ethical approach to data usage. This proactive stance positions them as leaders in ethical data-handling, demonstrating to stakeholders that they prioritize the welfare and rights of individuals, ultimately contributing to a healthier data ecosystem.

Protecting Individual Privacy

One of the primary reasons for limiting data collection is to protect individuals' privacy. When organizations collect only the necessary data, they significantly reduce the potential for misuse or unauthorized access to personal information. Excessive data collection heightens the risks of data breaches and leaks, which can have devastating consequences for individuals, including identity theft, financial loss, and reputational damage. For instance, companies that collect sensitive information, such as Social Security numbers or financial data, without a clear and justified need can expose themselves and their customers to significant harm. By adopting a data minimization approach, organizations can substantially decrease the volume of sensitive information they retain, thereby reducing the likelihood of breaches and enhancing overall data security. This proactive stance not only protects individuals but also mitigates potential legal and financial repercussions for the organizations themselves.

Additionally, limiting data collection aligns with the growing public demand for transparency and ethical data practices. Consumers are increasingly aware of their rights regarding personal information and are more likely to engage with organizations that demonstrate a commitment to privacy. By minimizing the data collected, organizations can build trust and foster stronger relationships with their customers, enhancing brand loyalty and reputation in the long run. Moreover, regulatory frameworks such as the GDPR and the CCPA emphasize the importance of data minimization, encouraging organizations to adopt responsible data-handling practices. By embedding data minimization into their operational strategies, organizations not only comply with these legal requirements but also position themselves as responsible stewards of personal information, ultimately benefiting both individuals and the broader society.

Respecting Autonomy and Rights

Limiting data collection respects individuals' autonomy and rights. Today's consumers are increasingly aware of how their data is collected, stored, and used. When organizations gather only what is necessary and communicate transparently about their data practices, they empower individuals to make informed decisions about their data. This respect for personal autonomy is essential in fostering a positive relationship between consumers and organizations.

For example, when a social media platform collects user data solely to enhance user experience rather than for targeted advertising or resale to third parties, it demonstrates ethical responsibility and a commitment to user privacy. Such practices build trust and encourage users to engage with the platform more freely, knowing their information is handled ethically. This trust is foundational to long-term customer relationships and brand loyalty, as consumers increasingly gravitate toward companies that prioritize ethical data practices.

Prioritizing data minimization also serves to enhance accountability within organizations. By limiting the scope of data collection, organizations can streamline their data management processes, making it easier to ensure compliance with privacy regulations and ethical standards. When companies maintain less data, they reduce the complexity of managing that information and lower the risks associated with data breaches or unauthorized access. This focus on accountability not only protects consumer interests but also reinforces the organization's reputation as a responsible data steward. As more organizations embrace data minimization as part of their core values, they contribute to the establishment of a more ethical data landscape, where individuals' rights are respected, and trust in digital interactions is fortified.

Streamlining Data Practices

A focus on data minimization encourages organizations to adopt a more thoughtful approach to data collection and processing. By critically evaluating what data is truly necessary for their operations, organizations can streamline their processes and eliminate unnecessary complexities associated with managing large datasets. This reflection not only leads to better data governance but also helps to reduce the operational costs related to data storage and management. Organizations can prioritize quality over quantity by concentrating on relevant data, enabling them to derive more meaningful insights while maintaining ethical standards. This thoughtful approach to data can also foster innovation, as teams can focus their efforts on improving products and services rather than navigating the challenges posed by unwieldy datasets.

Additionally, implementing data minimization can enhance an organization's ability to respond to regulatory requirements and changing market demands. With an increasing emphasis on data privacy laws, such as the GDPR and CCPA, organizations that practice data minimization are better positioned to comply with these regulations. By limiting data collection to only what is essential, organizations can reduce their legal risks and demonstrate a commitment to ethical data practices. This proactive stance can also serve as a competitive advantage, as consumers are more likely to choose brands that prioritize their privacy and demonstrate responsible data stewardship. As organizations navigate an evolving regulatory landscape, a focus on data minimization can prove invaluable in building resilience and trust with stakeholders.

Competitive Advantage in Ethical Practices

In an era where consumers are increasingly concerned about data privacy and ethical considerations, organizations that embrace data minimization can distinguish themselves in the marketplace. By prioritizing ethical data practices, businesses can gain a competitive edge, as consumers are more inclined to trust and engage with brands that demonstrate transparency and responsibility in their data-handling. This commitment to ethical standards fosters an environment where customers feel secure in their interactions, ultimately encouraging them to choose brands that respect their privacy. By limiting data collection and being explicit about data usage, organizations can align their practices with consumer expectations, which can lead to enhanced brand loyalty and an improved reputation in a crowded market.

Moreover, as consumers become more educated about their rights and the implications of data usage, organizations that champion data minimization are well positioned to attract and retain customers. This proactive approach not only helps organizations comply with evolving data protection regulations but also reinforces their commitment to ethical principles, contributing positively to the broader narrative of responsible data practices within the industry. By fostering a culture of trust through ethical data-handling, organizations can cultivate long-term relationships with their customers, ensuring sustainability in a landscape where consumer choices are increasingly driven by ethical considerations. Ultimately, adopting data minimization is not just a strategic move; it's a pathway to building a more responsible and trustworthy digital ecosystem that benefits both businesses and consumers alike.

The Moral Imperative of Data Minimization

Data minimization is a vital principle in ethical data practices that emphasizes the importance of limiting data collection to what is necessary. By actively reducing the volume of data collected, organizations can protect individual privacy, respect personal autonomy, enhance data governance, and build trust with consumers. This approach not only mitigates risks associated with data breaches and misuse but also creates an environment where consumers feel valued and respected. As data privacy concerns continue to grow, adopting a data minimization strategy will be essential for organizations aiming to navigate the ethical landscape of data usage responsibly and effectively.

Furthermore, through thoughtful data practices, organizations can not only comply with existing regulations but also contribute positively to society by ensuring that data is used ethically and responsibly. Embracing the principle of data minimization is not merely a legal obligation but a moral imperative that reflects an organization's commitment to ethical standards and respect for individual rights. By prioritizing ethical data practices, organizations can foster a culture of accountability, ultimately positioning themselves as leaders in the industry. In doing so, they not only protect the interests of individuals but also pave the way for a more sustainable and ethical data ecosystem that benefits all stakeholders involved.

CHALLENGES OF DATA MINIMIZATION

Balancing Act: Overcoming Hurdles in Data Minimization

While data minimization is an essential principle in data ethics, its implementation presents various practical challenges for organizations. These challenges can arise from technological limitations, such as outdated systems that are not designed to support selective data collection or the integration of new technologies that complicate existing data management processes. Operational factors also come into play, including organizational inertia that can lead to a reluctance to change longstanding data collection practices, as well as the pressures to gather more data for competitive advantage.

Additionally, cultural factors, such as a lack of awareness or understanding of ethical data practices among employees, can hinder efforts to prioritize data minimization. Understanding these hurdles is crucial for organizations seeking to uphold ethical standards in their data practices while also navigating the complexities of modern data environments.

As the demand for data-driven insights continues to grow, organizations must find a way to balance their operational needs with ethical considerations, ensuring that they collect only the data necessary for their objectives. This balancing act requires a commitment to reevaluating data collection strategies, training staff on the importance of data ethics, and fostering a culture that values responsible data-handling. By addressing these practical challenges head-on, organizations can create frameworks that not only comply with legal requirements but also embrace ethical principles. Ultimately, overcoming these hurdles will enable organizations to harness the power of data while safeguarding individual privacy and maintaining public trust, laying the groundwork for a more ethical data landscape in the future.

The Complexity of Data Ecosystems

One significant challenge organizations face in implementing data minimization is the inherent complexity of data ecosystems. Many organizations operate with diverse data sources, including customer interactions, social media, third-party vendors, and internal systems. This complexity makes it difficult to establish clear guidelines regarding what data is necessary for specific purposes. For instance, in a customer relationship management (CRM) system, organizations may collect a wide range of customer data, from basic contact information to detailed purchasing history. Determining which pieces of information are essential for providing services without infringing on privacy rights requires careful consideration. This often involves balancing operational needs with ethical considerations, which can be a daunting task. As a result, organizations may inadvertently find themselves collecting more data than is strictly necessary, counteracting the goal of data minimization.

This difficulty in delineating what constitutes essential data can lead to significant ethical dilemmas, potentially resulting in privacy violations. Organizations might face situations where they justify excessive data collection under the guise of operational efficiency, inadvertently exposing sensitive information to risks associated with data breaches or misuse. Additionally, the pressure to harness data for competitive advantage can lead to a culture that prioritizes data accumulation over responsible usage. Consequently, stakeholders may experience a disconnect between organizational practices and ethical standards, leading to diminished trust among consumers.

To navigate this complexity effectively, organizations must adopt comprehensive data governance frameworks that clearly define data collection criteria and ensure that all employees understand the importance of adhering to data minimization principles. By doing so, organizations can mitigate the risks associated with excessive data collection and foster an environment of ethical responsibility in their data practices.

Legacy Systems and Business Practices

Another challenge arises from existing business practices and legacy systems that may not be designed with data minimization in mind. Many organizations have historically adopted data collection practices based on the assumption that more data is better. This mentality can be difficult to shift, as departments may resist changes that impact their established workflows or objectives. For instance, marketing teams often rely on extensive customer data for targeted campaigns, believing that having access to more information will enhance their ability to reach potential customers effectively. Changing these practices may necessitate rethinking strategies and resource allocation, leading to pushback from teams accustomed to operating within a certain framework. Additionally, legacy systems may not support selective data collection or deletion, creating technical obstacles to implementing data minimization principles effectively.

As a result, organizations may need to invest significantly in updating their infrastructure to align with ethical data practices, which can be both time-consuming and costly. Transitioning to new systems that facilitate data minimization may require significant capital investment, as well as ongoing training for employees to adapt to new technologies and practices. This shift not only represents a logistical challenge but also necessitates a cultural transformation within the organization, encouraging teams to embrace a philosophy of responsible data use. Resistance to changing long-standing practices can create internal friction and hinder progress toward adopting data minimization effectively.

To overcome these hurdles, organizations must engage in comprehensive change management efforts that communicate the long-term benefits of data minimization and cultivate a shared understanding of its importance across all departments. By fostering collaboration and encouraging innovation in data practices, organizations can position themselves for success while upholding ethical standards.

Cultural Resistance to Change

Cultural resistance within organizations can significantly impede the adoption of data minimization principles, as employees often view data as a valuable asset for driving decision-making and enhancing services. This perspective can lead to a reluctance to limit data collection, with many believing that having more data will result in more informed strategies and better outcomes. As a result, tension may arise between data governance initiatives aimed at restricting data collection and the desire for comprehensive data insights that many teams prioritize. This friction can create an environment where ethical considerations are overshadowed by the pursuit of operational efficiency, making it challenging to implement necessary changes. To successfully navigate this resistance, organizations must undergo a cultural shift that prioritizes ethical data practices and highlights the importance of protecting individual privacy as a fundamental value.

Overcoming this resistance requires a multifaceted approach, including training programs, awareness campaigns, and strong support from leadership to advocate for data minimization. By equipping employees with the knowledge and tools to understand the implications of excessive data collection, organizations can foster a greater appreciation for ethical data-handling practices. Additionally, leadership must actively demonstrate their commitment to these principles by integrating them into the organization's core values and strategic objectives.

Implementing such cultural changes takes time and concerted effort, but the payoff is significant. Creating a workplace culture that values ethical data-handling as much as operational efficiency is essential for fostering a data minimization mindset among all employees. By reinforcing the idea that responsible data use can coexist with data-driven decision-making, organizations can cultivate an environment that supports both ethical standards and business goals.

Regulatory Compliance Complexities

Regulatory compliance introduces another layer of complexity to data minimization efforts, as organizations must navigate a labyrinth of guidelines that can differ significantly by region, industry, and data type. Regulations such as the GDPR provide essential frameworks for data collection practices; however, the interpretation and application of these rules can be challenging. Organizations may struggle to determine which data is necessary to collect to remain compliant while simultaneously adhering to data minimization principles.

This uncertainty can lead to a situation where organizations inadvertently over-collect data to ensure they meet compliance requirements, which directly contradicts the ethical aim of minimizing data collection. Consequently, this confusion can not only result in a bloated data repository but also increase the risk of potential privacy violations, as organizations may mishandle or fail to adequately protect the excessive data they accumulate.

Additionally, the evolving nature of data protection regulations adds to the challenges organizations face in their compliance efforts. As regulations are updated or new laws are enacted, organizations must constantly adapt their data practices to align with these changes. This continuous need for adjustment can be overwhelming and resource-intensive, leading to potential gaps in compliance. Organizations may find themselves in a reactive mode, scrambling to update their data management strategies rather than proactively fostering an ethical data culture. The rapid pace of regulatory change can also create uncertainty about what constitutes compliant behavior, further complicating organizations' efforts to implement data minimization effectively. As a result, organizations must invest in ongoing training, legal counsel, and robust data governance frameworks to navigate the intricate regulatory landscape while ensuring that their data practices remain ethical and aligned with the principles of data minimization.

Customer Perceptions and Expectations

Organizations may encounter practical challenges related to customer perceptions and expectations in their efforts to implement data minimization. In an era where consumers are increasingly vigilant about their data privacy, organizations must carefully navigate the delicate balance between collecting data for service improvement and respecting individual privacy rights. Customers may view limited data collection as a barrier to personalized service or responsiveness, leading to concerns about their experience with the organization. For instance, if a retail company restricts its data collection to align with ethical standards, customers may feel that the recommendations or services provided are less tailored to their preferences. Therefore, organizations must proactively communicate the rationale behind their data practices to reassure customers that their privacy is being prioritized without compromising the quality of service.

Striking the right balance between data minimization and customer expectations necessitates thoughtful communication and transparency regarding data practices, which can often be challenging to achieve consistently. Organizations should focus on educating customers about the benefits of data minimization, emphasizing how it safeguards their privacy and enhances trust in the organization. This communication can be supplemented with regular updates about how customer data is handled and the measures in place to protect their information.

Building a strong rapport with customers and offering assurances regarding data privacy can help organizations mitigate potential challenges stemming from customer skepticism. Achieving this balance requires ongoing effort, adaptability, and a commitment to prioritizing ethical data practices in every aspect of the organization's operations. By fostering a culture of transparency and ethical responsibility, organizations can enhance customer loyalty and trust while adhering to data minimization principles.

Navigating Challenges to Uphold Ethical Standards

While data minimization is a vital principle in ethical data practices, its implementation is fraught with challenges for organizations. The complexity of data ecosystems, legacy systems, cultural resistance, regulatory compliance, and customer perceptions all contribute to the difficulties organizations face in limiting data collection. To navigate these challenges successfully, organizations must adopt a proactive approach, investing in training, infrastructure, and clear communication strategies to foster a culture of ethical data management. By addressing these practical challenges, organizations can work toward effective data minimization while upholding their commitment to privacy and ethical responsibility.

Ultimately, embracing data minimization not only aligns organizations with ethical practices but also enhances their long-term viability in a data-driven economy. By prioritizing the ethical handling of data, organizations can build stronger relationships with customers and stakeholders, fostering trust and loyalty that contribute to sustainable growth. As data privacy continues to be a significant concern for consumers, organizations that successfully implement data minimization principles will position themselves as responsible data stewards, paving the way for ethical innovation and enhanced corporate reputation in the increasingly complex data landscape.

CHAPTER 8

DATA BIAS

UNDERSTANDING DATA BIAS

Types of Bias

Bias in data is a significant concern that affects the integrity and reliability of data-driven decisions, often leading to skewed or unjust outcomes. Understanding the various types of bias is crucial for organizations, data scientists, and policymakers to ensure that data is used ethically and accurately. Bias can arise from multiple sources, such as how data is collected, the algorithms employed to analyze it, and the subjective interpretations of individuals handling the results. For instance, selection bias occurs when the sample of data does not accurately represent the population, leading to results that disproportionately favor certain groups. Algorithmic bias, on the other hand, can stem from the inherent biases present in the data used to train machine learning models, causing these systems to reinforce or amplify societal inequality. These biases compromise the quality of insights derived from data, often producing misleading conclusions that can influence important decisions across sectors such as healthcare, criminal justice, and education.

Addressing bias in data is not merely an academic exercise but has profound real-world implications for equity, fairness, and justice. For example, in hiring algorithms, unchecked bias can result in discriminatory outcomes against marginalized groups, further perpetuating systemic inequality. In criminal justice, biased data can lead to unfair sentencing or over-policing in certain communities. By exploring key types of bias—such as confirmation bias, where analysts unintentionally interpret data in ways that confirm their preconceived notions, or survivorship bias, where conclusions are drawn from incomplete datasets—organizations can develop a more comprehensive understanding of how bias can infiltrate data analysis and decision-making processes.

Proactively identifying, addressing, and mitigating bias is essential for fostering more ethical, equitable, and just data-driven practices. Through ongoing vigilance and ethical consideration, organizations can improve the reliability of their data insights while promoting fairness in their decisions.

Selection Bias

Selection bias is one of the most prevalent forms of bias encountered in data collection and analysis, significantly affecting the accuracy and generalizability of findings. It occurs when certain individuals or groups are systematically excluded from the sample, leading to an unrepresentative dataset that skews the results. This bias can manifest in various research contexts, including survey studies, clinical trials, and observational research. For instance, in a public health study focused primarily on participants from urban areas, rural populations may be underrepresented, resulting in findings that fail to capture the health needs or outcomes of those living in non-urban settings. This lack of representation distorts the conclusions drawn from the data, making it difficult to accurately apply the results to broader populations. Selection bias can also occur unintentionally through self-selection, where individuals who choose to participate in a study may differ in important ways from those who do not, further skewing the results.

The impact of selection bias is significant, as it can lead to erroneous generalizations and hinder a true understanding of how various factors affect different segments of the population. In contexts such as healthcare, education, or social policy, this bias can result in misinformed decisions that fail to address the needs of underrepresented groups. To mitigate selection bias, researchers must adopt more rigorous sampling methods that are comprehensive and inclusive, ensuring that all relevant groups are adequately represented.

Employing random sampling techniques, stratified sampling, or oversampling of underrepresented populations can help improve the validity of the findings. Additionally, researchers should be transparent about their sampling processes and actively work to identify and address any potential sources of bias throughout their studies. By doing so, they not only enhance the credibility of their research but also promote equity by ensuring that all voices and perspectives are considered.

Algorithmic Bias

Algorithmic bias refers to the systematic and unfair discrimination that can emerge from the use of algorithms in data analysis and machine learning, often reflecting and perpetuating existing societal biases. This bias arises when the data used to train algorithms is skewed by historical prejudices or imbalances, leading to biased outputs and decisions. For example, if a hiring algorithm is trained on historical data that reflects gender or racial disparities, it may unknowingly favor certain demographics over others, perpetuating inequality in recruitment processes.

In another case, predictive policing algorithms trained on crime data from over-policed neighborhoods may unfairly target marginalized communities, reinforcing systemic biases in law enforcement. Such examples highlight the significant ethical concerns surrounding algorithmic bias, particularly in high-stakes fields such as criminal justice, healthcare, education, and employment, where biased algorithms can cause direct harm to individuals and exacerbate social inequality.

Addressing algorithmic bias requires a comprehensive and proactive approach to mitigate its impact. One crucial step is to diversify the training datasets, ensuring they include a wide range of perspectives and are free from historical inequity. Regularly auditing algorithms for potential bias is another critical measure, as it allows organizations to identify and correct any patterns of unfairness before they cause harm. Additionally, involving diverse stakeholders—such as ethicists, community advocates, and individuals from underrepresented groups—in the design, development, and implementation of AI systems can provide valuable insights into how these technologies might affect different populations. This inclusive approach is essential for ensuring that technology becomes a tool for empowerment, rather than a mechanism for perpetuating discrimination. By committing to ethical AI development, organizations can foster greater accountability and fairness in the deployment of machine learning systems, building a more equitable digital future.

Confirmation Bias

Confirmation bias is a pervasive cognitive bias that influences how individuals interpret and analyze data by favoring information that aligns with their preexisting beliefs or expectations. This bias can manifest in various contexts, from scientific research to business decision-making, often resulting in the selective gathering or interpretation of data that supports an individual's hypothesis while disregarding or minimizing conflicting evidence. For example, a researcher who strongly believes in a particular theory may unconsciously highlight data that supports their view while overlooking data that contradicts it. This selective focus can distort the overall analysis, leading to skewed conclusions and, in some cases, decisions that are not based on the full spectrum of available data. Such outcomes can be particularly detrimental in fields such as healthcare, where biased conclusions might lead to ineffective treatments, or in policy-making, where incomplete data could result in misguided regulations.

To mitigate the impact of confirmation bias, individuals and organizations must adopt strategies that promote objectivity and critical thinking. One effective approach is to intentionally seek out diverse perspectives and actively question assumptions throughout the data collection and analysis processes. This practice encourages a more holistic view of the data and reduces the likelihood of overlooking important but contradictory information.

Additionally, fostering a culture of collaboration and peer review can be instrumental in identifying potential bias, as it introduces alternative viewpoints that may challenge existing preconceptions. By encouraging open dialogue and rigorous evaluation, organizations can ensure that conclusions are based on a more comprehensive and accurate understanding of the data, leading to better-informed decisions and outcomes.

Other Types of Bias

In addition to selection and algorithmic bias, other significant forms of bias can emerge during the data collection process, each of which can compromise the integrity and reliability of the data.

Measurement Bias

This occurs when data is inaccurately collected or recorded, often due to faulty instruments, poorly constructed survey questions, or untrained data collectors. For instance, leading questions in a survey can influence respondents' answers, while faulty measuring devices in scientific experiments can yield erroneous results. This type of bias is particularly concerning because it can skew the data in subtle ways, leading to inaccurate analyses and misguided conclusions. Addressing measurement bias requires careful design of data collection instruments, thorough training for data collectors, and regular calibration or validation of tools to ensure consistent and accurate data recording.

Survivorship Bias

This is another form of bias that can significantly distort analyses by focusing only on the "survivors" or successes in a dataset, while ignoring the failures or those that did not make it through the selection process. This can lead to overly optimistic or skewed conclusions about the factors that lead to success. For example, analyzing only successful startups without considering the thousands of startups that failed can give a false impression that success is more common or easily achievable than it truly is.

Recall Bias

This type of bias often affects survey data when participants are asked to remember past events or experiences. Human memory is fallible, and participants may inadvertently misremember or omit details, leading to unreliable data.

These forms of bias emphasize the critical need for rigorous data validation methods and a comprehensive approach to analysis, which includes examining the full range of available data—both successes and failures—and cross-referencing collected information with objective records whenever possible to ensure accurate and unbiased results.

Broader Implications of Bias

The presence of bias in data extends beyond individual studies, posing significant risks to society at large, especially when it informs policies that shape public welfare. Biased data can lead to misinformed or harmful policies that disproportionately affect marginalized and vulnerable communities. For example, if data used in policy decisions systematically underrepresents certain racial or socioeconomic groups, the resulting policies may fail to address the needs of those populations, exacerbating existing inequality. In health, education, or criminal justice systems, such bias can perpetuate cycles of disadvantage, further marginalizing those already at risk. The consequences of these biases are far-reaching, potentially reinforcing social stratification and limiting opportunities for affected groups to thrive.

To mitigate these risks, policymakers must adopt inclusive data practices that prioritize fairness and representation. This involves engaging with diverse community stakeholders to ensure that data reflects the varied experiences, needs, and challenges faced by all segments of the population. Participatory research methods, in which community members are actively involved in the data collection and analysis process, can offer valuable insights and help identify bias that might otherwise go unnoticed. By creating a more comprehensive and inclusive approach to data gathering, policymakers can develop more equitable and effective policies, ensuring that decisions are grounded in a fuller understanding of the issues and that they serve the public in a way that promotes justice and fairness.

VALUE-LADEN BIAS

Value-laden bias in data analysis arises from the values, beliefs, and assumptions of individuals involved in the data collection, analysis, and interpretation processes. This bias can influence how research questions are framed, what data is selected, and how results are interpreted, often reflecting subjective viewpoints that may skew conclusions. This can compromise the objectivity and reliability of the analysis, reinforcing certain perspectives while overlooking important aspects of the data. Addressing this bias is crucial for promoting more equitable and comprehensive analyses. By fostering awareness and incorporating diverse perspectives, analysts can achieve more balanced insights, ultimately leading to better-informed decisions and policies that reflect the needs of all stakeholders.

The Influence of Values and Beliefs

Value-laden bias in data analysis arises from the inherent beliefs and values of individuals involved in the research process. This bias can shape the framing of data, the questions posed, and the types of analyses conducted. For instance, analysts' perspectives on social justice may lead them to prioritize data that highlights systemic inequality, while those with a more individualistic viewpoint might focus on personal accountability and achievements. The framing of questions can significantly affect the direction of the analysis; if analysts choose to emphasize certain societal values, they may inadvertently limit the scope of their inquiry. Consequently, this can create a skewed understanding of the issues at hand, ultimately influencing policy recommendations and decision-making processes.

Personal bias can manifest in various stages of data analysis, from hypothesis formation to data interpretation. For example, an analyst who strongly believes in the efficacy of a specific intervention may unconsciously select data that supports that belief while discounting evidence that suggests otherwise. This can lead to confirmation bias, where the analyst seeks out information that reinforces their preexisting notions, thereby neglecting contrary data. Such bias can cloud judgment and reduce the objectivity required for rigorous analysis, resulting in a flawed understanding of the underlying issues.

The implications of value-laden bias extend beyond individual analyses. When analysts share their findings with stakeholders or the public, their biases may inadvertently shape narratives around critical issues. Policymakers and decision-makers rely heavily on data to inform their strategies, and if that data is influenced by personal bias, the decisions made may not reflect the broader societal needs or realities. As a result, fostering awareness of this kind of bias is essential to promote a more balanced and inclusive approach to data analysis.

The Choice of Data and Metrics

The selection of data sources and metrics is a crucial aspect of data analysis that can reflect value-laden bias. Analysts may consciously or unconsciously choose specific datasets that align with their beliefs, leading to a distorted representation of reality. For example, in public health research, an analyst may prioritize data on certain health outcomes that align with their focus on individual behaviors, such as smoking rates, while neglecting to incorporate data that examines social determinants of health, such as access to healthcare or income disparity. This selective emphasis can result in incomplete analyses that fail to address the broader factors influencing health outcomes.

Furthermore, the choice of metrics can significantly impact how findings are interpreted. For instance, an organization evaluating the effectiveness of an educational program may focus solely on standardized test scores as a metric of success. While test scores provide valuable information, they do not capture other essential aspects of educational experiences, such as student engagement, social-emotional development, or long-term outcomes. By prioritizing certain metrics over others, analysts may inadvertently convey a narrow understanding of the program's impact, potentially leading to misguided conclusions and decisions.

This selective approach to data and metrics can also perpetuate existing biases within organizations and society. When organizations consistently use metrics that reflect particular values, they may reinforce a culture that prioritizes certain outcomes over others, further entrenching value-laden bias in decision-making. For instance, in the corporate world, if performance metrics focus solely on short-term financial gains, companies may overlook crucial factors such as employee well-being or environmental sustainability, ultimately leading to detrimental long-term consequences. Recognizing and addressing the bias inherent in data selection and metric choice is essential to promote a more holistic understanding of the issues being analyzed.

Interpretation and Communication

The interpretation and communication of data findings are critical stages in the data analysis process where value-laden bias can significantly influence outcomes. Analysts often have the power to frame results in ways that align with their beliefs, which can shape stakeholders' understanding of the data. For example, an analyst may choose to highlight certain statistical trends while downplaying others, framing the narrative to support a specific agenda. This selective emphasis can lead to a distorted perception of the data, which can influence decision-makers who rely on these interpretations to guide policy or business strategies.

Moreover, the communication of results can be impacted by the language used to describe findings. Analysts may employ terminology that carries implicit bias, framing issues in ways that evoke particular emotional responses. For instance, referring to a population as "at-risk" rather than "marginalized" can carry different connotations, potentially influencing how stakeholders perceive the needs and capabilities of that group. Such language choices can inadvertently reinforce stereotypes and perpetuate bias, making it essential for analysts to be mindful of the implications of their word choices when communicating results.

Additionally, the lack of transparency in the data analysis process can exacerbate value-laden bias. When analysts do not disclose the methods, assumptions, or limitations of their analyses, stakeholders may accept the findings at face value without critically evaluating their validity. This can lead to the unintentional endorsement of biased conclusions, ultimately influencing public discourse and policy decisions based on flawed data interpretations. To counteract this, analysts should prioritize transparency and encourage critical engagement with their findings, fostering a culture of accountability and inclusivity that supports informed decision-making.

BIAS AND ITS CONSEQUENCES

The Ethical and Societal Impact of Flawed Data

Bias in data has profound implications for decision-making processes at both the individual and societal levels, influencing everything from business strategies to public policy. As organizations increasingly rely on data-driven insights to guide their actions, understanding the ways in which bias can distort these insights is critical. Biased data can lead to flawed decisions, inaccurate predictions, and ineffective strategies, affecting everything from product development to resource allocation.

Beyond the technical inaccuracies, bias in data also has deeper ethical ramifications, as it can perpetuate existing inequality and reinforce harmful stereotypes. In sectors such as healthcare, criminal justice, and employment, biased data can result in outcomes that disproportionately disadvantage certain groups, exacerbating systemic inequity and leading to unfair treatment.

The consequences of biased data extend far beyond incorrect conclusions; they shape the societal landscape in ways that can harm marginalized communities. When data fails to accurately represent diverse populations or is used without critical reflection, it can reinforce structural disadvantages and perpetuate cycles of exclusion. For example, biased algorithms in hiring or policing can result in discrimination against minority groups, further entrenching social injustice.

By recognizing the sources and impacts of data bias, organizations and policymakers can take proactive steps to address these challenges. This includes diversifying datasets, auditing algorithms, and involving a wide range of stakeholders in the decision-making process. In doing so, they can work toward more equitable and responsible data practices that benefit society as a whole.

The Impact on Individual Decision-Making

At the individual level, bias in data can have serious consequences, leading to flawed decisions that directly impact people's well-being. In healthcare, for instance, biased data can result in unequal treatment recommendations based on demographic factors such as race, gender, or socioeconomic status. Medical algorithms trained primarily on data from one demographic group may fail to provide accurate assessments or treatment plans for individuals from other groups, compromising the quality of care they receive.

For example, a study revealed that algorithms used to predict heart disease outcomes were often less accurate for women, as they had been trained largely on data from male patients. This disparity can lead to misdiagnoses or inappropriate treatment recommendations, putting certain populations at higher risk for adverse health outcomes. The reliance on biased data not only jeopardizes patient safety but also exacerbates existing health inequity by perpetuating unequal access to effective care.

Moreover, the long-term consequences of biased healthcare data can extend beyond individual cases to affect broader public trust in the medical system. When certain populations experience inadequate care or consistently encounter misdiagnoses due to algorithmic bias, their confidence in healthcare providers and institutions may be significantly undermined. As patients become aware of these limitations, they may grow reluctant to seek medical help, further widening the gap in health outcomes between different demographic groups. This hesitation can intensify existing health disparity, as marginalized communities may avoid preventative care or necessary treatments, ultimately increasing the burden on healthcare systems and diminishing overall public health. Therefore, addressing bias in healthcare data is not only an ethical obligation but also a critical step in building more equitable and trustworthy healthcare systems.

Societal Implications of Bias

On a broader societal scale, bias in data can reinforce and perpetuate systemic inequality, exacerbating issues such as discrimination and social injustice. In areas such as criminal justice, the use of biased data in predictive policing algorithms often leads to the disproportionate targeting of marginalized communities. These algorithms, trained on historical arrest data, may predict higher crime rates in specific neighborhoods, often those with higher concentrations of minority populations. As a result, these areas become subject to increased police presence and surveillance, while the root causes of crime, such as poverty, lack of access to education, and systemic inequality, remain unaddressed. This not only leads to over-policing but also deepens the marginalization of already vulnerable groups, further perpetuating cycles of discrimination.

The impact of this bias extends beyond individual interactions with law enforcement, affecting entire communities and their relationship with legal institutions. A report by the Human Rights Data Analysis Group highlights how the reliance on biased crime data disproportionately results in the arrests of minority groups, feeding a vicious cycle in which these communities are more heavily scrutinized and criminalized. This, in turn, damages trust between residents and law enforcement, creating an environment of fear, resentment, and mistrust.

Over time, this strained relationship undermines social cohesion, making it more difficult for communities to work collaboratively with law enforcement and other public institutions to address underlying issues. In this way, biased data not only has immediate consequences but also contributes to long-term societal divisions that hinder progress and justice.

Economic Consequences of Bias

Biased decision-making can have significant economic repercussions, particularly in the realm of employment. When hiring algorithms are influenced by biased data, they may systematically disadvantage qualified candidates from underrepresented groups, leading to missed opportunities for both individuals and organizations. A study by the National Bureau of Economic Research, for example, revealed that resume-screening algorithms were more likely to favor candidates with traditionally male-associated names over equally qualified candidates with female-associated names.

Such bias not only perpetuates gender inequality in the workforce but also undermines efforts to promote diversity and inclusion. As a result, organizations may fail to tap into the broad range of skills, experiences, and perspectives that diverse talent pools offer. This can limit innovation, creativity, and problem-solving capabilities within companies, ultimately affecting their competitiveness and ability to adapt to new challenges in a globalized market.

Beyond the immediate impact on hiring, the economic implications of biased decision-making extend to an organization's reputation and long-term success. Consumers and clients are increasingly aware of social responsibility, and companies that are perceived as biased or discriminatory in their hiring practices may face a backlash from both stakeholders and the public. This can lead to a loss of business, as well as difficulties in attracting and retaining top talent from diverse backgrounds.

Additionally, companies that fail to embrace diversity may miss out on market insights and opportunities that arise from understanding different customer demographics. In an era where inclusivity is becoming a key differentiator for business success, organizations that do not address bias in their decision-making processes risk stagnation and losing out on the benefits of a truly diverse workforce.

Implications for Public Policy

The consequences of bias in data also significantly impact public policy, where decisions made by government agencies may fail to address the needs of all citizens when based on flawed or biased information. For instance, when housing policies are influenced by biased data, they may disproportionately benefit wealthier areas while neglecting low-income or minority communities. This perpetuates cycles of poverty, disenfranchisement, and inequality.

Research by the Urban Institute has highlighted how biased housing data can lead to inequitable zoning laws that prioritize affluent neighborhoods over the creation of affordable housing in underserved areas. This imbalance not only exacerbates economic disparity but also reinforces social segregation, further marginalizing already vulnerable populations. Inaccurate or incomplete data leads to policy decisions that fail to address the root causes of social issues, leaving systemic inequality unchallenged.

Such misaligned policies can also erode public trust in governmental institutions, as citizens who feel overlooked or ignored in the policymaking process may become disillusioned with the system. When individuals perceive that their voices and concerns are not adequately represented, they are less likely to engage in democratic processes, leading to reduced civic participation and voter apathy. This decline in engagement can further diminish the accountability of public officials, creating a vicious cycle where biased policies continue to be implemented without adequate scrutiny or opposition.

To prevent these negative outcomes, policymakers must ensure that the data informing their decisions is accurate, representative, and inclusive, promoting fairness and equity for all constituents. By addressing bias in public policy, governments can strengthen trust, increase civic engagement, and create more effective solutions to societal challenges.

Addressing Bias for Ethical Data Practices and Decision-Making

Addressing bias in data is critical for ensuring ethical and accurate data practices that lead to fair and just decisions. Bias such as selection bias, algorithmic bias, and confirmation bias can compromise data integrity and result in misguided or harmful outcomes. Organizations, researchers, and policymakers must remain vigilant in identifying and mitigating these biases through rigorous data collection, inclusive algorithm design, and critical analysis practices. This proactive approach not only enhances the reliability of data-driven decisions but also promotes a more equitable society, where decisions are made based on accurate, representative, and unbiased data. As data becomes more integral to decision-making across sectors, the ethical implications of bias must be a priority for all stakeholders involved.

To address these biases effectively, fostering a culture of awareness and responsibility is essential. Continuous education and training for data practitioners, policymakers, and researchers are vital in promoting ethical data practices. Institutions must advocate for policies that prioritize transparency and accountability in data use, ensuring that ethical considerations are embedded in every stage of data-handling. By creating an environment that emphasizes the importance of fairness and inclusivity, organizations can leverage data as a tool for social good, driving progress while safeguarding the rights and dignity of individuals. Engaging with affected communities and diversifying data sources can further support efforts to mitigate bias, ultimately leading to more informed and equitable decisions.

Furthermore, ethical decision-making in data practices requires the concerted efforts of multiple stakeholders, including data scientists, policymakers, and community organizations. Collaborative initiatives such as ethical review boards and algorithm audits can help identify bias early and ensure diverse perspectives are considered. This holistic approach strengthens the credibility of organizations, builds trust with stakeholders, and fosters accountability. As the use of data continues to shape policies and strategies, recognizing and addressing bias is not only a technical challenge but a moral imperative, paving the way for data to become a powerful tool for empowerment and inclusivity. Ultimately, the commitment to ethical data practices can lead to a more just and equitable society.

CHAPTER 9

DATA BIAS MITIGATION

STRATEGIES FOR FAIRNESS

Mitigating Bias in Data-Driven Decision-Making

As organizations increasingly adopt data-driven decision-making, the need to identify and address bias in data processing has never been more critical. Bias can infiltrate every stage of the data lifecycle—from collection to analysis and interpretation—leading to skewed conclusions and unintended consequences. Data may reflect historical inequality, algorithmic models can reinforce existing disparity, and subjective interpretations can lead to decisions that perpetuate systemic bias. Such flawed processes not only compromise the quality and accuracy of insights but can also result in decisions that are unethical and damaging to society, especially when they reinforce discrimination or marginalize vulnerable groups.

To counteract these risks, a range of bias mitigation techniques has been developed. These methods focus on both identifying the sources of bias and taking concrete action to correct them. For example, data collection strategies can be refined to ensure diverse representation, while algorithmic audits can detect and mitigate bias in models. Fairness constraints can be built into AI systems, and interpretive practices can be adjusted to prevent misinformed conclusions.

Additionally, fostering a culture of fairness and inclusivity within organizations is crucial to ensuring that decision-making processes align with ethical standards. By adopting these practices, organizations can work toward more equitable and just data practices, improving outcomes and building trust with stakeholders.

Data Auditing as a Foundational Technique

One of the foundational techniques for bias mitigation is data auditing, a critical process that involves a systematic evaluation of data sources, collection methods, and processing algorithms to identify potential bias early in the data lifecycle. This process entails a thorough examination of how data is gathered, ensuring that it accurately represents the target population and does not favor certain groups over others. For example, sampling methods must be scrutinized to determine whether they introduce bias by overrepresenting or underrepresenting particular demographics. If an organization is collecting customer data for a new product launch, it is essential that the sample reflects the diversity of the target market to prevent skewed results that may lead to flawed business decisions.

By understanding the composition of their datasets, organizations can proactively address any imbalances before they impact outcomes. For instance, in healthcare research, if a dataset heavily represents a specific demographic, it can introduce selection bias, leading to recommendations that may not be applicable to other populations. In such cases, researchers can seek additional data sources to achieve a more balanced representation, ensuring that findings are not only more reliable but also equitable. This practice enhances the inclusiveness of data-driven decisions and minimizes the risk of perpetuating disparity, helping organizations create more fair and robust models and outcomes.

Algorithmic Auditing for Bias Identification

Algorithmic auditing is a vital technique for identifying and addressing bias in data processing, ensuring that the models and systems used for analysis and decision-making produce fair and equitable outcomes. This process involves a systematic evaluation of algorithms to uncover patterns that may disadvantage specific demographic groups. By applying fairness metrics, organizations can assess whether algorithms disproportionately affect certain populations, providing a clearer picture of how different groups are treated.

For instance, in machine learning applications, bias detection tools can be employed to evaluate model performance across various demographics, highlighting disparities that might otherwise go unnoticed. Such audits allow organizations to maintain transparency and uphold ethical standards by identifying potential risks before they escalate.

Continuous algorithmic auditing ensures that any identified bias can be addressed promptly, promoting accountability and minimizing harm. As bias can emerge or evolve over time due to changing data patterns or shifts in societal dynamics, organizations must adopt a pro-active approach to regularly audit their algorithms. By integrating real-time monitoring and adjusting models accordingly, organizations can prevent biased outcomes from becoming ingrained in their decision-making processes. This practice not only fosters trust among stakehold-ers but also reinforces the ethical use of data, ensuring that algorithmic decisions are fair, unbiased, and reflective of an organization's commit-ment to inclusivity and equality.

Diverse Data Practices for Mitigation

In addition to auditing, adopting diverse data practices is a crucial strategy for mitigating bias. This approach involves assembling diverse teams for data collection, analysis, and decision-making, as varied perspectives can help identify and challenge potential bias that might otherwise go unno-ticed. Homogeneous groups are more likely to have blind spots, while teams with diverse backgrounds, experiences, and viewpoints can criti-cally examine assumptions and practices. For example, members from different cultural, gender, or socioeconomic backgrounds may spot biases in data or algorithms that others might miss. By incorporating these per-spectives, organizations can improve the accuracy and fairness of their data practices, leading to more robust and ethical outcomes.

Beyond team composition, organizations should also prioritize diver-sity in the data sources they use. Relying on a single or limited set of data sources can inadvertently introduce bias, especially if the data reflects only a narrow demographic. By actively seeking out data from multi-ple and varied sources, organizations can create richer, more balanced datasets that better represent the populations they serve. This reduces the risk of bias related to specific demographic groups and enhances the inclusiveness of the decision-making process. Together, the combi-nation of diverse teams and data sources fosters an environment where ethical data practices are more likely to thrive, ensuring that decisions are informed by a broad range of viewpoints and experiences.

Bias Correction Techniques

Bias correction techniques are instrumental in addressing and mitigat-ing biases during data analysis, ensuring that the insights drawn are both fair and representative. One common method is reweighting, a statistical approach where different weights are assigned to data sam-ples to correct imbalances. This technique is particularly useful in situ-ations where certain demographic groups are underrepresented. For example, in survey research, if a minority population is under-sampled, researchers can adjust the weights of those responses to reflect their actual proportions in the broader population. By rebalancing the data in this way, organizations can improve the representativeness of their analyses, reducing the risk of biased conclusions and ensuring more accurate decision-making.

In machine learning, bias correction can be achieved through techniques such as adversarial training, where models are designed to minimize biased outcomes. In adversarial training, models are trained not only to optimize performance but also to detect and penalize bias that may arise during the learning process. This helps the model adjust its predictions to avoid favoring one group over another. These bias correction methods allow organizations to move beyond merely identifying bias—they actively work to eliminate it. The result is a more equitable decision-making framework where the potential for unfair outcomes is significantly reduced, leading to data-driven decisions that are both just and inclusive.

Cultivating a Culture of Transparency and Accountability

Fostering a culture of transparency and accountability within organizations is vital for sustained bias mitigation, as it encourages a proactive approach to identifying and addressing bias in data practices. Open dialogue about data processes, potential bias, and the impact of data-driven decisions should be promoted at all levels of the organization. Creating platforms where employees can share their experiences with data, voice concerns, and offer insights into bias they observe can significantly improve awareness. These discussions can also help in identifying blind spots that may not have been previously considered.

Training programs focused on recognizing, understanding, and mitigating bias can further empower employees, providing them with the tools needed to be vigilant and responsible in their use of data. By cultivating this level of awareness and accountability, organizations can take deliberate steps toward ethical decision-making.

Moreover, transparency in data reporting and decision-making processes is essential for building trust with both internal and external stakeholders. When organizations are open about how they handle data, how decisions are made, and how bias is addressed, they demonstrate a commitment to ethical practices. This transparency fosters trust, not only among employees but also with customers, partners, and the wider community. It signals that the organization is serious about accountability and is taking active measures to mitigate biases in its operations. When employees feel confident in raising concerns about biases they encounter without fear of retribution, organizations are better positioned to address these issues quickly and effectively, ensuring a more ethical and equitable environment for all.

Mitigating Bias for Fair Data Practices

In conclusion, addressing bias in data processing is a multifaceted challenge that requires a combination of techniques and cultural shifts. Through data and algorithmic auditing, diverse data practices, bias correction methods, and a commitment to transparency, organizations can significantly reduce bias and promote fairness in their data practices. By prioritizing these bias mitigation techniques, organizations not only enhance the reliability of their data-driven decisions but also contribute to a more equitable and just society. The integration of these strategies can lead to better outcomes for individuals and communities affected by data-driven policies and practices, ultimately strengthening the integrity of organizations and fostering public trust.

Ultimately, the goal of bias mitigation is not just compliance with ethical standards but fostering an inclusive environment that recognizes the value of every individual's experience and perspective. Organizations that embrace bias mitigation not only safeguard their reputations but also create opportunities for innovation and growth by tapping into the diverse insights of their teams and stakeholders. As the landscape of data continues to evolve, the commitment to ethical data practices and bias mitigation will remain vital to ensuring that data serves as a force for good, driving positive change in society while respecting and valuing all individuals.

PRACTITIONERS' ROLE IN PROMOTING FAIRNESS

The Ethical Responsibility of Practitioners

In today's data-driven world, professionals in fields such as data science, AI, and data analytics bear a profound ethical responsibility. Their work directly influences decisions that impact individuals, communities, and entire societal structures. Beyond technical proficiency, these practitioners must prioritize fairness, transparency, and inclusivity in the systems they design and deploy. This responsibility extends to identifying and mitigating bias within data and algorithms, ensuring that the outcomes of their work are equitable and socially just.

The decisions made by data and AI practitioners have far-reaching consequences, shaping critical areas such as healthcare, education, hiring, criminal justice, and financial lending. A single flawed algorithm can perpetuate, or even exacerbate, existing inequality, making it essential for professionals to adopt a robust ethical framework. This framework must prioritize fairness and transparency while carefully considering the societal implications of their work. By embracing this ethical responsibility, practitioners can help create systems that are not only technically sound but also equitable and inclusive.

As the demand for data-driven insights grows, so too does the need for practitioners to advocate for fairness and uphold ethical guidelines. Their role extends beyond organizational interests to fostering public trust in data-driven systems. Ethical data practices enhance societal confidence in technology, mitigating risks associated with bias and misuse. This trust is critical in ensuring that technological advancements are embraced rather than feared.

Looking to the future, the ethical responsibilities of data practitioners will only increase as technologies such as AI and machine learning become more prevalent. The potential for bias in automated systems is greater than ever, making it crucial for practitioners to actively counteract these risks. By prioritizing fairness and social responsibility, they can help ensure that data-driven decision-making benefits all individuals, particularly those from marginalized or underrepresented communities. Ultimately, promoting ethical data practices is not only a professional obligation but a moral imperative that can drive positive societal change and foster equity across all sectors of society.

Ethical Responsibility in Data and Algorithm Design

At the core of ethical responsibility in data practices is the understanding that data and algorithms are not neutral; they are imbued with the values, assumptions, and biases of the individuals and organizations that design them. Practitioners in fields such as data science and AI must recognize their role as active participants in shaping these values and take ownership of the potential consequences of their work. This means understanding that bias can emerge at every stage of the data lifecycle—during data collection, processing, and analysis. For example, when datasets are disproportionately drawn from a specific demographic, the resulting models may be skewed, leading to decisions that disproportionately favor or disadvantage certain groups. Acknowledging these risks is the first step in fostering a more equitable and responsible approach to data use.

To effectively mitigate bias, practitioners must adopt a vigilant and critical mindset regarding the data they work with and the algorithms they develop. This requires a proactive approach to identifying potential sources of bias and addressing them before they can manifest in real-world outcomes. Moreover, a commitment to continuous education on ethical data practices is essential, as the landscape of technology and its societal impact evolves rapidly. Practitioners must stay informed about emerging ethical issues, such as how their decisions affect marginalized groups or perpetuate inequality, and make adjustments to their processes as needed. By doing so, they can contribute to the creation of more inclusive and fair systems that better serve diverse populations.

Advocating for Transparency and Accountability

Practitioners in data science, AI, and analytics have an ethical responsibility to champion transparency and accountability in their work. Transparency entails openly communicating the limitations, assumptions, and potential bias inherent in the data and algorithms they employ, as well as explaining how their decisions might affect different stakeholders. By being transparent, practitioners build trust with users, customers, and the public, offering them a clear understanding of how their data is being used and the possible risks involved. For instance, if a company utilizes an AI-powered hiring tool, it should disclose how the algorithm was trained, what data sources were used, and any potential bias that might impact the selection process. This level of openness allows individuals to make informed decisions and fosters confidence in the system's fairness and integrity.

Accountability is equally crucial, requiring practitioners to put in place mechanisms for regular oversight and evaluation of their data practices. Ensuring that data-driven systems are ethically compliant and fair should not be a one-time task but an ongoing process. This could involve the formation of interdisciplinary teams composed of ethicists, sociologists, and representatives from the affected communities. These teams would offer diverse perspectives, scrutinizing the ethical implications of the technology and holding practitioners accountable for their decisions. By promoting such structures for accountability, practitioners not only safeguard against unintended harm but also ensure that their work aligns with broader societal values and ethical standards.

Prioritizing Inclusivity in Data Practices

In addition to promoting transparency, practitioners must make inclusivity a core principle in their data practices. This involves deliberately seeking out diverse data sources and actively considering the perspectives of marginalized and underrepresented communities. By integrating these voices into their work, practitioners can design algorithms and systems that are more reflective of the populations they serve, ultimately fostering greater fairness and equity. For example, in healthcare analytics, using data from a broad range of demographic groups ensures that treatment algorithms are not only accurate but also applicable to patients of different ages, races, genders, and socioeconomic backgrounds. Inclusivity in data sourcing helps to prevent the marginalization of certain groups and reduces the risk of biased outcomes, creating more equitable systems overall.

Engaging directly with community stakeholders is a vital step toward building inclusive data practices. Practitioners should take the time to understand the needs, concerns, and lived experiences of these communities, allowing them to inform the development of technology that aligns with real-world challenges. Collaborating with community members not only strengthens the ethical foundation of data work but also empowers those affected by technological decisions, giving them a voice in shaping systems that impact their lives. This participatory approach enriches the design process by providing valuable insights and perspectives, leading to solutions that are both more just and more effective. Inclusivity, when embedded in data practices, thus helps bridge the gap between innovation and social responsibility.

Advocating for Ethical Guidelines and Best Practices

Practitioners should also take on the role of advocates for ethical guidelines and best practices within their organizations and across their industries. This involves actively supporting the creation of ethical frameworks that prioritize fairness, transparency, and equity in data-driven processes. By promoting these frameworks, practitioners can help shape organizational policies and cultures that place ethical considerations at the forefront of decision-making. For instance, establishing a formal code of ethics for data scientists within a company can provide clear guidance on how to handle complex ethical dilemmas, such as ensuring fairness in AI-driven hiring algorithms or avoiding biased predictions in financial systems. These internal frameworks serve as a foundation for ethical accountability, helping practitioners navigate the evolving challenges posed by data-intensive technologies.

Beyond individual organizations, this advocacy should extend to industry-wide initiatives focused on promoting fairness and ethical responsibility in data usage and AI applications. Practitioners can drive collaboration among companies, academic institutions, and regulatory bodies to share best practices, develop common ethical standards, and work toward consistent, equitable data practices across sectors. As the field of data science rapidly evolves, these frameworks will be essential in ensuring that ethical considerations keep pace with technological advancements. By working collectively to define and uphold these standards, practitioners can help safeguard against harmful bias and inequality, ensuring that the benefits of data and AI technology are equitably distributed across society.

CHAPTER 10

BIAS IN COMPUTER SYSTEMS

UNDERSTANDING BIAS IN COMPUTER SYSTEMS

Unpacking Bias in Computer Systems

Bias in computer systems presents a critical challenge that affects both the fairness and reliability of technology. Many algorithms are trained on historical data that often contains embedded bias, reflecting existing social inequalities and prejudices. When this biased data is used without careful examination or corrective measures, it can lead to unfair and harmful outcomes. For example, algorithms used in hiring processes may favor certain demographic groups over others, while those used in loan approvals might perpetuate patterns of discrimination against minorities. Even content recommendation systems, when skewed by biased data, can reinforce harmful stereotypes or limit diverse perspectives. These biased outcomes not only harm individuals directly but also exacerbate broader societal inequality, further entrenching systemic issues and diminishing public trust in technological systems that are expected to be objective and impartial.

Addressing bias in computer systems demands a multifaceted approach that includes a thorough evaluation of data quality, ensuring diverse representation, and making deliberate design choices to avoid reinforcing prejudices. Practitioners must critically assess the datasets they use, recognizing that data sourced from historically privileged groups or skewed environments can lead to biased models. Incorporating diverse perspectives during the design and development of algorithms is equally essential, as it ensures that the technology serves a wider array of users fairly.

Moreover, bias mitigation techniques, such as re-sampling data, adjusting algorithmic parameters, or implementing fairness checks, can help reduce unintended prejudices in outcomes. Ultimately, the responsibility to address bias lies with both the developers and the organizations deploying these systems, as intentional actions toward fairness and equity are necessary to create technology that genuinely benefits all members of society.

Biased Training Data

A major source of bias in computer systems is the use of biased training data, which is a foundational issue in machine learning. Machine learning models learn by identifying patterns from historical data, which they use to make predictions, categorize information, or provide recommendations. If the training data contains embedded prejudices or underrepresents certain groups, though, the model is likely to replicate and even reinforce these biases. For example, if a dataset used to train a facial recognition system predominantly features light-skinned individuals, the system may struggle to accurately recognize people with darker skin tones. Such bias has real-world implications, as it can lead to misidentification, wrongful accusations, or exclusion from critical services. The reliance on biased training data can thus result in technologies that unfairly impact marginalized communities, further entrenching societal disparity.

The consequences of biased training data extend far beyond facial recognition. In hiring algorithms, models trained on historical hiring data may favor candidates from certain demographic groups, perpetuating gender, racial, or socioeconomic discrimination. Similarly, biased data in loan approval systems can lead to unjust denials for individuals from underrepresented or marginalized groups, reinforcing financial inequity. Systems built on biased data not only amplify existing inequality but also risk eroding trust in technology, as the individuals and communities most affected are often already disadvantaged.

To address this issue, practitioners must prioritize the inclusion of diverse and representative data in training processes, as well as implement techniques to detect and mitigate bias. Ensuring fairness in data is key to developing systems that promote equality rather than exacerbating inequality.

Lack of Diversity in Development Teams

Bias can also emerge from the lack of diversity within the teams responsible for designing and developing computer systems. When development teams are not diverse, they may inadvertently overlook the ways their systems could affect people with different backgrounds, experiences, or needs. This unintentional bias often arises because developers, consciously or unconsciously, encode their own assumptions, preferences, and experiences into the design of a system. The result is technology that may function well for individuals who share characteristics with the creators, but it can be exclusionary or discriminatory toward others. For instance, when a team is predominantly composed of individuals from one demographic, they might fail to account for how their system will interact with users from different cultural, ethnic, or linguistic backgrounds. This lack of perspective can result in products that are neither inclusive nor fair, disproportionately affecting those outside the development team's experience.

A clear example of this issue is seen in speech recognition software that struggles with accents, dialects, or gendered speech patterns. These systems are often trained and tested on a narrow range of voices, typically those of individuals who speak in standard dialects or have neutral accents. As a result, people with regional accents or non-native English speakers often find these systems inaccurate or unresponsive. Similarly, gender bias can emerge in systems that are not designed to accommodate variations in pitch and tone, leading to poorer performance for women or individuals with non-binary vocal characteristics. These oversights are often the result of development processes that fail to incorporate diverse voices and perspectives during the design phase. Addressing this bias requires assembling diverse teams that reflect the broader society, as well as engaging with communities and users throughout the development process to ensure that products are inclusive and effective for all.

The Societal Impact of Algorithmic Bias

Algorithmic bias is not just a technical issue; it is deeply intertwined with societal challenges and has far-reaching consequences in critical areas such as law enforcement, healthcare, and finance. When biased algorithms are deployed in these sectors, they have the potential to perpetuate and even amplify existing social inequality. For instance, in law enforcement, predictive policing algorithms, which are designed to forecast criminal activity, often rely on historical crime data that disproportionately targets certain racial or ethnic communities. Because this data reflects longstanding bias in the criminal justice system, these algorithms can reinforce discriminatory practices, directing more police attention to already over-policed areas. This creates a harmful feedback loop where biased predictions lead to biased policing, further entrenching racial profiling and exacerbating the marginalization of disadvantaged groups.

The consequences of algorithmic bias extend beyond technical inaccuracies to contribute directly to systemic inequalities. In healthcare, for example, biased algorithms used in medical diagnostics or resource allocation may lead to unequal treatment of patients from underrepresented populations. This can result in poorer health outcomes for certain demographic groups, further widening the gap in healthcare access and quality. Similarly, in finance, biased credit-scoring algorithms may disadvantage individuals from lower-income or minority backgrounds, making it harder for them to access loans or credit.

These types of bias do not just reflect errors in data or algorithms but also mirror deeper societal inequity. As a result, algorithmic bias can exacerbate existing social divides, reinforcing structures of privilege and oppression. Addressing this issue requires more than just technical fixes; it demands a comprehensive approach that recognizes the societal implications of biased algorithms and prioritizes fairness and equity in their development and deployment.

Mitigating Bias in Computer Systems: A Dual Approach

Addressing bias in computer systems demands a two-pronged approach: improving data quality and establishing robust ethical guidelines. Ensuring that data used to train algorithms is representative of diverse populations is a crucial first step. Techniques such as auditing datasets to identify and rectify imbalances, debiasing data through statistical adjustments, and implementing fairness checks throughout the development process can help mitigate the risk of biased outcomes.

These methods aim to prevent the exclusion or misrepresentation of certain demographic groups, ensuring that algorithms perform equitably across a wide range of users. Moreover, incorporating fairness checks during both the training and deployment phases helps to catch and correct potential bias before it can cause harm. By prioritizing diverse and high-quality data, developers can create systems that reflect the complexities of the real world, minimizing unintended bias and fostering greater inclusivity.

In addition to improving data quality, transparency and accountability are key elements in ensuring fairness in computer systems. Developers and organizations must be open about how their algorithms are trained, what data is used, and how decisions are made. This transparency allows external stakeholders—such as ethicists, regulators, or the affected communities themselves—to scrutinize and challenge potential bias in the system.

Continuous testing and refinement of algorithms are essential, as bias may emerge over time or in specific contexts. Developers should remain committed to regularly auditing their models, particularly when they are applied to sensitive areas such as healthcare, finance, or criminal justice. Although addressing bias is a complex and ongoing challenge, the adoption of these practices can significantly enhance fairness, building more trustworthy and equitable systems that serve all segments of society.

Community Engagement and Participatory Design

Bias mitigation efforts must also involve active feedback from stakeholders, particularly those directly affected by the technologies being developed. Community engagement and participatory design are essential for identifying sources of bias that may be invisible to developers but highly evident to users. Engaging with diverse communities throughout the development process allows practitioners to gather insights from a wide range of perspectives, ensuring that the technology does not inadvertently harm or exclude particular groups.

This collaborative approach is crucial because developers, no matter how well intentioned, may have blind spots when it comes to understanding the lived experiences of marginalized or underrepresented communities. By incorporating stakeholder feedback early and often, developers can proactively address potential issues of fairness, ensuring that the system reflects the needs of all users.

Including diverse perspectives in the design process leads to more inclusive and equitable systems. For example, when underrepresented communities are actively involved in the creation of algorithms, their unique challenges and concerns are more likely to be addressed. This can result in technology that is not only more effective but also more just. In the case of AI in healthcare, for instance, engaging with minority groups may reveal health disparity that would otherwise be overlooked, prompting the development of algorithms that account for these differences.

Similarly, involving women, non-binary individuals, and those from various cultural backgrounds in the design of voice recognition or hiring algorithms can help ensure these systems work fairly for all users, regardless of gender or ethnicity. By incorporating a participatory design approach, developers can create more equitable technologies that better serve the diverse populations they aim to assist.

Accountability and Ethical Considerations

Bias in computer systems brings to the forefront critical issues of accountability and transparency. Algorithms are frequently viewed as impartial decision-makers, which can obscure the fact that they often reflect the bias present in the data and design choices of the developers who create them. This illusion of objectivity makes it difficult to trace and hold accountable those responsible for biased outcomes, particularly when the inner workings of these algorithms are opaque. Without transparency, biased decisions can go unchecked, affecting marginalized communities in various areas. To address this, ethical frameworks and guidelines for responsible AI are essential. These frameworks provide a roadmap for developers and companies to recognize their role in mitigating bias, ensuring that fairness is a fundamental consideration in every stage of the development process.

Establishing clear standards for explainability is another crucial step in promoting accountability and transparency. When algorithms are explainable, it becomes easier for users, stakeholders, and regulators to understand how decisions are made and to identify where bias may arise. Explainability allows individuals to scrutinize the factors that influence algorithmic decisions, offering a clearer pathway to address and correct biases. This is particularly important in high-stakes sectors such as healthcare, finance, and criminal justice, where biased outcomes can have significant consequences.

By implementing these standards, developers can provide greater visibility into their models' decision-making processes, enabling more informed discussions around bias and fairness. Ultimately, transparency and accountability go hand in hand in ensuring that algorithms are not only technically accurate but also ethically responsible and equitable in their impact.

Toward Fairer Computer Systems

Completely eliminating bias from computer systems may be an unrealistic goal, but reducing its impact is both necessary and attainable. Bias in technology often mirrors the broader societal biases embedded in the data and structures from which these systems are developed. Therefore, addressing bias in technology requires not only technical solutions but also a commitment to social change. Techniques such as auditing data, debiasing algorithms, and implementing fairness checks are vital technical measures. These techniques alone, though, are not sufficient.

Ethical considerations must be integrated into every stage of the development process, from design to deployment. By fostering an environment of accountability—where developers and companies take responsibility for the fairness of their systems—and by promoting transparency, the harmful effects of bias can be mitigated. These efforts, combined with a holistic understanding of the social contexts in which technology operates, are key to reducing bias in meaningful ways.

The fight against bias in technology is an ongoing process, but through awareness, vigilance, and inclusive practices, more equitable systems can be built. Actively seeking diverse perspectives, both within development teams and from the communities affected by these technologies, is essential to this effort. Diversity brings a broader range of experiences and viewpoints that can help identify potential bias and address it proactively.

This collaborative approach not only helps in reducing bias but also ensures that the technology is better suited to serve the diverse populations it impacts. While achieving total bias elimination may not be possible, continual refinement of these systems, informed by ethical guidelines and inclusive practices, can lead to fairer and more just outcomes. By remaining committed to these principles, the technology sector can play a critical role in advancing equity and justice in society.

FRAMEWORK FOR ANALYZING BIAS IN COMPUTER SYSTEMS

Bias in computer systems is a pervasive issue that can affect fairness, equality, and social justice. Understanding and addressing biases in technology requires a structured approach to analyzing how these biases arise and manifest. One way to understand bias in computer systems is through a framework that identifies three primary types of biases: preexisting bias, technical bias, and emergent bias.

Preexisting Bias

Preexisting bias refers to bias that originated before the technical development of a system. This bias may stem from individuals involved in the design process or the broader societal context in which these individuals operate. Preexisting bias is embedded in the algorithms and data used in computer systems, affecting the outputs and decisions made by these technologies. Understanding preexisting bias is crucial for developing fair and equitable systems, especially as reliance on AI and machine learning continues to grow in various sectors, including healthcare, criminal justice, and finance.

Bias Originating from Individuals

Bias originating from individuals is influenced by the values, experiences, and perspectives of those who create or interact with technology. This type of bias often operates at an unconscious level, subtly shaping the design decisions made during the development process. For instance, if a development team lacks diversity—whether in terms of gender, ethnicity, socioeconomic background, or life experience—the members may unintentionally introduce assumptions that favor certain groups over others. This homogeneity can result in blind spots where the needs and perspectives of marginalized groups are overlooked.

Additionally, individual biases can manifest in various stages of technology development, including data collection, processing, and representation. For example, the way questions are framed in surveys or the metrics chosen for evaluation can reflect the biases of the designers. A team that predominantly comprises individuals from a particular demographic may prioritize features and functionalities that resonate with their experiences, thereby neglecting the needs of users from different backgrounds. This lack of diverse perspectives can lead to biased outcomes, as the algorithms may fail to incorporate important nuances relevant to underrepresented groups, ultimately perpetuating existing inequality.

Bias Originating from Society

Bias that arises from society is reflective of existing social and cultural inequalities. These types of bias are often deeply ingrained in societal structures, influencing the data used to train algorithms. Historical records, societal norms, and prevalent stereotypes contribute to the datasets that serve as the foundation for many AI and machine learning models. For instance, facial recognition systems have been shown to perform poorly for people of color, primarily because the training datasets contain disproportionately more images of light-skinned individuals. This discrepancy not only highlights the bias embedded in the data but also reveals the underlying social inequality that persists in society.

Moreover, societal bias can be exacerbated by the algorithms themselves, leading to a cycle of discrimination and exclusion. For example, predictive policing algorithms may disproportionately target specific communities based on historical crime data that reflects systemic bias in law enforcement practices. As a result, these algorithms can perpetuate stereotypes and reinforce existing disparities, further entrenching societal bias into the fabric of technological systems.

Addressing Preexisting Bias

Addressing preexisting bias requires a multifaceted approach that considers both individual and societal influences. By promoting diversity within development teams and critically examining the data used to train algorithms, we can work toward creating technologies that are more inclusive and equitable. Awareness of preexisting bias is essential for fostering a culture of responsibility among technologists, ensuring that the systems they create reflect the complexities and diversities of the real world.

Technical Bias

Technical bias arises from the design and implementation of computing systems, influenced by the inherent limitations of hardware, software, and peripherals. These constraints can lead to unintended consequences in how data is processed, analyzed, and represented. For instance, the choice of algorithms and the precision with which calculations are performed can significantly affect outcomes. When algorithms are designed, developers must make decisions regarding data representation, including choices about rounding numbers, categorizing information, and employing sampling techniques. Each of these decisions carries the potential to introduce bias into the system if not carefully considered. For example, if a dataset is rounded in a way that consistently favors higher values, this could skew results and lead to misleading conclusions, especially in scenarios such as financial assessments or risk analysis.

The biases stemming from technical design can also be exacerbated by the social contexts in which algorithms are developed. When algorithms are designed without a comprehensive understanding of the cultural or socioeconomic dynamics of their intended user base, the resulting applications may fail to account for the nuances that differentiate various groups. For instance, an algorithm developed to assess creditworthiness based on data from a specific demographic may not translate effectively to another group with distinct economic behaviors and cultural norms. In such cases, the algorithm could generate biased assessments, unfairly disadvantaging individuals from different backgrounds who may not conform to the initial assumptions made during the design phase. This misalignment underscores the importance of contextual awareness in algorithm development to ensure that the technology serves diverse populations fairly.

Furthermore, the mathematical models that underlie algorithms play a crucial role in shaping their outcomes. Many algorithms rely on statistical techniques that can inadvertently reinforce existing bias if the underlying data is flawed or unrepresentative. For example, if a predictive model is trained on historical data that reflects past discriminatory practices, it may perpetuate that bias in its predictions and recommendations. As a result, marginalized groups may continue to face unequal treatment in areas such as employment, lending, and law enforcement.

To combat technical bias, developers must not only ensure robust data collection and processing methods but also engage in ongoing assessments of algorithmic performance across diverse populations. By fostering a culture of accountability and inclusivity in technology development, we can mitigate the effects of technical bias and work toward creating more equitable systems.

Emergent Bias

Emergent bias refers to the misalignment that occurs when a system is designed without adequate foresight regarding future changes in its context of use. This type of bias typically arises after the system's design is completed, as it becomes increasingly disconnected from evolving societal norms, population dynamics, or cultural values. The inherent assumption during the design phase is that the system's utility and relevance will remain static; however, this is often far from reality.

As society progresses and perspectives shift, previously accepted solutions can become obsolete or problematic, resulting in systems that may no longer function effectively or fairly within their intended environments. Recognizing emergent bias is crucial for ongoing evaluation and adaptation of technology to meet the needs of an ever-changing society.

One prominent example of emergent bias is evident in automated hiring systems. Initially, these systems were designed to enhance objectivity in the recruitment process, leveraging algorithms to evaluate candidates based on predefined criteria. As societal awareness of the importance of diversity in the workforce has grown, however, these systems have faced scrutiny for perpetuating bias, particularly against applicants from underrepresented backgrounds. The original framework of these hiring algorithms may have seemed unbiased at the time of their creation; yet, as social norms shifted toward inclusivity and diversity, the inherent bias in the algorithms became increasingly apparent. This underscores the necessity for continual assessment and refinement of such systems to ensure alignment with evolving social values.

Emergent bias can also arise from changes in the user population that the system was not designed to accommodate. For example, consider a health monitoring system initially tailored for younger individuals, which may rely on specific physiological metrics or lifestyle factors typical of that demographic. When this system is subsequently utilized by older adults, who have different physical characteristics and health conditions, it may perform inadequately or yield misleading results. This mismatch can lead to emergent bias, ultimately resulting in health disparity or inappropriate medical advice for older users.

To mitigate emergent bias, it is essential for designers and developers to maintain a flexible approach, regularly revisiting and updating systems to reflect shifts in user demographics and societal understanding. By doing so, they can ensure that their technologies remain relevant, effective, and equitable for diverse populations.

Addressing the Complexity of Bias in Computer Systems

Bias in computer systems is a multifaceted issue that can arise at various stages—from the conception of the idea to its use in society. A framework for analyzing bias must consider preexisting, technical, and emergent sources of bias. By understanding these different forms of bias, developers, policymakers, and other stakeholders can take more proactive measures to mitigate bias in computer systems, promoting fairness and inclusivity in technology. Addressing bias in technology is crucial for ensuring that computer systems work equitably for all members of society, regardless of background or identity.

CHAPTER 11

TRANSPARENCY AND ACCOUNTABILITY

TRANSPARENCY IN DATA PRACTICES

Navigating Data Ethics: The Role of Transparency

Transparency in data ethics is fundamentally about openness and clarity in how data collection, processing, and usage practices are communicated to various stakeholders, including consumers, regulatory bodies, and the general public. This principle encompasses providing accessible and comprehensible information regarding the types of data being collected, the methods of its collection, the algorithms that process this data, and the rationale behind the decisions that stem from these processes.

When organizations embrace transparency, they allow individuals to have a clear understanding of how their data is being managed and utilized. This empowerment is crucial, as it enables users to make informed choices about their participation and consent regarding data usage, fostering a sense of agency over their personal information.

Moreover, transparency in data ethics necessitates an acknowledgment and communication of the potential limitations, bias, and risks associated with the data and algorithms employed. By openly discussing these factors, organizations can help mitigate misunderstandings and build trust among stakeholders. For example, if a company uses an algorithm to determine creditworthiness, disclosing the data sources, the criteria used in the algorithm, and any known bias can help consumers understand the potential impacts on their financial opportunities.

This visibility not only cultivates trust but also enhances accountability, as organizations become answerable for their data practices and the implications they have for individuals and communities. Ultimately, transparency in data ethics is vital for creating a more equitable digital landscape, where individuals are informed participants in their data journeys, and organizations are held to higher standards of responsibility and integrity.

Transparency for Trust

The importance of transparency in data practices cannot be overstated, as it serves as a foundation for building trust, promoting accountability, and ensuring ethical conduct in an increasingly data-driven world. As individuals become more aware of the vast amounts of personal data being collected and analyzed, concerns regarding data usage, privacy, and security have grown significantly.

Organizations that prioritize transparency in their data practices actively demonstrate respect for individuals' rights and autonomy. By openly sharing how data is collected, used, and stored, they alleviate fears of misuse and exploitation, thus fostering a climate of trust. This trust is essential for maintaining healthy relationships between businesses, governments, and the public, as it encourages individuals to engage with data-driven services and technologies without apprehension.

Moreover, the absence of transparency can have detrimental effects, leading to feelings of exploitation and deception among data subjects. When individuals are kept in the dark about how their information is managed, they may become distrustful of organizations and skeptical of technology as a whole. This erosion of trust can damage an organization's reputation and undermine public confidence in digital systems, potentially stifling innovation and progress. In contrast, when organizations embrace transparency, they not only enhance their credibility but also contribute to broader societal confidence in technology.

By establishing clear communication about data practices, organizations can encourage informed participation from individuals, ensuring that data is managed ethically and responsibly. Ultimately, fostering transparency in data practices is not just a best practice; it is a crucial step toward building a more equitable and trustworthy digital ecosystem.

Promoting Accountability Through Transparency

Transparency is fundamental in promoting accountability within organizations, particularly concerning data practices. When organizations commit to openly communicating their data practices, they effectively invite scrutiny from various stakeholders, including regulatory bodies, advocacy groups, and the general public. This openness serves as a critical mechanism for evaluating the fairness, legality, and ethical implications of how data is collected and utilized.

By subjecting their practices to external examination, organizations are held accountable for their actions, making it less likely for unethical practices—such as discrimination, data misuse, or invasion of privacy—to occur. This accountability fosters a culture of responsibility, where organizations recognize that their decisions and actions have tangible effects on individuals and communities.

Furthermore, transparency about algorithmic decision-making processes is particularly important for identifying potential biases or unintended consequences that may arise. When organizations disclose how algorithms operate and the data on which they are based, it allows stakeholders to analyze the outcomes critically and spot areas of concern. For instance, if a hiring algorithm shows a pattern of bias against certain demographic groups, transparency enables stakeholders to highlight these issues and advocate for corrective measures.

This level of accountability not only mitigates the risk of harm to individuals but also empowers organizations to refine and enhance the quality and fairness of their products and services. By fostering a culture of transparency and accountability, organizations can cultivate public trust while ensuring their practices align with ethical standards and social responsibility.

Empowering Individuals Through Transparency

Transparency plays a vital role in empowering individuals by granting them greater control over their personal information. When organizations clearly communicate how data is collected, processed, and utilized, individuals gain insights that enable them to make informed decisions regarding their data-sharing practices. For instance, if consumers are aware that a company intends to share their personal information with third parties, they can assess their comfort level with such practices and decide whether to proceed or opt out altogether.

This capacity to choose is crucial for upholding privacy rights and autonomy, as it allows individuals to assert their preferences and boundaries regarding their personal data. By promoting transparency, organizations not only respect individual rights but also cultivate a more ethical approach to data management.

This level of agency is fundamental to ensuring that consent is genuinely informed. When individuals are kept in the dark about how their data is used, they may unknowingly consent to practices that compromise their privacy or expose them to unwanted data collection. Transparency serves as a safeguard for personal freedom, ensuring that people are not subjected to data practices without their knowledge or consent.

Furthermore, when individuals feel empowered to make choices about their data, they are more likely to engage positively with organizations, fostering trust and loyalty. In an era where personal data is a valuable asset, transparency in data practices becomes essential for creating a respectful and ethical relationship between organizations and the individuals they serve. Ultimately, by prioritizing transparency, organizations can not only enhance their reputation but also contribute to a more equitable digital landscape where personal freedom is safeguarded.

Business Case for Transparency in Data Practices

In addition to promoting accountability and empowering individuals, transparency in data practices offers significant practical benefits for organizations themselves. By adopting transparent data practices, organizations can enhance their reputation and gain a competitive advantage in the marketplace. As public awareness of data privacy issues increases, consumers are more inclined to engage with companies that prioritize ethical data use and openly communicate their practices.

Transparency is increasingly viewed as a marker of integrity, and businesses that demonstrate this commitment often find that they attract a more loyal customer base. This loyalty not only fosters long-term relationships but can also translate into increased customer retention and advocacy, as satisfied customers are likely to share their positive experiences with others.

Moreover, transparent communication regarding data practices can help organizations mitigate legal risks and avoid potential penalties. By ensuring compliance with data protection laws and regulations—such as the GDPR in the EU, which requires clear communication about how individuals' data is processed—organizations can safeguard themselves against legal repercussions. Proactively adhering to these regulations demonstrates a commitment to ethical practices and responsible data management, which can further enhance an organization's standing in the eyes of consumers and regulators alike. In this way, transparency not only builds trust with customers but also fortifies an organization's legal and ethical foundation, creating a sustainable business model that is both socially responsible and commercially viable. Ultimately, the integration of transparent practices can lead to a stronger, more resilient organization that is well positioned to navigate the complexities of the modern data landscape.

The Cornerstone of Ethical Data Practices

In conclusion, transparency is a cornerstone of ethical data practices, promoting trust, accountability, individual empowerment, and compliance. By providing clear and comprehensible information about data collection, usage, and algorithms, transparency allows stakeholders—including consumers, regulatory bodies, and advocacy groups—to evaluate and engage with data practices in an informed manner. This understanding is crucial in an era where individuals are increasingly concerned about how their personal information is handled and used.

Moreover, transparency fosters a culture of openness and respect within organizations, enhancing their credibility and reputation in the eyes of the public. Ultimately, by prioritizing transparency, both individuals and organizations can cultivate healthier relationships built on mutual respect and informed decision-making, ensuring that ethical standards are upheld in our data-driven world.

EXPLORING BARRIERS TO DATA TRANSPARENCY

Navigating Obstacles

Achieving transparency in data use is vital for fostering trust and accountability; however, it presents numerous challenges for organizations. As data collection and analytics evolve, the processes involved become increasingly intricate, making it difficult to maintain clarity about how data is gathered, processed, and utilized. These challenges arise from various sources, including technological limitations, organizational silos, and the complexities of legal frameworks that govern data protection and privacy.

For instance, the rapid pace of technological advancement may outstrip an organization's ability to implement transparent practices, leading to confusion about data usage and increasing the risk of compliance failures. Consequently, understanding these obstacles is crucial for organizations aiming to develop effective strategies that enhance transparency and, by extension, trust in their data-driven systems.

Furthermore, organizations must navigate a landscape where data governance and compliance requirements are constantly evolving, adding another layer of complexity to achieving transparency. Legal frameworks, such as the GDPR or CCPA, impose stringent requirements for transparency, yet these regulations can be difficult to interpret and implement in practice.

Additionally, organizations may face internal resistance to transparency initiatives, especially if there is a culture of secrecy or fear surrounding data practices. To overcome these barriers, organizations must invest in training and resources that promote a culture of openness, enabling employees to understand the importance of transparent practices. By addressing both external and internal challenges, organizations can develop practical strategies to improve transparency, thereby fostering greater trust and accountability in their data practices.

The Complexity of Data Systems and Algorithms

One of the primary challenges in achieving transparency is the complexity of data systems and algorithms. In today's data-driven landscape, processing and analyzing vast amounts of information often involves sophisticated machine learning models, neural networks, and intricate data flows, which can be difficult for a general audience to grasp. These advanced algorithms, particularly those utilizing deep learning techniques, are frequently described as *black-boxes* due to their opaque decision-making processes; even the engineers who develop these systems may struggle to fully understand how certain outputs are derived from inputs. This inherent opacity presents a significant obstacle for practitioners attempting to provide clear and comprehensible explanations about how and why specific decisions are made, as the intricacies of these models may obscure the logic behind their predictions.

For transparency to be genuinely effective, it must be presented in a manner that is easily understandable to the public. Unfortunately, the technical complexity of modern data systems often hinders the ability to communicate information clearly. Simplifying these explanations without sacrificing essential details poses a challenging task that requires considerable effort and specialized skills. Organizations must invest in developing clear communication strategies that distill complex information into digestible formats, utilizing visual aids or analogies that resonate with non-technical audiences.

Furthermore, this process may involve cross-disciplinary collaboration, bringing together data scientists, communication experts, and stakeholders to ensure that transparency initiatives are accessible and effective. By addressing these challenges head-on, organizations can improve public understanding of their data practices and foster greater trust in their systems.

Organizational Reluctance to Share Information

Another significant barrier to achieving transparency is the organizational reluctance to share information. Many companies are apprehensive that being fully transparent about their data practices could expose them to competitive disadvantages, public criticism, or increased regulatory scrutiny. For example, revealing the specifics of how data is utilized may provide competitors with valuable insights into proprietary strategies or highlight vulnerabilities in data governance that could be exploited.

Moreover, transparency regarding algorithmic decision-making may uncover bias or shortcomings within their systems, leading to potential reputational damage and loss of consumer trust. As a result, organizations often adopt a defensive posture, choosing to withhold critical information to safeguard their interests rather than embracing a culture of openness.

Additionally, organizations may be wary of exposing themselves to liability if transparency reveals non-compliance with data regulations or unethical practices. In such scenarios, revealing information about data-handling processes could lead to significant legal repercussions, including fines or sanctions from regulatory bodies. This fear of accountability can further entrench a culture of secrecy, causing organizations to prioritize risk management over ethical transparency. Consequently, the reluctance to share information can impede the development of trust between organizations and their stakeholders, ultimately undermining efforts to foster ethical data practices.

To overcome these challenges, organizations must recognize the long-term benefits of transparency and invest in creating a supportive environment that encourages open communication while addressing valid concerns about competitive intelligence and regulatory compliance. By doing so, they can work toward more ethical and responsible data practices that benefit both the organization and the public.

Challenges from Data Privacy Regulations

Data privacy regulations and compliance requirements significantly complicate efforts to achieve transparency. While laws such as the GDPR are designed to promote transparency in data-handling practices, they also impose strict guidelines on how personal data can be communicated. Organizations must navigate a complex landscape where they are tasked with being open about their data practices while adhering to regulations that mandate confidentiality for specific types of information.

This balancing act can be particularly challenging, as any attempt to provide detailed explanations about data processing could inadvertently expose sensitive information or violate individuals' privacy rights. For example, sharing the methodologies or datasets used in analytics could lead to the identification of personal data, creating ethical and legal dilemmas for organizations.

Moreover, this paradox creates a dilemma for organizations, as they must strive to be transparent while simultaneously protecting user privacy. The complexity lies in determining the appropriate level of detail to share without infringing on privacy rights, leading to uncertainty and inconsistency in transparency initiatives. Organizations might err on the side of caution and withhold information, which can hinder public understanding and trust in their data practices.

To address these challenges, companies should invest in developing clear communication strategies that align with privacy regulations, focusing on conveying essential information without compromising confidentiality. This may involve employing anonymization techniques, aggregating data insights, or utilizing plain language to explain complex processes. By proactively navigating these regulatory challenges, organizations can foster a culture of transparency that respects individual privacy while also meeting legal obligations.

Limited Public Understanding of Data

The limited public understanding of data and technology significantly compounds the challenges of achieving transparency. Even when organizations make concerted efforts to communicate openly about their data practices, the average individual often lacks the technical literacy needed to fully grasp the intricacies of data usage and processing. This gap between the information provided by organizations and the public's ability to understand it can result in misunderstandings, misconceptions, and a general sense of mistrust. For instance, a company may disclose its responsible use of data analytics, yet the public's unfamiliarity with data science concepts can foster fears of privacy invasion or potential misuse. Without clear comprehension, the audience may misinterpret the intentions behind data practices, which can ultimately lead to increased skepticism and hesitancy regarding technology.

Bridging this knowledge gap necessitates not only transparency but also robust educational efforts aimed at enhancing data literacy among the public. Organizations need to recognize that communicating complex technical concepts in a straightforward and relatable manner is essential for fostering trust and understanding. This could involve developing user-friendly resources, such as infographics, tutorials, or community workshops, that explain how data is collected, processed, and used in everyday applications.

Additionally, engaging in proactive outreach initiatives that invite public participation and feedback can help demystify data practices and promote a more informed dialogue between organizations and the communities they serve. By prioritizing education alongside transparency, organizations can empower individuals to engage meaningfully with data-driven technologies, alleviating concerns and building a more informed society.

Resource Constraints

Achieving transparency in data practices can be resource-intensive, posing significant challenges for many organizations. Developing comprehensive and user-friendly documentation of data-handling processes, training staff to effectively address public inquiries about data usage, and establishing mechanisms for ongoing communication with stakeholders necessitate considerable investments of time, money, and effort.

For instance, organizations must ensure that documentation is not only accurate but also accessible to individuals with varying levels of technical understanding. This requires collaboration among technical teams, legal experts, and communications professionals, which can be a daunting task. Moreover, ongoing training for staff to ensure they are knowledgeable about data practices and capable of engaging meaningfully with the public is essential, but it also diverts resources from other critical business functions.

For many organizations, particularly smaller ones, the cost of implementing and maintaining transparency initiatives can be prohibitively high when compared to other business priorities. The need for regular audits of data systems to assess fairness, the development of explainable AI tools, and the production of clear, concise disclosures can strain limited budgets and resources.

Additionally, organizations may struggle to balance transparency efforts with the demands of their operational objectives, leading to the perception that investing in transparency is a lower priority. This challenge is further compounded by the competitive landscape, where organizations may feel pressure to allocate resources toward immediate profit-generating activities rather than long-term ethical considerations. As a result, fostering a culture of transparency may require innovative approaches to resource management and a commitment to prioritizing ethical practices over short-term gains, ultimately benefiting both the organization and its stakeholders in the long run.

Overcoming Challenges to Build Trust

In conclusion, while transparency in data use is vital for ethical data practices, organizations encounter numerous challenges that hinder their ability to be fully open about their data activities. The complexity of modern technology often makes it difficult to convey how data is collected, processed, and utilized, leaving many stakeholders confused or skeptical.

Additionally, organizational reluctance to share sensitive information due to fears of competitive disadvantage or regulatory scrutiny can lead to a culture of secrecy. Regulatory compliance further complicates matters, as organizations must navigate stringent laws that protect individual privacy while still striving for transparency. Coupled with limited public understanding of data practices and technology, these factors create a challenging landscape for organizations trying to be transparent about their data usage.

Addressing these challenges requires a multifaceted approach that combines technical solutions, regulatory support, and an intentional effort to foster a culture of openness within organizations. Technical innovations, such as explainable AI and user-friendly data disclosures, can help demystify complex processes and enhance public understanding. Additionally, regulatory bodies must provide guidance and support that encourages transparency without compromising privacy rights, creating an environment where organizations feel empowered to share information.

At the same time, organizations should prioritize internal education and training to cultivate a culture of openness among employees, promoting the importance of ethical data practices. Overcoming these obstacles is essential for building trust among stakeholders and ensuring that data-driven technologies serve all members of society in a fair and ethical manner, ultimately leading to more equitable outcomes.

ACCOUNTABILITY IN ETHICAL DATA USE

Assigning Responsibility

In the evolving landscape of data usage and technology, assigning responsibility for ethical data practices is crucial for ensuring fairness, accountability, and public trust. Ethical data usage encompasses a range of activities, from collecting and processing personal data to making decisions through machine learning algorithms. Given the complexity of these processes, it is essential to delineate clear lines of accountability at each stage.

This means recognizing that responsibility for ethical data practices cannot rest on a single individual or role; instead, it must be distributed among multiple stakeholders within an organization. This includes not only data scientists and developers who create and implement algorithms, but also company leadership who set the tone for ethical culture, legal teams who ensure compliance with regulations, and external regulators who oversee adherence to ethical standards.

Moreover, this collective approach to accountability allows a more comprehensive understanding of the ethical implications of data practices. When stakeholders at various levels are engaged in discussions about data ethics, they can collaboratively identify potential bias, address ethical dilemmas, and implement best practices for data usage. This multidimensional framework for accountability fosters an organizational culture that prioritizes ethical considerations, thereby enhancing trust among consumers and the broader public.

Furthermore, as technology continues to evolve, establishing shared responsibility for ethical data practices ensures that organizations are better equipped to respond to new challenges and emerging risks in the data landscape. By embracing a culture of accountability, organizations can build stronger relationships with their stakeholders, ultimately leading to more equitable and responsible data practices.

The Role of Data Practitioners

Data practitioners, such as data scientists, data engineers, and software developers, play a pivotal role in ensuring ethical data usage. These individuals are directly involved in designing and implementing data-driven systems, making them the first line of defense against unethical practices. Their work encompasses a wide range of responsibilities, from data collection and preprocessing to algorithm design and model deployment.

As such, it is imperative that data practitioners remain vigilant about the ethical implications of their actions at every stage of the data lifecycle. This means actively preventing bias in data, ensuring fairness in algorithmic outcomes, and respecting individual privacy while developing innovative data solutions. By recognizing the significance of these ethical considerations, practitioners can influence the integrity of the entire data ecosystem.

To effectively fulfill their responsibilities, data practitioners need to be adequately trained in data ethics and equipped to identify potential ethical issues as they arise. This training should encompass not only technical skills but also a robust understanding of the social and ethical ramifications of data use. Workshops, continuous education, and collaborative discussions with ethicists can provide practitioners with the knowledge and tools necessary to navigate complex ethical dilemmas.

Additionally, fostering an organizational culture that prioritizes ethics encourages data practitioners to engage in open dialogue about the potential consequences of their work. By embedding ethical considerations into their daily operations, data practitioners can ensure that their contributions to data-driven technologies are responsible, fair, and aligned with societal values. This proactive approach ultimately enhances public trust in data systems and promotes a more equitable technological landscape.

Leadership Accountability in Ethical Data Usage

Organizational leadership, including executives and managers, holds significant accountability for ethical data usage within their companies. As the architects of company culture, they play a critical role in establishing policies, frameworks, and resources that promote ethical behavior throughout the organization. By prioritizing ethical data usage as an integral component of their broader business strategy, leaders can ensure that ethical considerations are woven into the fabric of decision-making processes.

This commitment not only involves setting clear expectations for how data should be handled but also fostering an environment where employees feel empowered to voice concerns about ethical dilemmas. Through their leadership, executives can cultivate a culture of accountability that reinforces the importance of ethical practices in all aspects of data management.

Moreover, organizational leaders are responsible for ensuring compliance with data protection regulations and industry standards, which requires a proactive approach to transparency and stakeholder communication. By openly discussing data usage practices and potential risks, they can build trust with customers, clients, and regulators alike. Allocating resources for ongoing ethical training and auditing is also crucial, as it equips employees with the knowledge and skills necessary to navigate the complex ethical landscape of data usage.

Ultimately, the actions and values of organizational leaders significantly shape the ethical landscape of their companies, influencing employee behavior and reinforcing the commitment to ethical data practices. When leadership exemplifies a strong ethical stance, it sets a powerful precedent, encouraging a culture of integrity and responsibility that permeates the entire organization.

The Role of Legal and Compliance Teams

Legal and compliance teams play a pivotal role in maintaining ethical standards within organizations by ensuring that data practices adhere to existing laws and regulations. Their responsibilities extend beyond mere compliance; they guide data projects to align with relevant legislation, such as the GDPR and CCPA. By interpreting and applying these laws, compliance teams help organizations understand their legal obligations and the ethical implications of their data usage. This proactive approach is essential in fostering a culture of accountability, as it ensures that data practices are not only lawful but also ethical, promoting principles of fairness, transparency, and respect for individual rights.

In addition to providing legal guidance, compliance teams are responsible for conducting regular audits of data practices and responding to potential ethical breaches. This oversight creates a structured framework for monitoring and evaluating ethical data usage, allowing organizations to identify areas for improvement and mitigate risks. By systematically reviewing data-handling processes and ensuring they align with ethical guidelines, compliance teams help safeguard against violations that could harm individuals or damage the organization's reputation. Their role is crucial in establishing trust among stakeholders, as it demonstrates a commitment to ethical practices and the protection of personal information. Ultimately, the collaboration between legal, compliance, and other teams within an organization is essential for creating a robust ethical data framework that supports responsible data usage and fosters public confidence.

The Role of Regulators and Policymakers

Assigning responsibility for ethical data usage extends beyond individual organizations; regulators and policymakers play a crucial role in the broader ecosystem. Governments and regulatory bodies establish the legal frameworks within which data usage must operate, setting minimum standards for data ethics and guiding the behavior of organizations. This external oversight is essential for ensuring that companies adhere to ethical practices and are held accountable for their data-handling.

By creating and enforcing policies that govern how organizations collect, use, store, and share data, regulators help to mitigate risks associated with data misuse and promote responsible practices. This regulatory framework is vital for fostering a culture of accountability within the industry, as it reinforces the idea that organizations must prioritize ethical considerations in their data activities.

Moreover, regulators serve as advocates for the public interest, ensuring that organizations respect individuals' privacy rights and that data practices do not lead to societal harm. They provide a necessary check on the power of organizations, helping to balance the interests of businesses with the rights of individuals and the well-being of communities. By actively engaging with stakeholders, including consumer advocacy groups, industry representatives, and the public, regulators can develop policies that reflect the diverse needs and concerns of society.

This collaborative approach not only enhances the effectiveness of data regulations but also fosters trust between the public and organizations. Ultimately, the involvement of regulators and policymakers is essential in creating a comprehensive ethical framework for data usage that promotes fairness, transparency, and accountability across the entire data ecosystem.

Societal Influence on Ethical Data Usage

Society as a whole plays a pivotal role in driving ethical data usage, with consumers and advocacy groups acting as influential stakeholders in this endeavor. Consumers have become increasingly aware of their data privacy rights and ethical considerations related to data-handling. By voicing their expectations and concerns, they can exert significant pressure on organizations to prioritize ethical data practices. This consumer demand for accountability compels businesses to adopt more transparent and fair data usage policies. As individuals make informed choices about which companies to support based on their ethical track records, organizations are incentivized to align their practices with public sentiment to retain customer loyalty and trust.

Advocacy groups and non-governmental organizations (NGOs) further amplify these public concerns by monitoring corporate practices and highlighting instances of unethical behavior. These organizations often serve as watchdogs, conducting research, raising awareness, and campaigning for stronger regulations to protect individuals' rights in the digital age. Their efforts can lead to increased scrutiny of data practices and foster a culture of accountability among organizations.

By collaborating with consumers and other stakeholders, advocacy groups can drive meaningful change and encourage organizations to adopt more responsible data practices. This collective societal influence not only steers data usage toward more ethical outcomes but also reinforces the idea that organizations are accountable to the communities they serve, ultimately contributing to a more equitable and just data ecosystem.

Collective Responsibility in Ethical Data Practices

In conclusion, the responsibility for ethical data usage is a multifaceted endeavor that is shared across various levels within and outside an organization. At the ground level, data practitioners play a critical role in embedding ethics into their technical processes, ensuring that their work reflects considerations of fairness, accountability, and transparency. They must be vigilant about potential bias and actively work to mitigate them throughout the data lifecycle.

Simultaneously, organizational leaders are tasked with creating a culture that prioritizes ethical behavior, developing policies that guide data practices, and fostering an environment where ethical considerations are integrated into strategic decision-making. Together, these groups create a foundational framework for ethical data usage within organizations.

Moreover, legal and compliance teams serve as crucial guardians of ethical standards by ensuring that organizations adhere to relevant regulations and industry standards. They provide the necessary oversight to prevent legal violations while promoting best practices in data management. On a broader scale, policymakers play an essential role in establishing the regulatory environment that governs data practices, ensuring that ethical considerations are enshrined in law.

Ultimately, ethical data usage is a collaborative effort that requires the active participation of all stakeholders—data practitioners, organizational leaders, legal experts, policymakers, and society at large. By recognizing and embracing this shared responsibility, organizations and individuals can more effectively address ethical challenges and promote data practices that are fair, transparent, and accountable, ultimately leading to data-driven technologies that benefit individuals and society as a whole.

TOOLS FOR ENSURING DATA ACCOUNTABILITY

Building Accountability in Data Management

Ensuring accountability in data usage is a critical aspect of ethical data management, especially as data-driven decision-making becomes more integral to various sectors. With the growing reliance on data analytics, the need for robust frameworks that hold individuals and organizations accountable for their data practices is paramount. These frameworks can include comprehensive data governance policies that outline specific roles and responsibilities regarding data-handling.

Additionally, implementing technical tools such as audit logs, data lineage tracking, and automated compliance checks can provide a clear trail of data usage and decision-making processes. Such measures not only promote ethical behavior but also foster trust with consumers and stakeholders who increasingly demand transparency and responsible data practices.

Practical approaches for ensuring accountability can be broadly categorized into technical tools, organizational practices, and regulatory measures. Technical tools, such as data quality assessments and algorithmic auditing software, help identify and mitigate potential bias and inaccuracies in data processing. Organizational practices may include regular training sessions for staff on data ethics, as well as the establishment of ethics review boards to oversee data projects.

On the regulatory side, governments can enact laws and standards that require organizations to adhere to specific ethical guidelines, providing a structured framework for accountability. Collectively, these strategies create a comprehensive system of checks and balances, ensuring that data is used responsibly and ethically across all levels of an organization. This multifaceted approach not only mitigates risks associated with data misuse but also enhances public confidence in data-driven technologies.

Technical Tools for Accountability

Audit Trails

Audit trails are one of the most effective technical tools for ensuring accountability in data usage. An audit trail involves maintaining a record of every action taken with data, from collection to deletion, including any modifications and transfers. These records provide a clear history of how data has been handled, which helps in detecting any misuse or unauthorized access.

Regular audits of these trails allow organizations to monitor compliance with data policies and regulations, identify potential vulnerabilities, and take corrective action as needed. Audit trails are particularly useful in ensuring that data-handling aligns with privacy regulations, such as the GDPR, and in providing evidence in the event of an investigation.

Algorithmic Transparency and Explainability

Algorithmic transparency and explainability are also crucial tools for accountability, especially in data-driven decision-making systems that use complex algorithms or machine learning models. Explainability tools, such as LIME (Local Interpretable Model-agnostic Explanations) and SHAP (SHapley Additive exPlanations), are designed to make the outputs of complex algorithms more understandable for stakeholders.

These tools help practitioners identify the key factors influencing a particular decision, ensuring that the models operate fairly and without hidden bias. By making algorithmic processes more transparent, organizations can ensure that individuals affected by automated decisions understand the basis for those decisions and can challenge or appeal them if necessary.

Organizational Practices for Accountability

Data Governance Frameworks

Data governance frameworks are another powerful organizational approach to ensuring accountability. A robust data governance framework establishes clear policies, roles, and responsibilities for data-handling within an organization. It typically involves the formation of a data ethics committee or similar body responsible for overseeing data practices, ensuring that all processes align with ethical standards.

These committees can help ensure accountability by reviewing data projects, providing guidance on ethical issues, and monitoring compliance with data management policies. Data governance frameworks also outline data stewardship roles, ensuring that specific individuals are accountable for maintaining data quality, security, and privacy throughout the data lifecycle.

Ethical Impact Assessments

Ethical impact assessments are also effective tools for promoting accountability. Similar to environmental impact assessments, ethical impact assessments involve evaluating the potential effects of data projects on individuals and society. This process helps organizations identify potential risks, such as bias or discrimination, and ensures that adequate safeguards are in place before launching a data initiative.

Ethical impact assessments require teams to document the expected outcomes and the steps taken to mitigate any risks, thereby creating a culture of accountability. These assessments not only help in identifying issues early but also provide a documented record of ethical considerations that can be referenced if questions arise about a particular data project.

Training and Education for Data Practitioners

Training and education are essential for fostering accountability among data practitioners and decision-makers, as they lay the foundation for a robust ethical framework within organizations. It is crucial that all employees involved in data processing understand the ethical principles guiding their work and the specific data policies of their organization. Comprehensive training programs that focus on data ethics, privacy concerns, and the regulatory landscape equip individuals with the knowledge they need to navigate the complexities of data management responsibly.

These programs can include interactive workshops, case studies, and discussions about real-world scenarios that highlight the potential consequences of unethical data practices. By promoting awareness and understanding of ethical considerations, organizations can cultivate a culture that prioritizes accountability and encourages employees to take ownership of their roles in data-handling.

Additionally, the implementation of certification programs in data ethics can further enhance accountability by formalizing the skills required for ethical data management. These certifications not only validate the expertise of data practitioners but also signal to organizations the importance of adhering to ethical standards in their operations. When individuals achieve certification, they are more likely to feel a heightened sense of personal responsibility and commitment to ethical practices. This, in turn, fosters a proactive approach to identifying and addressing potential ethical dilemmas before they escalate into larger issues.

Furthermore, the presence of certified professionals within an organization can enhance its credibility and reputation, demonstrating a commitment to ethical data usage that resonates with consumers, stakeholders, and regulatory bodies. Ultimately, by investing in training and certification, organizations can create a more accountable workforce capable of navigating the challenges of ethical data management.

Regulatory Measures and Compliance

Regulatory measures and compliance are essential external tools that significantly contribute to ensuring accountability in data management. Laws such as the GDPR in the EU and the CCPA in the United States impose stringent requirements regarding the handling of personal data, effectively holding organizations legally accountable for any failures in compliance. These regulations often encompass mandates for transparency, requiring organizations to disclose how they collect and use personal information, as well as the necessity for obtaining user consent before processing their data.

By enshrining data subject rights within these laws, regulators compel organizations to respect individuals' autonomy and privacy, thus reinforcing accountability in their data practices. Compliance with such regulations is not merely a legal obligation; it fosters a culture of responsibility within organizations, prompting them to prioritize ethical data management.

Moreover, the threat of regulatory fines and penalties for non-compliance serves as a powerful incentive for organizations to uphold ethical standards and establish robust internal accountability mechanisms. Significant financial repercussions can arise from violations, motivating companies to invest in compliance programs, staff training, and auditing processes to prevent data breaches or misuse.

The potential for public scrutiny and reputational damage associated with non-compliance further amplifies the pressure on organizations to adhere to ethical data practices. Consequently, regulatory frameworks not only protect consumers but also encourage organizations to take proactive measures to safeguard data integrity. By establishing clear legal expectations and consequences for unethical behavior, these regulations enhance accountability, ensuring that organizations operate transparently and responsibly in their handling of personal information.

Fostering a Culture of Accountability

In conclusion, tools for ensuring accountability in data usage encompass a wide range of approaches that span technical, organizational, and regulatory domains. Technical tools such as audit trails and algorithmic explainability are vital for providing transparency in data processes and decision-making. Audit trails help organizations track data access and modifications, making it easier to identify any potential misuse or ethical breaches. Algorithmic explainability enables stakeholders to understand how data-driven decisions are made, which is crucial for recognizing bias and ensuring fairness.

Complementing these technical tools are organizational practices, such as implementing robust data governance frameworks and conducting ethical impact assessments, which guide ethical decision-making and promote a responsible culture. Training programs aimed at educating employees about data ethics and their roles in upholding these standards are also essential for fostering accountability within organizations.

Moreover, regulatory measures play a critical role in reinforcing accountability by establishing clear legal expectations for data practices. Laws such as the GDPR and CCPA provide frameworks that mandate transparency and ethical behavior, holding organizations accountable for their data usage. The combination of these various tools ensures that organizations not only comply with legal standards but also embrace a culture of responsibility and ethical conduct.

By integrating technical, organizational, and regulatory tools into their data management practices, organizations can navigate the complexity of ethical data usage more effectively. This commitment to accountability not only respects individuals' rights but also enhances public trust, ultimately contributing to a more ethical digital landscape where data is used responsibly and ethically for the benefit of all stakeholders.

CHAPTER 12

ETHICAL AI: TACKLING BIAS AND FAIRNESS

BIAS IN AI

Bias in AI: Sources and Solutions

Bias in AI systems poses a significant concern, especially as these technologies increasingly permeate everyday decision-making processes across various sectors, including recruitment, lending, and healthcare. When AI systems are trained on historical data that reflects existing prejudices or inequity, they can produce unjust or harmful outcomes. This can reinforce societal inequality and perpetuate discrimination against marginalized groups. For instance, an AI-driven recruitment tool may favor candidates from certain demographics if its training data primarily consists of successful applicants from those backgrounds. As AI continues to be integrated into critical areas of life, it becomes imperative to identify and understand the sources of bias to mitigate its impact and promote the ethical usage of AI technology.

The origins of bias within AI algorithms are multifaceted, encompassing biased data, flawed algorithmic design, human involvement, and broader societal inequality. Biased data can arise from historical injustices that are reflected in the datasets used to train these algorithms. If an algorithm is fed data that underrepresents certain populations or contains discriminatory patterns, its outputs will likely reflect that bias.

Furthermore, algorithmic design choices, such as the selection of features or the weight assigned to specific variables, can introduce bias if not carefully considered. Human involvement in the development and deployment of AI systems also plays a critical role; decisions made by designers and engineers can inadvertently introduce personal bias.

Lastly, societal inequality can influence the data available for AI training, perpetuating cycles of discrimination. By comprehensively addressing these sources of bias, stakeholders can work toward creating more equitable AI systems that do not exacerbate existing disparities.

Biased Training Data

One of the primary sources of bias in AI is biased training data, which significantly influences how AI algorithms learn and make predictions. AI models rely heavily on the data they are trained on, meaning that if the training datasets contain bias—such as underrepresenting certain racial or gender groups—this bias will likely manifest in the AI's outcomes. For example, facial recognition technologies have been shown to have higher error rates for individuals with darker skin tones, primarily because the training datasets predominantly feature lighter-skinned individuals.

This lack of representation not only undermines the effectiveness of such technologies but also raises serious ethical concerns about fairness and inclusivity. The implications of biased training data extend beyond just performance metrics; they can lead to real-world consequences for marginalized groups who may be unfairly targeted or misidentified.

Furthermore, historical data may also contain bias that reflects past prejudices or discriminatory practices, which, if uncorrected or unacknowledged, become ingrained in AI models. For instance, in hiring algorithms, if historical data shows a preference for certain demographic profiles, the AI may learn to replicate these preferences, thereby disadvantaging qualified candidates from underrepresented groups. The perpetuation of bias such as this can reinforce systemic inequality, making it crucial for developers and organizations to critically evaluate the datasets used in training AI systems.

Strategies such as diversifying training data, employing bias detection methods, and continuously updating datasets can help mitigate such bias. Ultimately, addressing the issue of biased training data is essential to ensure that AI technologies operate fairly and equitably across all segments of society.

Algorithmic Design Choices

Algorithmic design itself can be a significant source of bias, stemming from the choices made during the development of an algorithm. The selection of features, weighting, and evaluation metrics can all inadvertently introduce bias that affects the algorithm's performance. For instance, if a creditworthiness prediction algorithm relies on features such as neighborhood location or occupation, it may disproportionately disadvantage specific socioeconomic groups.

These design decisions can lead to a scenario where the algorithm perpetuates existing inequality, rather than leveling the playing field. Developers must be aware that the features they choose to include carry inherent bias and that this bias can skew results, ultimately impacting real lives. As such, it's essential to evaluate the ethical implications of feature selection to ensure that algorithms do not reinforce harmful stereotypes or systemic discrimination.

Moreover, bias can arise not just from data but also from the assumptions and decisions made during the algorithm's development process. For instance, developers may prioritize metrics such as accuracy or efficiency without adequately considering fairness or equity, resulting in systems that may perform well statistically but yield biased outcomes in practice. This focus on performance metrics can create a false sense of security regarding the algorithm's fairness, masking the potential for discriminatory practices that may affect marginalized populations.

By emphasizing fairness as a core objective during the design phase, organizations can proactively identify and address potential bias. Incorporating diverse perspectives in the design process can also help developers recognize and mitigate bias that might otherwise go unnoticed, fostering more equitable AI systems that serve the broader community without perpetuating existing inequality.

Human Involvement in the AI Lifecycle

Another significant source of bias in AI arises from human involvement at various stages of the model lifecycle. From data collection and labeling to algorithm design and model deployment, each step is vulnerable to the influence of human bias. For instance, data labeling, often conducted by humans, can inadvertently introduce bias if the labelers harbor implicit or explicit prejudices. Such bias can skew the data's representativeness, affecting how accurately the AI model learns from it.

Additionally, the way a problem is framed by developers—deciding what the AI should predict and which features are deemed significant—can reflect subjective bias. This decision-making process is not purely objective; it is inherently shaped by the developers' cultural, social, and personal experiences, which may lead to an AI system that fails to equitably address the needs and values of diverse groups.

Furthermore, human bias can manifest in the deployment and ongoing use of AI models. Even if a model is initially developed with ethical considerations in mind, bias can re-emerge when humans interpret the results or apply the AI's recommendations. For example, if a hiring algorithm is used, recruiters may inadvertently favor candidates that align with their own biases, despite the model's intention to mitigate discrimination. This underscores the importance of not only acknowledging human involvement in the AI lifecycle but also implementing training and awareness programs to help individuals recognize and confront their biases.

By fostering a culture of critical reflection around human influence, organizations can create safeguards against the perpetuation of bias in AI systems and work toward solutions that genuinely serve the interests of all stakeholders.

Societal Inequality

Societal inequality is a significant root cause of bias in AI systems, as these technologies often reflect and reinforce the existing biases found within the societies they aim to serve. When certain groups are marginalized or discriminated against in various social contexts, the data collected about those groups is likely to mirror those disparities. For example, data derived from a biased criminal justice system may reveal disproportionately high arrest rates for specific racial groups. These figures do not reflect inherent behavioral tendencies but rather the outcomes of systemic discrimination and social injustice.

When AI models are trained on such skewed data, they are likely to generate biased predictions that perpetuate these disparities. Consequently, the use of AI in decision-making processes can inadvertently support a cycle of discrimination, exacerbating the disadvantages faced by already marginalized communities.

Moreover, this cycle of bias can lead to a compounding effect where AI systems not only reinforce existing societal inequities but also amplify them. As AI becomes increasingly integrated into critical sectors, such as recruitment, lending, and law enforcement, biased algorithms can result in significant consequences for affected individuals and communities. For instance, an AI-driven hiring system might favor candidates who fit the profiles of historically successful applicants, inadvertently sidelining qualified candidates from underrepresented backgrounds.

This can entrench socioeconomic disparity, as those from marginalized groups may find it increasingly challenging to access opportunities that would allow them to break the cycle of disadvantage. To combat these issues, it is essential for developers and organizations to critically assess the social contexts in which their AI systems operate, ensuring that data collection and algorithmic processes actively seek to counteract societal bias rather than reinforce it.

Addressing Bias in AI

In conclusion, bias in AI systems can arise from various sources, including biased training data, algorithmic design choices, human involvement, and entrenched societal inequality. Each of these factors contributes to the likelihood that AI systems will produce unfair or discriminatory outcomes, often exacerbating existing societal disparity. For example, biased training data can lead to models that misrepresent the characteristics and needs of underrepresented groups, while algorithmic design choices can inadvertently prioritize certain demographics over others.

Additionally, human involvement in data collection, labeling, and decision-making processes can introduce subjective bias that reflects the diverse perspectives and experiences of individuals, further complicating the quest for fairness. Therefore, it is imperative to recognize that bias in AI is not merely a technical flaw; it is a manifestation of broader societal issues that demand careful attention and intervention.

To effectively address bias, we must adopt a comprehensive approach that includes a critical examination of the data used in AI systems, the incorporation of diverse perspectives during the design process, and ongoing efforts to identify and correct bias throughout the AI lifecycle. Engaging stakeholders from various backgrounds can help ensure that AI systems are designed with a more equitable lens, promoting inclusivity and fairness.

Moreover, organizations must implement robust auditing and monitoring processes to assess the impact of their AI systems on different demographic groups continually. By understanding and addressing the sources of bias in AI, we can work toward developing technologies that are not only ethical and fair but also genuinely beneficial for all members of society, ultimately fostering a more just and equitable future.

ENSURING FAIRNESS IN AI

The Importance of Fairness in AI

As AI systems become increasingly integrated into key areas of human life, including healthcare, employment, finance, and criminal justice, ensuring fairness in AI decision-making has become paramount. The stakes are high in these domains, as biased AI systems can lead to significant and often irreversible consequences for individuals and communities. Fairness in AI involves designing and implementing systems that treat all individuals and groups impartially, without introducing or reinforcing bias or discrimination.

This commitment to fairness necessitates a multifaceted approach, integrating not only advanced technical methodologies but also a thorough understanding of the social contexts in which these systems operate. Such a holistic perspective is essential to mitigate the potential harm that can arise from automated decision-making processes, particularly for marginalized or vulnerable populations who may already face systemic inequality.

Ethical guidelines for fair AI encompass a variety of strategies, ranging from technical interventions to governance policies and stakeholder engagement, all aimed at mitigating bias and promoting equitable outcomes. Technical interventions can include developing algorithms that are transparent and interpretable, ensuring that stakeholders can understand how decisions are made and hold systems accountable. Additionally, rigorous testing and validation processes must be put in place to identify and address bias in training data and model outputs.

On the governance side, organizations should establish policies that prioritize ethical considerations in AI development and deployment, including regular audits and assessments of AI systems to ensure compliance with fairness standards. Furthermore, engaging with a diverse range of stakeholders—including community representatives, ethicists, and domain experts—can enrich the decision-making process and ensure that AI technologies reflect a broader spectrum of values and perspectives. By implementing these comprehensive strategies, we can move toward AI systems that not only enhance efficiency and productivity but also uphold the principles of fairness and justice.

Diverse and Representative Datasets

One essential strategy for promoting fairness in AI is the use of diverse and representative datasets. Training data serves as the foundation upon which AI models are built, and if this data is biased or unrepresentative, it can lead to unfair outcomes that disproportionately affect certain groups. To counteract this, it is crucial to ensure that the data used to train AI models reflects the diversity of the population it serves, encompassing different genders, races, ages, and socioeconomic backgrounds.

By doing so, we can create models that function effectively across all demographic groups, reducing the risk of perpetuating existing inequality. This requires meticulous planning and oversight during the data collection process to ensure inclusivity. Organizations must also engage in continuous efforts to identify and address any gaps in the data, which may necessitate revisiting and revising data collection methods.

Moreover, addressing data representation issues may involve employing various techniques to enhance dataset diversity. For instance, oversampling underrepresented groups can ensure that the model receives adequate exposure to these populations during training. Similarly, generating synthetic data can help create a more balanced dataset, filling in the gaps where real-world data is scarce. These strategies not only help in mitigating bias but also improve the model's overall robustness and accuracy, ensuring that its predictions and decisions are fair and equitable.

Additionally, organizations should regularly audit their datasets to assess their representativeness and make necessary adjustments, thereby fostering a culture of ongoing improvement. By prioritizing diverse and representative datasets, we can significantly enhance the fairness of AI systems and build greater trust among users and stakeholders.

Bias Detection and Mitigation Tools

Bias detection and mitigation tools are essential for promoting fairness in AI systems, as they enable developers to identify and address bias that may arise during the model training process. Techniques such as fairness metrics serve as valuable evaluation tools, helping to assess whether AI models produce biased outcomes that may disadvantage specific groups.

Metrics such as demographic parity, equal opportunity, and disparate impact provide quantifiable measures of fairness, allowing organizations to pinpoint areas where inequalities may exist. By systematically applying these metrics during the model evaluation phase, developers can gain insights into how their algorithms perform across different demographics and make informed decisions about necessary adjustments.

Once bias is detected, a range of algorithmic techniques can be employed to mitigate it effectively. Methods such as reweighting, debiasing, or adversarial training can help adjust the model's predictions to ensure fairness without significantly compromising accuracy. Regular audits and fairness evaluations are crucial for maintaining equity, both during the development phase and after deployment.

Continuous monitoring is particularly vital for AI models that learn from real-time data, as new input can introduce bias that was not present during initial training. By establishing a robust framework for bias detection and mitigation, organizations can ensure that their AI systems remain fair and responsive to evolving societal norms, ultimately fostering greater trust and accountability in their AI-driven solutions.

Transparency and Explainability

Transparency and explainability are fundamental components in the quest for fairness in AI systems, as they promote trust and accountability among users and stakeholders. Transparency involves providing clear and accessible information about how AI systems operate, including the data sources, algorithms, and decision-making processes employed. This openness is crucial for demystifying AI technology and fostering public confidence in its use.

When stakeholders understand how decisions are made, they can better assess the reliability and fairness of the outcomes produced by these systems. Additionally, being transparent about the potential risks and limitations of AI helps set realistic expectations and encourages responsible usage.

Explainable AI (XAI) techniques play a vital role in making AI systems more interpretable, allowing developers and users to comprehend the rationale behind specific decisions. By leveraging XAI methods, organizations can provide insights into how various factors contribute to an AI model's predictions or classifications. This understanding is essential for identifying and rectifying bias embedded in the decision-making process.

If AI systems are opaque, stakeholders may struggle to pinpoint the causes of biased outcomes, making it challenging to implement effective solutions. Therefore, creating XAI systems, which are accessible even to non-technical users, is imperative for ensuring fairness. It enables meaningful oversight and facilitates discussions around ethical considerations, ultimately leading to better-informed decision-making and enhanced accountability in AI applications.

Stakeholder Involvement and Governance

Stakeholder involvement is a fundamental aspect of promoting fairness in AI systems, as it brings together diverse perspectives that can help identify potential bias and ethical concerns. Engaging with various stakeholders—including users, affected communities, domain experts, and ethicists—during the design, development, and deployment phases ensures that the AI system addresses the needs and values of the individuals it impacts.

By involving those who may be affected by the technology, organizations can gain valuable insights into how AI systems operate in real-world contexts. Methods such as co-design sessions, focus groups, and community consultations allow stakeholders to voice their concerns, share their experiences, and contribute to shaping the AI system in a way that is fair and equitable.

Furthermore, establishing ethical AI committees or working groups can provide structured oversight throughout the AI development process, ensuring that fairness is prioritized at every stage. These committees should include a diverse array of members, such as data scientists, ethicists, and representatives from various parts of the organization, to create a holistic approach to ethical AI design. By fostering a collaborative environment where multiple viewpoints are considered, organizations can better address potential bias and ethical dilemmas.

This collective decision-making process enhances accountability and strengthens the commitment to fairness, ultimately leading to AI systems that are more reflective of the diverse society they serve. Such stakeholder engagement not only improves AI systems but also builds trust and transparency, contributing to the overall success and acceptance of AI solutions in society.

Monitoring and Updating AI Systems

Regular monitoring and updating of AI systems are crucial for ensuring fairness, particularly for those systems deployed in dynamic environments where conditions and societal norms can shift rapidly. AI models can experience performance degradation over time, which may result in biased or unfair outcomes if they are not regularly evaluated.

To mitigate this risk, organizations should implement comprehensive mechanisms for ongoing monitoring, allowing them to track the performance of AI systems continuously. This involves not only assessing the accuracy and efficiency of the models but also examining their impact on various demographic groups to ensure that no group is adversely affected. By systematically analyzing how different populations are treated by AI, organizations can identify emerging bias and take corrective action before it leads to significant harm.

In addition to ongoing monitoring, organizations should prioritize retraining models with updated data to reflect changes in the social context and user behavior. Incorporating feedback from affected stakeholders is equally vital, as it provides insights into the real-world implications of AI decisions. Conducting regular fairness audits can help organizations assess the ethical implications of their AI systems and identify areas for improvement.

These practices, when combined, form a robust framework for maintaining fairness over the long term. By committing to continuously evaluating and updating their AI systems, organizations can adapt to evolving societal expectations and enhance the overall fairness of their technological solutions, thereby fostering trust and accountability in AI deployment.

Building Ethical AI Systems

In conclusion, promoting fairness in AI systems is a complex challenge that necessitates a holistic approach incorporating technical, organizational, and social strategies. Organizations must prioritize the use of diverse and representative datasets to ensure that their AI models reflect the wide array of human experiences and perspectives. Implementing bias detection and mitigation tools is equally essential, as these mechanisms enable organizations to identify and rectify bias that may inadvertently arise during the AI development process.

Furthermore, promoting transparency and explainability ensures that stakeholders can comprehend how decisions are made, fostering a sense of accountability among developers and users alike. Engaging with a broad spectrum of stakeholders throughout the design and deployment phases helps to illuminate potential bias and align AI systems with the needs and values of the communities they serve.

Moreover, establishing clear accountability frameworks and ensuring regular monitoring of AI systems are critical for maintaining fairness over time. By embedding these practices into their operations, organizations can continuously assess the performance of their AI models and adapt them to changing social contexts. Fair AI systems not only enhance the individual experiences of those affected by them, ensuring equitable treatment across diverse groups, but they also contribute to broader societal well-being.

By building trust and reducing discrimination, fair AI promotes inclusive progress, which is vital in an increasingly digital world. Ultimately, a commitment to fairness in AI development can lead to more ethical technologies that uplift society as a whole, paving the way for a future where AI serves as a tool for positive change rather than a source of division.

ACCOUNTABILITY FOR AI DECISIONS

Complexity of Accountability in AI Systems

Assigning responsibility in AI is a multifaceted challenge, particularly when addressing the intricacies of black-box models. These models, which include complex architectures such as deep learning neural networks, operate in ways that are not readily interpretable, even to the engineers and data scientists who create them. This inherent opacity complicates the process of understanding how specific decisions are made within the model, making it difficult to pinpoint the source of errors or bias when they occur.

Consequently, when an AI system produces a biased or harmful outcome, the lack of transparency poses significant hurdles in determining accountability. This raises critical questions: is the developer responsible for the design choices made? Does accountability rest with the data scientist for the quality and representation of the training data? Or should the organization deploying the model bear responsibility for its outcomes? Such ambiguity in assigning responsibility can have profound implications, eroding trust among users and stakeholders and complicating compliance with regulatory frameworks.

Moreover, the challenges of accountability in AI systems extend beyond individual actors and can impact broader ethical standards within the industry. When the lines of responsibility are blurred, organizations may be less motivated to implement robust oversight mechanisms or ethical guidelines, leading to a culture where AI systems are deployed without sufficient scrutiny. This lack of accountability can diminish public trust in AI technologies, as users may feel vulnerable to the consequences of decisions made by systems they do not understand.

Furthermore, it can create legal and regulatory risks for organizations, particularly as governments and policymakers begin to establish stricter guidelines around AI usage and accountability. As a result, it is essential for stakeholders to work collaboratively to enhance the interpretability of AI systems and develop clear frameworks for assigning responsibility. By doing so, they can not only foster a culture of accountability but also ensure that AI technologies are used ethically and responsibly, ultimately benefitting society as a whole.

Decoding Decision-Making in Black-Box AI Models

One of the primary challenges in assigning responsibility with black-box models is the inherent difficulty in understanding the decision-making process. In complex AI systems, particularly those employing deep learning, decisions are derived from intricate patterns detected across vast datasets. For instance, a deep learning model used for loan approval might analyze hundreds of variables—such as income, credit history, and spending habits—to determine whether an applicant is creditworthy. Understanding why it reached a particular decision, however—whether to approve or deny the loan—poses a significant challenge.

The lack of interpretability in these models means that even the developers may not fully grasp how different features contributed to the final output. This opacity complicates accountability, especially when errors occur, such as when a model unjustly denies loans to specific demographic groups. In such cases, the absence of a clear causal link between the data inputs and the decision renders it nearly impossible to hold any individual or group responsible for the issue.

Moreover, the implications of this lack of interpretability extend beyond individual cases of bias or error; they can erode public trust in AI technologies as a whole. When users encounter AI-driven systems that make opaque decisions, they may feel marginalized or victimized, especially if these decisions negatively affect their lives, such as in financial or legal contexts. This sense of disenfranchisement can foster skepticism about the fairness and reliability of AI, leading to resistance against adopting such technologies.

Furthermore, organizations may face significant reputational risks if they cannot demonstrate accountability in their AI systems. Without clear mechanisms for understanding and rectifying bias, stakeholders—including consumers, regulators, and advocacy groups—may demand stricter regulations and oversight, pushing for greater transparency and ethical standards in AI deployment. Therefore, it is crucial for developers and organizations to invest in methods that enhance model interpretability, ensuring that decisions made by AI systems can be understood and scrutinized, thereby promoting accountability and trust in these powerful technologies.

Shared Responsibility Among Stakeholders

Another significant issue is the shared responsibility among multiple stakeholders involved in the lifecycle of an AI system. AI models are rarely developed, trained, and deployed by a single individual; rather, they emerge from a collaborative effort that includes data scientists, software engineers, domain experts, and business leaders. Each stakeholder contributes a unique perspective and set of skills to the project, but this collaborative approach can lead to a diffusion of responsibility.

For instance, while data scientists are tasked with training the model using the data, they often have little control over the quality and representativeness of the data provided to them. Similarly, business leaders may prioritize certain outcomes, such as efficiency or profitability, without fully considering the ethical implications of their decisions. This fragmented chain of responsibility complicates the task of pinpointing who should be held accountable when negative outcomes arise. As a result, accountability may become diluted, making it challenging to address issues and rectify mistakes.

This complexity often leads to what is known as "responsibility washing," where no single party claims full accountability for the AI system's actions or outcomes. This lack of clear accountability can undermine public trust in AI technologies, as stakeholders and users may feel that no one is genuinely responsible for the decisions made by these systems. Furthermore, it can create a culture of complacency within organizations, where individuals believe that their roles are insulated from the ethical ramifications of AI applications.

To combat this issue, organizations must establish clear accountability frameworks that delineate roles and responsibilities at each stage of the AI lifecycle. This may include developing comprehensive guidelines for ethical decision-making, implementing regular reviews of the AI system's impact, and fostering an environment where stakeholders are encouraged to voice ethical concerns. By creating a culture of shared responsibility and accountability, organizations can ensure that all stakeholders are aligned in their commitment to ethical AI practices, ultimately enhancing the integrity and trustworthiness of AI technologies.

Regulatory and Ethical Uncertainty

The problem of assigning responsibility is further compounded by regulatory and ethical uncertainty. Existing legal and regulatory frameworks are often ill equipped to address the unique challenges posed by black-box AI models, which defy traditional accountability structures. These frameworks typically rely on the assumption that decision-making processes can be understood and explained in a straightforward manner, but with AI systems, particularly those utilizing deep learning, the intricate and often opaque nature of their decision-making makes it difficult for regulators to ascertain liability in the event of harm.

For instance, if an autonomous vehicle is involved in an accident, it raises complex questions about accountability: should the manufacturer of the vehicle bear responsibility, or should it lie with the software developer who designed the AI algorithms, or even the vehicle owner? This ambiguity in existing laws creates a challenging landscape for accountability, leaving stakeholders unsure of their legal and ethical responsibilities.

Moreover, the uncertainty surrounding accountability in AI can deter organizations from proactively considering ethical implications during the development and deployment of their systems. When companies perceive that liability is ambiguous or ill-defined, they may be less inclined to prioritize ethical considerations, fearing that taking proactive measures may expose them to undue risk without clear legal protections. This hesitation can stifle innovation and impede the adoption of responsible AI practices.

Furthermore, the absence of well-defined regulatory guidance creates a vacuum, hindering efforts to foster responsible AI deployment and encouraging a reactive rather than proactive approach to ethics. As AI technologies continue to evolve and permeate various sectors, there is an urgent need for regulatory bodies to establish clear, comprehensive guidelines that address the intricacies of AI systems. Doing so would not only help clarify accountability but also encourage organizations to engage more rigorously with ethical standards, fostering a culture of responsibility that aligns with societal expectations.

Algorithmic Bias and Unintended Consequences

Algorithmic bias and unintended consequences pose significant challenges when it comes to assigning responsibility within AI systems. This bias can emerge from various sources, including flawed training data, biased algorithmic design, and even unforeseen interactions between different features within the model. For instance, if an AI hiring tool yields biased outcomes that disadvantage candidates from certain backgrounds, determining the origin of that bias becomes a complex task.

Was the bias introduced by the dataset used for training, the selection of features that the model considers, or the inherent design of the algorithm itself? Each stage of the model development presents opportunities for bias to creep in, and the black-box nature of some AI systems complicates the process of tracing bias back to its source. As a result, holding a specific individual or team accountable for biased outcomes becomes increasingly difficult, especially when multiple parties are involved in the model's lifecycle.

Moreover, the occurrence of unintended consequences adds another layer of complexity to responsibility assignment in AI systems. AI models may misinterpret data patterns or draw incorrect inferences that lead to harmful outcomes, often in ways that are not immediately apparent. In opaque models, such as deep neural networks, developers might not even recognize that a problem exists until it manifests in a tangible way, making it harder to implement preventive measures proactively. This unpredictability further complicates accountability, as it may not be evident who should have identified the potential for bias or unintended behavior.

The diffusion of responsibility across various stakeholders, combined with the challenges of identifying the root cause of bias and misinterpretation, underscores the need for more robust frameworks and practices that can address these issues. Without clear guidelines for accountability, organizations may struggle to manage the ethical implications of AI systems effectively, potentially leading to widespread harm and the erosion of public trust.

Navigating Challenges in AI Responsibility

Addressing the challenges of assigning responsibility in black-box models necessitates a combination of technical advancements and organizational strategies. One effective approach is to enhance model interpretability through XAI techniques, which can illuminate the decision-making processes underlying AI systems. Techniques such as SHAP and LIME are instrumental in providing insights into how specific inputs influence outcomes, thereby facilitating the identification of accountability points.

By making the decision-making process more transparent, organizations can better understand where potential bias or errors originate, allowing them to take corrective actions more efficiently. This transparency can empower stakeholders, including developers and users, to engage critically with AI systems, fostering an environment where accountability is prioritized and encouraged.

In addition to technical improvements, it is crucial for organizations to establish clear guidelines and ethical frameworks that govern AI development and deployment. Defining roles and responsibilities at each stage of the AI lifecycle helps to mitigate the diffusion of accountability that often occurs when multiple stakeholders are involved. By assigning specific responsibilities—such as data collection, model training, and performance evaluation—to designated teams or individuals, organizations can create a clearer line of accountability.

Furthermore, regulatory bodies should play an active role in creating AI-specific laws and guidelines that address the unique challenges posed by opaque models. These regulations should focus on ensuring that developers and organizations adhere to consistent ethical standards, thereby fostering a culture of accountability in AI practices. By implementing both technical and organizational interventions, stakeholders can better navigate the complexities of responsibility in AI, leading to more ethical and transparent AI systems.

Toward a More Accountable AI Landscape

In conclusion, assigning responsibility in AI systems, particularly those involving black-box models, is fraught with challenges due to their inherent lack of transparency, shared responsibility among multiple stakeholders, and regulatory uncertainty. The complexity of AI decision-making processes can obscure accountability, making it difficult to pinpoint who is responsible for biased or harmful outcomes. Addressing these challenges necessitates a concerted effort to enhance model interpretability, utilizing techniques that provide insights into how decisions are made.

Additionally, establishing clearer ethical guidelines and developing regulatory frameworks tailored to the intricacies of AI is essential for ensuring accountability. By tackling these issues head-on, organizations and policymakers can foster a more accountable AI landscape, ensuring that technology is used responsibly and ethically while safeguarding the rights and interests of individuals and society as a whole. Such proactive measures will help build trust in AI systems, ultimately promoting a more equitable and just technological future.

ETHICAL AI GOVERNANCE FRAMEWORKS

The Importance of Ethical AI Governance

As AI becomes an integral part of our daily lives, establishing governance frameworks is essential to ensure that AI systems are used responsibly and ethically. Ethical AI governance encompasses a set of principles and guidelines designed to promote the fair and just application of AI technologies across various sectors. These frameworks involve the implementation of comprehensive policies, practices, and tools that not only guide the development and deployment of AI but also ensure that these technologies respect human rights and the dignity of all individuals.

By providing a structured approach to navigating the complex challenges associated with AI, governance frameworks help organizations address critical issues such as bias, transparency, accountability, and privacy, ultimately fostering trust in AI systems among users and in society as a whole.

Moreover, effective AI governance frameworks can serve as a foundation for collaboration among diverse stakeholders, including policymakers, industry leaders, and civil society. These stakeholders can work together to create an ecosystem that encourages responsible innovation while minimizing potential risks associated with AI technologies. Engaging with affected communities and experts in the development of governance frameworks ensures that the policies implemented reflect a wide range of perspectives and concerns, leading to more equitable and inclusive AI systems.

Additionally, regular assessments and updates to these frameworks are necessary to adapt to the rapidly evolving nature of AI technology and its implications for society. By prioritizing ethical governance, we can harness the benefits of AI while safeguarding individual rights and promoting social good.

Risk Management and Impact Assessment

One well-established framework for ethical AI governance is risk management and impact assessment, which plays a crucial role in identifying and mitigating potential ethical risks associated with AI systems. This process involves conducting an AI ethics impact assessment before and during the deployment of these systems, allowing organizations to proactively address ethical concerns. Tools such as risk assessment matrices are employed to categorize potential risks based on their impact and likelihood, providing a structured approach to understanding the implications of AI technologies.

For instance, a predictive policing tool may raise significant privacy concerns due to its reliance on sensitive data; an effective impact assessment can reveal strategies to minimize these risks, such as limiting the scope of data collection or anonymizing sensitive information. By implementing these assessments early in the development process, organizations can lay a solid foundation for ethical AI deployment.

Furthermore, regular risk assessments throughout the lifecycle of the AI system are essential for ensuring that the technology continues to operate ethically within a dynamic environment. As societal norms, regulations, and technological capabilities evolve, the ethical implications of AI systems may change as well. Continuous monitoring and evaluation allow organizations to adapt their governance strategies in response to new risks or unforeseen consequences that may arise after deployment.

This ongoing process not only helps maintain ethical standards but also fosters a culture of accountability within the organization. By integrating risk management and impact assessment into their governance frameworks, organizations can better navigate the complexities of AI technologies while safeguarding individual rights and promoting public trust in AI systems.

AI Ethics Boards and Advisory Councils

AI ethics boards and advisory councils play a crucial role in fostering ethical governance within organizations, especially in sectors where the implications of AI technologies can significantly impact individuals and communities. By establishing independent ethics boards, organizations can draw on a diverse range of expertise, including ethicists, domain experts, and representatives from affected communities, ensuring that a variety of perspectives are considered in decision-making processes.

These boards are tasked with overseeing the development and deployment of AI systems, providing essential guidance on ethical considerations that align with established principles. This multidisciplinary approach allows organizations to evaluate the societal implications of their AI initiatives comprehensively, addressing potential risks to human rights and promoting fairness across all stakeholders involved.

In addition to providing oversight, advisory councils enhance accountability by offering an independent review of AI practices and policies. This external perspective can help organizations identify areas for improvement and ensure that their AI systems comply with ethical standards and regulatory requirements. By regularly assessing AI initiatives, advisory councils can provide actionable recommendations that align technological advancement with ethical imperatives, helping organizations navigate complex moral landscapes.

Furthermore, the involvement of diverse stakeholders fosters transparency and builds trust with the public, as communities can see that their concerns are being addressed in the development of AI technologies. Ultimately, AI ethics boards and advisory councils are instrumental in promoting responsible AI use, ensuring that technological progress serves the greater good while mitigating potential harm.

Transparency and Explainability Tools

Transparency and explainability tools are essential for ensuring responsible oversight of AI systems, as they create a framework for accountability throughout the AI development lifecycle. By documenting processes such as data collection practices, algorithmic design choices, and the rationale behind decisions, organizations can establish a clear audit trail that fosters trust among stakeholders. This transparency enables both internal teams and external auditors to critically evaluate AI systems, identifying potential bias or ethical concerns before deployment. Moreover, by making their methodologies transparent, organizations can demonstrate their commitment to ethical AI practices, addressing public apprehensions about AI's role in society.

XAI tools further enhance this transparency by breaking down complex models into more understandable components. Techniques such as SHAP and LIME allow stakeholders to see how specific features influence decisions made by AI systems, which is vital for informed oversight. This understanding is not limited to developers and auditors; end-users also benefit from insights into how decisions that affect them are made.

By promoting clarity in AI operations, organizations can empower users to make informed choices and provide meaningful feedback, thereby supporting transparency and informed consent. As a result, the integration of transparency and explainability tools not only improves accountability but also cultivates trust between AI systems and the people they impact, leading to more ethical outcomes.

Continuous Monitoring and Auditing

Continuous monitoring and auditing are essential practices for maintaining ethical AI governance in a landscape where AI models can change and adapt over time. As AI systems learn from real-time data, they can inadvertently develop bias or make decisions that deviate from established ethical standards. By implementing a framework for ongoing monitoring, organizations can swiftly identify when an AI system strays from expected behavior, allowing timely intervention to address any emerging issues. This proactive approach not only minimizes the risks associated with unintended consequences but also ensures that the AI systems remain aligned with organizational values and societal norms.

Periodic audits, encompassing both internal and external assessments, are critical for ensuring that AI systems adhere to ethical guidelines and operate fairly and effectively throughout their lifecycle. These audits should be comprehensive, evaluating not only the technical functionality of the AI system but also its broader impact on stakeholders. By considering factors such as user experience, potential bias, and social implications, organizations can gain a holistic understanding of how their AI systems affect various groups.

This multifaceted evaluation process encourages accountability and fosters trust among stakeholders, ultimately contributing to a more ethical and responsible approach to AI deployment. Continuous monitoring and regular audits serve as vital safeguards, helping organizations navigate the complexities of AI governance while ensuring that ethical standards remain a priority.

Stakeholder Engagement

Stakeholder engagement is a critical component of ethical AI governance that helps to create more inclusive and responsible AI systems. By involving a diverse range of stakeholders—such as employees, customers, affected communities, and regulatory bodies—organizations can gather valuable insights and perspectives that may otherwise be overlooked. Engaging stakeholders through public consultations, feedback mechanisms, or co-design sessions empowers them to participate actively in shaping the AI system, ensuring that their voices are heard and considered in the decision-making process. This collaborative approach not only enhances the relevance and applicability of the AI systems but also fosters a sense of ownership among stakeholders, increasing the likelihood of acceptance and trust in the technology.

Moreover, incorporating stakeholder input helps organizations identify and address potential ethical concerns early in the AI development process. Understanding the values, needs, and rights of those affected by AI technologies enables organizations to mitigate risks related to bias, discrimination, and privacy violations. By prioritizing stakeholder engagement, organizations can align their AI systems with the broader societal context, ensuring that the technologies they develop do not inadvertently reinforce existing inequality or harm marginalized communities.

This ongoing dialogue not only promotes transparency but also cultivates a culture of accountability, encouraging organizations to continuously evaluate their practices and adapt to the evolving ethical landscape of AI. Ultimately, stakeholder engagement enriches the ethical AI governance framework, paving the way for more equitable and responsible AI deployment.

Fostering Ethical AI Development

In conclusion, frameworks for ethical AI governance represent a comprehensive collection of tools and practices designed to promote responsible AI development and use. Elements such as risk management and impact assessments allow organizations to identify and mitigate potential ethical risks before they materialize, ensuring that AI systems operate within acceptable moral boundaries. The establishment of ethics boards adds an additional layer of oversight, providing diverse perspectives that enrich the decision-making process and uphold ethical standards.

Meanwhile, transparency tools enhance accountability by providing clear documentation of AI processes and decisions, which is essential for building trust with stakeholders. By integrating adherence to regulatory guidelines, continuous monitoring, and active stakeholder engagement into their governance frameworks, organizations can create a robust ethical foundation for their AI initiatives.

As AI technology continues to evolve, effective governance becomes increasingly critical in maintaining alignment with ethical principles and societal expectations. Organizations that prioritize ethical AI governance not only protect themselves from legal and reputational risks but also contribute positively to the broader societal narrative surrounding AI. By fostering an environment of trust, fairness, and accountability, these frameworks encourage innovation while ensuring that the deployment of AI technologies serves the public good.

Ultimately, the establishment of ethical AI governance frameworks is vital for navigating the complex challenges posed by AI, allowing society to harness its benefits while safeguarding against potential harm and injustice.

CHAPTER 13

ETHICAL IMPLICATIONS OF AI IN DECISION-MAKING SYSTEMS

AI IN AUTONOMOUS DECISION-MAKING

AI's Expanding Role in Critical Sectors

AI's expanding role in critical sectors such as healthcare, criminal justice, and finance is transforming how decisions are made, often with far-reaching consequences. In healthcare, AI systems are increasingly used for diagnostic purposes, drug discovery, personalized treatment plans, and even surgery assistance. These systems can analyze vast amounts of medical data and detect patterns that are difficult or impossible for human practitioners to identify. For example, AI-driven diagnostic tools have demonstrated proficiency in identifying conditions such as cancer or heart disease from imaging data. Relying on AI for such high-stakes decisions, however, raises ethical questions about trust, accuracy, and the extent to which humans should depend on these systems for life-critical decisions.

In criminal justice, AI is being used to predict criminal behavior, assess risk, and inform sentencing or parole decisions. Algorithms such as risk assessment tools are employed to predict the likelihood of reoffending and to guide judges in making decisions about bail or sentencing. While these systems are designed to reduce bias and improve efficiency, concerns about fairness and transparency have emerged. For example, some risk assessment algorithms have been criticized for perpetuating racial bias due to the historical data on which they are trained. This has raised ethical concerns about whether AI can truly be neutral in such sensitive applications and how to ensure that automated decisions do not result in unjust outcomes.

The finance sector has also seen significant AI adoption, particularly in areas such as credit scoring, fraud detection, and algorithmic trading. AI systems analyze vast quantities of financial data to predict market movements or assess the creditworthiness of individuals and businesses. While AI can process data far more efficiently than humans, the opacity of these systems can make it difficult for users to understand how financial decisions are made. For example, if an individual is denied a loan based on an AI-generated credit score, they may not have access to a clear explanation of why the decision was made. This lack of transparency not only raises ethical concerns but also poses regulatory challenges, particularly in relation to fairness and consumer protection.

Across these critical sectors, the shift toward AI-driven autonomous decision-making highlights both the potential benefits and significant ethical risks. While AI has the capacity to improve accuracy, efficiency, and outcomes in areas where human error or limitations can be costly, it also introduces new vulnerabilities. The lack of explainability in AI decision-making, the potential for embedded bias, and the challenge of assigning accountability in cases of error or harm are all important ethical considerations.

As AI continues to permeate these critical fields, ensuring that these systems operate transparently and fairly will be essential to maintaining public trust and protecting the individuals affected by their decisions.

Ethical Concerns in Life-Critical Decisions

When AI is tasked with making life-critical decisions, the ethical stakes are exceptionally high, as these decisions can directly affect the safety, health, and well-being of individuals. In the case of autonomous vehicles, for example, AI systems are responsible for making split-second decisions in complex, real-world environments, where mistakes can result in injury or loss of life. The ethical dilemma here revolves around how these systems should prioritize different outcomes.

The infamous *trolley problem* highlights a key concern: if an autonomous vehicle faces an unavoidable accident, how should it decide who or what to prioritize? Should it protect the occupants at all costs or minimize harm to pedestrians, even at the expense of the passengers? These scenarios expose the moral complexity of programming AI to make ethical judgments in critical situations.

In healthcare, AI-driven diagnostic systems and treatment planning tools are becoming integral to patient care. While these systems have the potential to greatly enhance accuracy and efficiency, their use raises ethical concerns about the delegation of decision-making power in life-or-death situations. For instance, an AI system might recommend a particular course of treatment based on statistical patterns, but there may be individual factors that it fails to account for, which a human doctor might recognize. If an AI system makes an incorrect diagnosis or treatment recommendation, the consequences could be dire. This raises the question of accountability—who is responsible when an AI system's decision leads to harm? Moreover, how do we ensure that AI's recommendations are transparent and understandable, allowing medical professionals and patients to make informed decisions?

Another key issue in life-critical AI decisions is the potential for bias in the data and algorithms that inform these systems. In healthcare, if AI systems are trained on data that overrepresent certain demographic groups while underrepresenting others, the resulting recommendations could be less effective, or even harmful, to those in the minority. Similarly, in autonomous vehicles, bias in data collection or in the prioritization algorithms could lead to inequitable outcomes for certain groups of people. The challenge is to ensure that AI systems are trained on diverse, representative datasets and that their decision-making processes are continually audited for fairness. Addressing bias is not just a technical issue; it is a profound ethical challenge that requires ongoing scrutiny to prevent AI from perpetuating or exacerbating existing inequality.

Ultimately, the ethical concerns in AI life-critical decisions are rooted in questions of trust, transparency, and accountability. Can people trust AI systems with their lives when the decision-making process is often opaque and the outcomes may not always be explained or justified? How can we ensure that these systems act in ways that align with societal values and ethical principles, especially when making complex moral decisions?

As AI continues to play a large role in critical sectors such as transportation and healthcare, the need for robust ethical frameworks, clear guidelines for accountability, and mechanisms for transparency will become increasingly urgent. These frameworks must strike a delicate balance between leveraging the capabilities of AI to improve decision-making and safeguarding the rights, dignity, and safety of individuals affected by these decisions.

Bias and Discrimination in Automated Decisions

Bias and discrimination in automated decisions are significant ethical challenges in AI, driven by the fact that AI systems are only as unbiased as the data and algorithms that underpin them. When AI models are trained on historical data that reflect societal bias—such as those based on race, gender, or socioeconomic status—they tend to replicate or even amplify that bias in their predictions and decisions. This is especially concerning in areas where AI systems are deployed to make critical decisions, such as recruitment, lending, criminal justice, and healthcare. For example, if a recruitment algorithm is trained on data that reflects past discriminatory practices, it may inadvertently favor candidates who resemble those who have historically been hired, disadvantaging qualified candidates from underrepresented groups. The result is a perpetuation of historical discrimination, posing serious risks to equity and justice.

One common source of bias in AI systems is imbalanced training data. When datasets used to train AI models are not representative of the diversity of the population, the system's decisions may disproportionately favor certain groups over others. In criminal justice, for example, risk assessment tools used to predict recidivism may be trained on historical arrest data that overrepresents certain racial or ethnic groups. Consequently, the algorithm may unfairly label individuals from these groups as high-risk, influencing decisions around bail, parole, or sentencing.

Similarly, in healthcare, if an AI diagnostic tool is trained predominantly on data from male patients, it may be less accurate when diagnosing conditions in female patients, leading to disparity in treatment outcomes. This imbalance in training data reinforces existing inequality, making it imperative to audit and adjust AI systems for fairness.

Algorithmic bias is not just about the data but also the design of the algorithms themselves. The assumptions made during the algorithm development process can introduce bias. For example, if an algorithm is designed to prioritize efficiency or profit over fairness, it may favor outcomes that are optimal in a narrow sense but discriminatory in practice. A credit-scoring algorithm might prioritize financial criteria that are more accessible to affluent individuals, systematically disadvantaging those from lower-income backgrounds, even if they have a strong record of repayment. This can lead to discriminatory practices in lending, where certain groups find it harder to access financial services despite being equally creditworthy. To prevent such outcomes, algorithm developers must consider ethical guidelines that go beyond technical performance, incorporating fairness as a key metric in their models.

Mitigating bias and discrimination in automated decisions requires proactive effort at every stage of AI development and deployment. This includes using more diverse and representative datasets, regularly auditing AI systems for biased outcomes, and employing techniques such as *fairness-aware machine learning*, which explicitly incorporates fairness constraints into the algorithm's design.

Additionally, transparency and explainability are crucial—organizations must be able to explain how their AI systems arrive at decisions and provide recourse for individuals who are adversely affected by biased outcomes. Addressing bias is not a one-time fix but an ongoing process of monitoring, improving, and evolving AI systems to ensure that they promote fairness and prevent discrimination. In the long term, the ethical success of AI depends on the commitment of organizations and developers to align technology with values of equity and justice.

HUMAN-AI COLLABORATION IN DECISIONS

In this section, we explore the ethical dynamics involved in integrating human oversight within AI-driven decision-making processes. This includes examining situations where human bias might either override or complement AI insights, impacting the fairness and reliability of outcomes.

The Role of Human Oversight in AI Systems

Human oversight is a critical element in ensuring the ethical deployment of AI systems, particularly as these technologies become more autonomous and integrated into decision-making processes. AI systems can process vast amounts of data and identify patterns that are beyond human capability, which makes them valuable for tasks such as diagnostics in healthcare, financial risk assessment, or autonomous driving. The complexity and opacity of these systems often mean their decisions are not fully understandable to the humans interacting with them. This raises the question: how do we maintain appropriate levels of human control and responsibility when AI systems are making increasingly independent decisions?

One of the central challenges in human oversight of AI systems is determining when and where human intervention is necessary. In certain situations, such as autonomous vehicles or algorithmic trading, decisions need to be made in milliseconds, which makes real-time human involvement impractical. In these cases, AI systems are often given significant autonomy to make decisions based on predefined criteria. This autonomy can, however, lead to ethical and safety concerns, especially when AI systems encounter scenarios they were not specifically programmed to handle, such as unexpected objects on the road in the case of self-driving cars or sudden market disruptions in trading algorithms. Human oversight is thus essential in the design, testing, and monitoring stages to ensure that AI behaves as expected under normal conditions and that fail-safe mechanisms are in place for unusual circumstances.

In regulated industries such as healthcare and criminal justice, human oversight becomes even more critical due to the life-altering consequences of AI decisions. AI systems used in medical diagnostics or legal risk assessments can greatly assist human professionals by processing vast amounts of data, but they must not replace human judgment entirely.

Physicians, judges, and other professionals rely on experience, empathy, and ethical reasoning to make decisions that balance facts with the nuances of human experience—something AI cannot fully replicate. Human oversight ensures that AI-generated insights are carefully evaluated and contextualized before being acted upon, reducing the risk of harmful or unjust outcomes. In healthcare, for instance, an AI may flag a potential cancer diagnosis, but it is the responsibility of the physician to confirm the diagnosis and consider the patient's overall condition before recommending treatment.

The ethical principle of human oversight in AI systems also relates to accountability. When AI systems make mistakes or cause harm, it can be difficult to assign blame. If a self-driving car causes a fatal accident or an algorithm denies someone access to a loan, who is responsible—the developer, the company, or the AI system itself? Ensuring that human oversight is integral to AI deployment allows for clear accountability.

Organizations deploying AI systems must implement procedures for human review, audit mechanisms, and clear points of accountability to ensure that there is always a responsible party who can intervene when necessary. Ultimately, while AI systems can automate tasks and enhance decision-making, human oversight is indispensable in ensuring that these systems operate ethically and in alignment with societal values, particularly in complex or high-stakes environments.

Augmenting Human Judgment with AI

The integration of AI into decision-making processes has the potential to significantly enhance human judgment by providing powerful tools for analysis, prediction, and optimization. AI systems can process vast amounts of data at speeds and scales far beyond human capability, enabling quicker and more accurate insights. In sectors such as healthcare, finance, and logistics, AI has become instrumental in augmenting human expertise.

For instance, in healthcare, AI-powered diagnostic systems assist doctors in analyzing medical images, identifying potential conditions with greater precision and speed than traditional methods. In finance, AI-driven models help analysts predict market trends or assess credit risks by sifting through vast datasets that would otherwise be unmanageable. These enhancements allow professionals to make more informed decisions, improve outcomes, and optimize performance across a wide range of industries.

The benefits of AI-augmented decision-making are not without ethical challenges. One key concern is the risk of over-reliance on AI systems, where human judgment becomes secondary to algorithmic outputs. While AI can enhance decision-making, it is still prone to errors, bias, or limitations, especially when the data it was trained on is flawed or incomplete.

If human decision-makers blindly follow AI recommendations without fully understanding the reasoning behind them, they may overlook critical nuances or context that an algorithm cannot capture. For example, in legal contexts, judges using AI tools for risk assessments in sentencing might rely too heavily on the algorithm's recommendation, disregarding the personal circumstances of a defendant. This over-reliance can lead to unjust outcomes, as AI systems lack the capacity for empathy, moral reasoning, and subjective judgment that are often essential in complex decision-making scenarios.

Another ethical challenge arises from the transparency, or lack thereof, of AI systems. Many AI algorithms, particularly those based on machine learning, operate as black-boxes, meaning that even the developers may not fully understand how the system arrived at a particular decision. This opacity creates a dilemma for human users who are expected to rely on AI recommendations but cannot scrutinize or interpret the underlying logic.

In fields such as healthcare or criminal justice, where decisions have profound impacts on individuals' lives, the inability to explain an AI's decision can lead to significant ethical and legal issues. Patients and defendants, for example, may demand to know why an AI system diagnosed them with a specific condition or deemed them a high risk for recidivism. Without transparency, it becomes difficult to ensure that the AI system is making fair, just, and unbiased recommendations, thus undermining trust in the technology.

To address these ethical challenges, a balanced approach is needed that preserves human autonomy in decision-making while leveraging AI's strengths. One effective strategy is adopting a model of *human-in-the-loop* systems, where AI assists by providing data-driven insights, but the final decision-making responsibility remains with human experts. This approach allows professionals to benefit from AI's analytical power while ensuring that human judgment, empathy, and ethical considerations are not displaced.

In healthcare, for example, an AI system might flag a potential diagnosis based on a patient's symptoms and medical history, but the doctor would still need to evaluate the recommendation in light of their clinical expertise and the patient's personal context. Similarly, in finance, while AI can assist in analyzing market trends or investment opportunities, human oversight ensures that broader economic and social considerations are factored into final decisions. This balance of AI and human judgment not only enhances decision-making but also addresses the ethical concerns of fairness, accountability, and transparency.

Ethical Dilemmas in Overriding AI Decisions

As AI systems become increasingly integrated into decision-making processes across various sectors, ethical dilemmas arise when human judgment conflicts with AI recommendations. This tension is particularly pronounced in high-stakes environments, such as healthcare, criminal justice, and finance, where the consequences of decisions can significantly impact human lives. For instance, in medical settings, AI algorithms may analyze patient data and suggest specific treatment protocols. A physician may override this recommendation, however, based on a patient's unique circumstances, historical context, or professional intuition.

This raises questions about the reliability of AI in critical areas, the responsibility of healthcare professionals to intervene, and the potential for conflict between algorithmic efficiency and nuanced human understanding.

The ethical implications of overriding AI decisions extend beyond individual cases; they also touch upon broader societal concerns about accountability and transparency. When human agents decide to disregard AI recommendations, it becomes crucial to assess the rationale behind such decisions. Are they based on sufficient expertise and data, or do they stem from bias or unfounded assumptions?

Additionally, if an overridden decision leads to negative outcomes, determining liability becomes complex. Should accountability rest with the AI developers, the organization employing the technology, or the individual who intervened? This ambiguity in responsibility can foster a culture of reluctance in trusting AI, potentially stymieing innovation and leading to hesitation in adopting valuable technological advancements.

Moreover, the issue of bias cannot be overlooked in the discussion of overriding AI decisions. AI systems are often trained on historical data, which may embed existing societal bias. When a human overrides an AI recommendation due to perceived bias in the algorithm, it can create a conflicting narrative about whose bias is more valid. For example, in recruitment, an AI may recommend candidates based on certain criteria that inadvertently favor one demographic group over another. If a recruitment manager chooses to disregard the AI's selection in favor of a more diverse candidate pool, the ethical dilemma centers on whether the override was a necessary correction to systemic bias or an overreach that could perpetuate other forms of inequity. This dilemma necessitates a critical examination of how bias is identified and rectified within both AI systems and human decision-making.

Lastly, the relationship between trust and transparency plays a significant role in navigating these ethical dilemmas. Trust in AI systems is contingent upon understanding their decision-making processes, which are often described as black-boxes. When users lack insight into how AI reaches its conclusions, it complicates the ability to confidently override these recommendations.

Therefore, fostering transparency in AI systems is essential for empowering human agents to make informed choices. This includes developing clearer explanations of AI reasoning and outcomes, enabling individuals to weigh the merits of AI recommendations against their expertise and ethical considerations. As society increasingly relies on AI, creating a framework that prioritizes both human judgment and algorithmic support will be vital in addressing the ethical tensions inherent in overriding AI decisions.

Bias from Human-AI Interactions

The interplay between human bias and AI outputs presents significant challenges in various domains, from hiring processes to law enforcement and healthcare. Human judgment is inherently influenced by individual experiences, societal norms, and cognitive bias, all of which can inadvertently seep into the data that train AI systems. For instance, if a recruiting AI is trained on historical hiring data reflecting biased practices, it may perpetuate that bias by favoring certain demographics over others. When human operators interact with AI outputs, their preconceived notions and preferences can further distort the interpretation of these results, resulting in decisions that reflect a mix of algorithmic bias and human fallibility. This cycle of bias complicates efforts to achieve fairness and equity in AI-driven decisions.

Moreover, the feedback loop between human users and AI systems can amplify existing bias. When users rely on AI recommendations, their trust in the technology can lead them to overlook or misinterpret potentially flawed output. For example, in predictive policing, if an AI model consistently flags certain neighborhoods as high-risk based on historical crime data, police officers may disproportionately focus their efforts in those areas, leading to a self-fulfilling prophecy. As officers act on AI recommendations, they reinforce the data patterns that underpin the algorithm, creating a cycle that can entrench systemic bias. The interplay of human and AI biases thus raises ethical concerns about the responsibility of individuals to critically assess AI outputs and the extent to which they can rely on algorithms to support their decision-making.

Additionally, cognitive bias can distort how humans perceive and utilize AI-generated information. For instance, confirmation bias may lead individuals to favor AI output that aligns with their beliefs while disregarding contradictory evidence. This can be particularly problematic in settings such as healthcare, where a clinician might trust an AI's diagnosis that supports their initial hypothesis but ignore recommendations that suggest alternative treatments. Such behavior not only undermines the effectiveness of AI but can also compromise patient care. The awareness of this bias is crucial for organizations seeking to enhance the synergy between human expertise and AI capabilities, emphasizing the need for training and education on the limitations and potential pitfalls of AI technologies.

To mitigate the influence of human bias on AI output, organizations must prioritize transparency and promote a culture of critical evaluation. This involves fostering an environment where users are encouraged to question AI recommendations and understand the underlying data and algorithms driving that output. Implementing mechanisms for regular audits and updates of AI systems can also help to identify and rectify bias, ensuring that human-AI interactions are informed by the most accurate and equitable data available. Ultimately, addressing the complexities of bias from human-AI interactions requires a concerted effort to bridge the gap between human intuition and algorithmic reasoning, paving the way for more balanced and fair decision-making processes.

ALGORITHMIC TRANSPARENCY AND EXPLAINABILITY

Algorithmic transparency and explainability are critical concepts in the ethical deployment of AI systems, reflecting the importance of understanding how these systems arrive at their decisions. As AI increasingly influences various aspects of life—from hiring practices to financial lending and healthcare diagnostics—stakeholders must be able to comprehend the mechanisms behind these automated processes. Transparency in AI algorithms not only fosters trust among users and affected parties but also empowers them to critically assess the fairness and reliability of the decisions being made.

When AI systems operate as black-boxes, shrouded in complexity and obscurity, it becomes challenging for individuals to understand the rationale behind outcomes that significantly impact their lives. Thus, there exists an ethical duty to ensure that AI systems are explainable, enabling users to grasp the underlying logic of decisions, identify potential bias, and hold organizations accountable for their automated processes. By prioritizing algorithmic transparency, stakeholders can promote ethical AI practices that prioritize fairness, accountability, and the protection of individual rights in an increasingly automated world.

The Black-Box Problem in AI

The black-box problem in AI refers to the inherent difficulty in understanding and interpreting how complex AI models, particularly those based on deep learning, arrive at their decisions. These models often consist of multiple layers of interconnected nodes, processing vast amounts of data in intricate ways. While they can yield remarkably accurate predictions, the mechanisms by which they do so remain opaque to users and even the developers who create them. This lack of transparency poses significant challenges across various domains, particularly in critical areas such as healthcare, finance, and criminal justice, where decisions can have profound consequences on individuals and communities.

One of the primary challenges of the black-box problem is the issue of accountability. When an AI system makes a decision—be it diagnosing a medical condition, approving a loan, or determining sentencing in a legal context—stakeholders need to understand the rationale behind that decision to ensure accountability and trust. The complexity of these models, however, makes it difficult to trace how input data is transformed into output decisions. As a result, when adverse outcomes arise from AI-driven processes, pinpointing responsibility becomes contentious. This ambiguity not only undermines trust in AI systems but also raises ethical questions about the reliance on such technology in high-stakes situations.

Furthermore, the black-box problem can perpetuate existing bias within AI systems. If users cannot comprehend how an AI model operates, they are ill equipped to identify potential sources of bias embedded in its decision-making process. For example, if a hiring algorithm systematically favors certain demographic characteristics, users may be unaware of this bias unless they can scrutinize the model's workings. The inability to access the "thought process" of AI models can lead to a false sense of confidence in their outputs, allowing bias to go unchecked and potentially resulting in discriminatory practices. Addressing the black-box problem is therefore crucial for ensuring fairness and equity in AI applications.

Efforts to mitigate the black-box problem have led to the development of various interpretability and explainability frameworks within the AI community. Techniques such as LIME and SHAP aim to provide insights into model behavior by highlighting the influence of specific input features on predictions. By offering users a clearer view of how decisions are made, these approaches help bridge the gap between AI technology and human understanding, but while these methods can enhance interpretability, they do not entirely resolve the black-box issue.

Continued research and innovation in AI transparency are essential to promote responsible AI use, ensuring that users can trust and effectively engage with these powerful technologies. Ultimately, fostering an environment of openness and understanding around AI decision-making is key to harnessing its potential while mitigating the risks associated with its deployment.

The Importance of Explainability in AI Systems

Explainability in AI systems refers to the ability to understand and interpret the reasoning behind the decisions made by these models. As AI becomes increasingly integrated into various aspects of society, from healthcare to finance to law enforcement, the importance of explainability cannot be overstated. Transparency in AI decision-making is essential for building trust among users, stakeholders, and the general public. When individuals understand how AI systems operate and arrive at their conclusions, they are more likely to have confidence in the technology, which is crucial for its widespread adoption and acceptance. This trust is particularly important in high-stakes scenarios where decisions can significantly impact lives, such as diagnosing medical conditions or determining eligibility for loans.

Explainability is integral to ethical accountability in AI systems. When decisions are made by algorithms, it becomes challenging to ascertain responsibility in the event of adverse outcomes. For example, if an AI system denies a loan application based on seemingly arbitrary criteria, the applicant may struggle to understand the reasoning behind the decision, leaving them without recourse for redress. Ensuring that AI systems are explainable allows organizations to demonstrate accountability, as it provides a clear rationale for decisions made on their behalf. This transparency not only helps mitigate potential harms but also encourages organizations to take ethical considerations seriously in the development and deployment of AI technology.

Additionally, explainability plays a crucial role in identifying and addressing bias present in AI systems. Many algorithms are trained on historical data, which may reflect existing societal bias. When users can examine the decision-making process of an AI model, they can better identify any potential bias that could lead to unfair or discriminatory outcomes. For instance, in hiring practices, an XAI system might reveal that certain demographic factors unduly influence candidate selection. By understanding these underlying mechanisms, organizations can take proactive steps to rectify bias and ensure that their AI systems operate fairly and equitably. This process is essential for fostering a culture of responsible AI use that prioritizes inclusivity and social justice.

Finally, the push for explainability is also gaining traction due to regulatory and legal pressures. As governments and regulatory bodies become more aware of the implications of AI technologies, they are increasingly advocating for transparency in AI decision-making. Policies such as the EU's AI Act emphasize the need for XAI systems, particularly in high-risk applications. Organizations that prioritize explainability not only align with emerging regulations but also position themselves as leaders in ethical AI practices. By investing in transparency and explainability, companies can enhance their reputation, gain a competitive edge, and contribute to the development of AI technologies that are not only innovative but also trustworthy and accountable.

Techniques for Improving AI Explainability

As the demand for transparent and trustworthy AI systems continues to grow, various techniques and tools have emerged to enhance AI explainability. These methods aim to illuminate the complex decision-making processes of AI models, making it easier for users to understand the rationale behind their outputs. One widely used technique is LIME, which provides insights into individual predictions by approximating the behavior of the AI model locally. By generating interpretable explanations for specific instances, LIME enables users to see which features were most influential in a particular decision, thus demystifying the black-box nature of many machine learning algorithms. This localized approach is particularly valuable in contexts such as healthcare, where understanding the factors leading to a diagnosis can significantly impact patient care and treatment.

Another effective technique for improving AI explainability is the use of SHAP, which draws from cooperative game theory to assign each feature an importance value for a given prediction. SHAP values provide a unified measure of feature contributions, allowing stakeholders to see not only which factors influenced a decision but also to what extent. This capability fosters a deeper understanding of AI models by revealing the interplay between different features and their combined effect on the output. For example, in a credit scoring model, SHAP can help explain how various attributes—such as income, credit history, and employment status—interact to influence a loan approval decision. By providing clear and consistent explanations, SHAP aids organizations in identifying potential bias and making informed decisions based on AI output.

Moreover, model-agnostic techniques allow for explanations regardless of the underlying AI model used, enhancing flexibility and accessibility. Techniques such as feature importance ranking and partial dependence plots can help visualize the relationship between features and predictions, offering intuitive insights into how models make decisions. For instance, partial dependence plots illustrate how varying a single feature while keeping others constant affects the predicted outcome, allowing users to grasp the model's sensitivity to specific variables. These visualization tools are invaluable for stakeholders who may lack deep technical expertise, as they translate complex model behavior into more comprehensible formats. The accessibility of these techniques fosters broader acceptance and trust in AI technologies among diverse user groups.

In addition to these individual techniques, organizations can adopt a holistic approach to AI explainability by incorporating explainability into the entire AI development lifecycle. This includes involving stakeholders in the design and evaluation phases to ensure that their needs for transparency and understanding are met. Engaging users early in the process can help identify critical aspects of decision-making that require explanation, guiding the selection of appropriate explainability methods.

Furthermore, establishing best practices for documentation and communication around AI systems can enhance user confidence and promote accountability. By prioritizing explainability from the outset, organizations can develop AI solutions that are not only effective but also transparent and trustworthy, ultimately paving the way for responsible AI deployment across various sectors.

Balancing Complexity and Usability

The integration of sophisticated AI models into various applications has revolutionized industries, enabling unprecedented levels of automation and efficiency. This complexity often poses significant challenges when it comes to explaining AI decision-making processes to non-experts. As AI systems become increasingly intricate—utilizing advanced techniques such as deep learning or ensemble methods—their decision-making pathways can become obscured, making it difficult for users to grasp how and why specific outcomes are generated. This complexity can lead to mistrust and apprehension among users, particularly in high-stakes environments where understanding the rationale behind decisions is crucial for ethical accountability and informed consent.

One of the primary trade-offs in AI development lies in the balance between model accuracy and interpretability. Sophisticated models often yield higher predictive performance, benefiting from the ability to process vast amounts of data and identify complex patterns. This enhanced performance typically comes at the cost of explainability. For example, while deep neural networks can achieve remarkable accuracy in image recognition tasks, their intricate structures render them largely incomprehensible to users. Conversely, simpler models such as decision trees or linear regression provide more intuitive explanations for their predictions but may lack the accuracy needed in complex scenarios. Striking the right balance requires careful consideration of the specific application and the audience's need for clarity versus performance.

To address this challenge, researchers and practitioners are exploring hybrid approaches that combine the strengths of both complex and interpretable models. For instance, using simpler, more interpretable models as surrogates for more complex models can offer a means of explanation without sacrificing performance. In this approach, the complex model's predictions are approximated by a simpler model, allowing stakeholders to understand the key drivers behind decisions while still benefiting from the sophisticated underlying system. This method not only enhances transparency but also facilitates trust, as users can see a clearer connection between input features and output predictions without having to navigate the intricacies of a complex model.

Furthermore, the development of user-centered design principles can significantly enhance the usability of AI systems without compromising their complexity. By involving non-expert users in the design process, developers can identify which aspects of the decision-making process are most critical for explanation and tailor the communication of these insights accordingly. Tools such as interactive visualizations, dashboards, and narrative explanations can bridge the gap between complex AI models and user comprehension, allowing individuals to engage with the technology meaningfully. Ultimately, balancing complexity and usability requires a multifaceted approach that recognizes the importance of both performance and transparency, ensuring that AI technologies are not only powerful but also accessible and trustworthy for all users.

ACCOUNTABILITY FOR AUTOMATED DECISIONS

Defining Responsibility in AI-Driven Decision-Making

As the reliance on AI systems grows, particularly in high-stakes decision-making scenarios, the question of accountability becomes increasingly critical—specifically, who holds responsibility when AI decisions go wrong? This issue is complex, as it involves various stakeholders, including developers who create the algorithms, operators who implement and manage the systems, and the AI systems themselves. Each of these parties may contribute to the outcomes produced by AI, complicating the assignment of liability. For instance, developers may be held accountable for flaws in the algorithmic design or biased training data, while operators might bear responsibility for improper use or failure to implement adequate oversight.

Additionally, there is a growing discussion about whether the AI systems themselves should be considered responsible for their actions. To ensure fairness in assigning liability, it is essential to establish clear frameworks that delineate the roles and responsibilities of each stakeholder involved. This requires comprehensive legal and ethical guidelines that address the complexities of AI accountability, promote transparency in decision-making processes, and protect the rights of individuals affected by automated decisions. Ultimately, developing a robust accountability framework is crucial for fostering trust in AI technologies and ensuring that individuals can seek recourse when faced with adverse outcomes stemming from automated decisions.

Accountability for AI Decisions

The question of accountability for decisions made by AI systems has become increasingly prominent as these technologies become integral to various sectors, including healthcare, finance, and law enforcement. As AI systems operate with varying degrees of autonomy, determining who bears responsibility for their outcomes poses significant legal and ethical challenges. Traditionally, accountability has rested with human agents—such as developers, organizations, or end-users—who design, implement, or deploy these systems. However, as AI capabilities expand, especially in high-stakes applications where decisions can have profound implications on individuals' lives, the lines of responsibility become blurred, necessitating a comprehensive examination of accountability frameworks in the context of AI.

One of the primary concerns surrounding AI accountability is the issue of liability in the event of adverse outcomes. For example, if an AI system incorrectly diagnoses a medical condition or unjustly denies a loan application, determining who is responsible can be complex. Should liability fall on the developers of the algorithm, who may argue that the system was functioning as intended? Or does accountability lie with the organizations that deploy the technology, who are responsible for its ethical implementation and oversight? Current legal frameworks often struggle to adequately address these questions, leading to calls for new regulations that specifically account for the unique challenges posed by AI. Establishing clear guidelines and standards for accountability is essential to ensure that affected parties have recourse and to maintain public trust in AI systems.

Ethical considerations also play a crucial role in discussions about AI accountability. Beyond legal liability, organizations must grapple with their moral obligations regarding the deployment of AI technologies. This includes fostering transparency about how AI systems operate, the data they rely on, and the potential bias embedded within their algorithms. Ethical frameworks, such as the principles of fairness, accountability, and transparency (FAT), can guide organizations in navigating the complexities of AI accountability. By prioritizing ethical considerations, organizations can build trust with users and stakeholders, demonstrating a commitment to responsible AI practices that prioritize human well-being and societal equity.

Furthermore, as AI continues to evolve, the concept of *algorithmic agency* has emerged, raising questions about the extent to which AI systems can be seen as autonomous decision-makers. In this context, it becomes essential to explore the potential for shared accountability models, where multiple stakeholders—including developers, organizations, users, and policymakers—collaborate to ensure responsible AI usage. This collaborative approach can help distribute responsibility while promoting a culture of ethical awareness and proactive risk management.

Ultimately, establishing clear lines of accountability for AI decisions requires ongoing dialogue among stakeholders, legal experts, ethicists, and technologists to create a robust framework that addresses the challenges and complexities of AI accountability in a rapidly evolving landscape.

Shared Responsibility Between Developers and Users

As AI systems increasingly permeate various sectors, the concept of shared responsibility emerges as a vital framework for understanding accountability in AI deployment. This framework recognizes that the complexities of AI decision-making require collaboration among multiple stakeholders, including developers, organizations, end-users, and policymakers. Rather than placing the burden of responsibility solely on one group, a shared responsibility model encourages collective ownership of both the benefits and risks associated with AI technologies. By fostering cooperation among these stakeholders, organizations can enhance the ethical deployment of AI while ensuring that decision-making processes are transparent and accountable.

Developers play a crucial role in the shared responsibility framework, as they are tasked with designing and building AI systems that are both effective and ethically sound. This involves not only creating algorithms that produce accurate results but also implementing safeguards to mitigate bias, enhance explainability, and ensure that the technology aligns with ethical guidelines. Developers must prioritize ethical considerations throughout the development lifecycle, including conducting thorough impact assessments and engaging in regular audits of AI systems. By taking proactive steps to understand the potential implications of their technologies, developers can contribute to a culture of accountability that extends beyond mere compliance with regulations, promoting the responsible use of AI in practice.

End-users, including organizations and individuals who deploy AI systems, also share in this responsibility. Their role involves understanding the capabilities and limitations of the technology they are using and ensuring that AI systems are applied in appropriate contexts. Users must engage with the outputs of AI systems critically, questioning the recommendations made and recognizing potential bias or inaccuracies. By fostering an informed user base, organizations can create a feedback loop that informs developers about real-world applications and challenges, ultimately leading to improved AI systems. This shared engagement enhances the effectiveness of AI technologies and promotes accountability across the deployment process.

Additionally, policymakers and regulatory bodies play a significant role in establishing the legal and ethical frameworks that guide AI deployment. By creating clear regulations that address issues of accountability, transparency, and bias, policymakers can set standards for shared responsibility that encompass both developers and users. Collaborative efforts, such as public-private partnerships, can facilitate dialogue among stakeholders, fostering a better understanding of the complexities involved in AI deployment.

Ultimately, a shared responsibility model not only promotes ethical AI practices but also cultivates trust among all stakeholders involved, creating a more equitable and transparent AI landscape that benefits society as a whole.

Ethical Frameworks for Assigning Liability

The rapid integration of AI into various sectors has necessitated the development of ethical frameworks for assigning liability in AI-driven systems, particularly when errors occur. As AI systems become more autonomous, determining accountability for adverse outcomes becomes increasingly complex. An effective ethical framework must address not only the legal aspects of liability but also the moral responsibilities of the various stakeholders involved—developers, organizations, users, and policymakers. Such frameworks are essential for promoting transparency, trust, and responsible AI deployment, ensuring that affected parties have avenues for redress when AI systems fail.

A foundational aspect of these ethical frameworks is the principle of transparency. Stakeholders must clearly understand how AI systems operate, including the algorithms used, the data on which they are trained, and the potential bias inherent in their design. Transparency empowers users to critically engage with AI outputs and fosters a culture of accountability among developers and organizations. When stakeholders have access to information about the decision-making processes of AI systems, it becomes easier to identify when and why errors occur. This openness also encourages organizations to adopt rigorous testing and validation practices, ensuring that AI systems are thoroughly evaluated before deployment and continuously monitored for performance and bias.

Another crucial element is the principle of proportionality, which involves balancing the level of responsibility assigned to stakeholders based on their degree of involvement and influence over the AI system. For instance, developers may bear greater responsibility for technical failures resulting from design flaws, while organizations that deploy these systems may be accountable for ensuring ethical use and oversight. End-users also play a role in this ecosystem, as their understanding and engagement with AI outputs can influence outcomes significantly. By establishing guidelines that reflect the varying levels of responsibility across stakeholders, ethical frameworks can promote a more equitable distribution of liability and encourage collaborative efforts to improve AI systems.

Moreover, ethical frameworks should incorporate the principle of redress, providing mechanisms for individuals and organizations affected by AI errors to seek remedies. This includes defining clear procedures for reporting issues, investigating errors, and determining appropriate compensation or corrective measures. Ensuring that users have access to avenues for recourse not only enhances trust in AI systems but also reinforces the ethical obligation of organizations to prioritize user welfare. By embedding these principles within ethical frameworks for assigning liability, stakeholders can work together to create a responsible AI landscape that emphasizes accountability, continuous improvement, and the protection of individuals' rights in the face of technological advancement.

Ultimately, developing and implementing robust ethical frameworks is vital for navigating the complexities of AI liability, fostering a culture of responsibility that keeps pace with the evolving capabilities of AI technologies.

Addressing Ethical Failures in AI

As AI systems increasingly influence critical decisions across various sectors, the potential for ethical failures has become a pressing concern. These failures can result in significant harm, whether through biased outcomes in hiring practices, erroneous medical diagnoses, or unjust legal penalties. Addressing this harm requires a multifaceted approach that combines mechanisms for redress with systemic changes to ensure accountability and prevent future occurrences. Central to this effort is the establishment of clear legal recourse for individuals and communities affected by AI decisions, which plays a crucial role in holding organizations accountable for the impact of their technology.

Legal recourse is essential for victims of AI-induced harm, as it provides a structured pathway for seeking justice and compensation. Individuals who have suffered due to erroneous decisions made by AI systems should have access to grievance mechanisms that allow them to challenge these outcomes effectively. This might include the right to appeal decisions made by AI-driven processes or the establishment of regulatory bodies that oversee AI systems and their implementation. Legal frameworks need to evolve to include provisions specifically addressing AI, ensuring that there are clear pathways for accountability. This evolution might involve developing laws that recognize AI systems as entities capable of causing harm, thereby establishing a legal basis for holding organizations responsible for their outcomes.

In addition to legal recourse, addressing ethical failures in AI also necessitates systemic changes within organizations. Companies must implement robust oversight mechanisms to monitor AI systems continuously and assess their impacts on various stakeholders. This includes conducting regular audits to identify and mitigate bias in AI algorithms, as well as fostering a culture of transparency that encourages employees to report ethical concerns related to AI deployments. Training programs focused on ethics in AI development and usage can also help raise awareness of potential pitfalls, ensuring that developers and users alike understand the implications of their decisions. By embedding ethical considerations into the organizational culture, companies can proactively prevent ethical failures before they occur.

Finally, addressing ethical failures in AI requires broader systemic changes that involve collaboration among stakeholders, including governments, industry leaders, and civil society organizations. This collaboration can lead to the development of industry-wide standards and best practices for AI deployment, promoting ethical accountability across the board. Public engagement and advocacy play vital roles in holding organizations accountable and demanding transparency from AI developers. By creating forums for dialogue between stakeholders, policymakers can better understand the challenges posed by AI technologies and formulate regulations that safeguard individuals' rights while promoting innovation.

Ultimately, a comprehensive approach that combines legal recourse with systemic changes is essential for effectively addressing ethical failures in AI, ensuring that technological advancements are aligned with societal values and the well-being of all individuals.

THE IMPACT ON WORKFORCE AND DECISION ROLES

AI's Impact on Workforce Roles

The introduction of AI into various industries is significantly reshaping the landscape of decision-making processes, raising essential ethical considerations about the future roles of human decision-makers. As AI systems become more sophisticated, they possess the ability to automate routine tasks and provide data-driven insights that can enhance the decision-making process. This shift has the potential to either replace human roles in certain contexts, particularly those involving repetitive or low-level decision-making, or augment them by providing support that enables professionals to focus on higher-order thinking and strategic judgment.

The ethical implications of this transformation are profound. Organizations must grapple with the potential for job displacement, the necessity of reskilling workers to adapt to new roles that require collaboration with AI, and the challenge of ensuring that human expertise remains integral to critical decision-making processes.

Additionally, there are concerns about the fairness and inclusivity of AI systems, as bias in algorithms can disproportionately affect certain groups of workers, further complicating the transition. Addressing these ethical considerations is vital for organizations as they navigate the complexities of integrating AI into their decision-making frameworks, ensuring that the human workforce is empowered rather than sidelined in this evolving landscape.

AI's Impact on Traditional Decision-Making Roles

The rise of AI is fundamentally transforming traditional decision-making roles across various industries, reshaping how decisions are made and who is responsible for them. Historically, decision-making processes relied heavily on human judgment, intuition, and experience. AI systems are increasingly being integrated into these processes, however, providing data-driven insights and automating routine tasks. This shift is altering the dynamics of decision-making by enabling faster, more accurate analysis while also raising questions about the future roles of human decision-makers. As a result, organizations must adapt to this evolving landscape to harness the benefits of AI while maintaining effective governance and oversight.

One of the most significant impacts of AI on decision-making is the enhancement of analytical capabilities. AI systems can process vast amounts of data at unprecedented speeds, uncovering patterns and insights that might be overlooked by human analysts. In industries such as finance, healthcare, and marketing, AI-driven tools are being used to inform investment strategies, diagnose medical conditions, and optimize customer targeting. By augmenting human intelligence with machine learning algorithms, organizations can make more informed decisions that enhance operational efficiency and drive innovation. This transformation necessitates a reevaluation of the skills required for decision-makers, as professionals must now be proficient in understanding and interpreting AI outputs to remain relevant in their roles.

Despite the advantages offered by AI, there are inherent challenges in its integration into decision-making processes. The reliance on AI systems can lead to a diminished role for human decision-makers, potentially resulting in a loss of critical thinking and judgment in favor of algorithmic recommendations. This shift raises concerns about accountability, particularly when decisions are made based on flawed or biased data inputs. In industries such as criminal justice and recruitment, where AI systems can perpetuate existing bias, the implications of over-reliance on technology can be profound and harmful. Consequently, organizations must strike a delicate balance between leveraging AI for efficiency and ensuring that human oversight remains integral to decision-making processes.

Furthermore, the evolving nature of decision-making roles necessitates a cultural shift within organizations. As AI takes on more analytical tasks, human decision-makers must focus on higher-order thinking skills, such as ethical considerations, empathy, and strategic vision.

Leadership will need to foster a collaborative environment where AI is viewed as a tool to support human judgment rather than replace it. This shift involves training and reskilling employees to work effectively alongside AI systems, emphasizing the importance of human intuition and contextual understanding in areas where technology may fall short.

By embracing this collaborative approach, organizations can fully leverage the strengths of both AI and human decision-makers, ensuring a more balanced and responsible decision-making process that aligns with ethical standards and societal values.

Automation vs. Human Expertise

The advent of AI and automation technologies has sparked a significant debate around the ethical implications of replacing or augmenting human decision-makers in various industries. As AI systems become increasingly capable of executing tasks that traditionally require human expertise, organizations face critical decisions about how to balance the efficiency gains offered by automation with the value of human insight and judgment. While AI can analyze data faster and often with greater accuracy, it lacks the nuanced understanding of context, ethical considerations, and emotional intelligence that human decision-makers bring to the table. This dichotomy raises essential questions about the role of human expertise in decision-making processes and the potential consequences of prioritizing automation over human involvement.

One of the primary ethical considerations surrounding automation is the potential for job displacement. As AI systems are integrated into workflows, there is a real concern that human workers may be rendered obsolete, leading to widespread unemployment and economic inequality. Industries such as manufacturing, customer service, and finance are particularly susceptible to this shift, where routine tasks can be easily automated.

Organizations, however, must recognize that the elimination of jobs can have detrimental effects on individuals and communities, fostering social unrest and widening economic divides. Ethical considerations in this context involve not only the obligation to protect jobs but also the responsibility to provide retraining and upskilling opportunities for displaced workers, enabling them to transition into new roles that leverage their unique human capabilities.

In contrast to concerns about job loss, there is also a strong case for augmenting human decision-makers with AI rather than replacing them entirely. AI can serve as a powerful tool to enhance human expertise, providing insights and analysis that empower individuals to make more informed decisions. In fields such as healthcare, AI-driven diagnostic tools can assist doctors in identifying conditions faster and more accurately, ultimately improving patient outcomes.

The ethical challenge, however, lies in ensuring that human oversight remains integral to the decision-making process. Reliance on AI without adequate human intervention can lead to blind spots, where critical ethical considerations or contextual factors are overlooked. Organizations must implement frameworks that prioritize collaboration between AI systems and human decision-makers, fostering a symbiotic relationship that enhances the overall quality of decisions.

Ultimately, the ethical considerations surrounding automation versus human expertise necessitate a nuanced approach that prioritizes both technological advancement and the well-being of individuals and society. Organizations must adopt ethical guidelines that govern the deployment of AI technologies, emphasizing the importance of human oversight and accountability in decision-making processes.

Additionally, engaging diverse stakeholders in discussions about the implications of AI on employment and expertise can help shape policies that mitigate the risks associated with automation. By recognizing the unique strengths of human decision-makers and leveraging AI as a complement rather than a replacement, organizations can navigate the complex landscape of automation while fostering a future that values both technological innovation and human insight.

Job Displacement and Reskilling in AI-Era Decision Systems

The rapid integration of AI into decision-making systems across various industries presents both opportunities and challenges, particularly concerning job displacement. As AI systems become more capable of performing tasks traditionally executed by humans, there is a growing concern that many workers may face redundancy. This disruption poses significant ethical questions regarding the responsibility of organizations and governments to prepare the workforce for an AI-driven future. A proactive approach is essential to address the skills gap created by automation, ensuring that workers are not left behind as industries evolve.

The need for new skills in the AI era is paramount. Many traditional roles are being transformed as AI technologies change the nature of work. Jobs that require routine, repetitive tasks are particularly vulnerable to automation, necessitating a shift toward positions that emphasize critical thinking, creativity, emotional intelligence, and complex problem-solving—skills that AI systems are not equipped to replicate.

Moreover, as AI technologies become integrated into various sectors, employees will increasingly need to understand how to work alongside these systems. This includes gaining proficiency in data analysis, machine learning basics, and AI ethics, empowering workers to leverage technology rather than compete with it. To facilitate this transition, educational institutions and training programs must adapt their curricula to equip students and current employees with the competencies required in an AI-driven economy.

Organizations bear an ethical obligation to invest in reskilling and upskilling their workforce in response to the changes brought about by AI. By taking a proactive stance on workforce development, companies can help mitigate the negative impacts of job displacement while fostering a culture of continuous learning. This might involve offering training programs, mentorship opportunities, and access to online courses focused on emerging technologies and soft skills.

Additionally, organizations can engage in partnerships with educational institutions and local governments to create community-based initiatives aimed at reskilling displaced workers. Such commitments not only benefit the employees but also enhance organizational resilience and adaptability in a rapidly changing job market.

Governments also play a critical role in addressing the challenges of job displacement and reskilling in the AI era. Policymakers should establish frameworks that support workforce development, including funding for training programs, tax incentives for companies that invest in employee education, and initiatives that promote lifelong learning. Furthermore, regulations should be enacted to ensure that the transition to an AI-driven economy is inclusive, providing support for vulnerable populations disproportionately affected by job displacement. By prioritizing reskilling and fostering an inclusive approach to workforce development, societies can navigate the challenges posed by AI and automation, ultimately creating a labor market that is not only resilient but also equitable and prepared for the future.

Ensuring Ethical Use of AI in Workforce Decisions

As organizations increasingly rely on AI to guide workforce decisions—such as recruitment, promotions, and compensation—ensuring ethical practices in these processes becomes paramount. The use of AI in human resources holds the potential for enhanced efficiency and objectivity; however, it also introduces significant risks related to fairness and transparency. AI systems can inadvertently perpetuate or even exacerbate existing bias if they are trained on flawed datasets or lack appropriate oversight.

Therefore, organizations must adopt ethical frameworks that prioritize fairness, transparency, and accountability in AI-driven workforce decisions to foster trust and maintain a diverse and inclusive workplace.

Fairness in AI applications is critical, particularly when it comes to employment decisions. Organizations must rigorously evaluate the data used to train AI systems to ensure that it is representative and free from bias that could lead to discriminatory outcomes. For instance, if an AI system is trained on historical hiring data that reflects gender or racial disparities, it may inadvertently replicate that bias in its recommendations. To combat this, organizations should implement bias detection and mitigation strategies throughout the AI development lifecycle, ensuring that fairness is a core consideration from the outset. Additionally, involving diverse teams in the development and evaluation of AI systems can help identify and address potential bias that may not be apparent to homogeneous groups.

Transparency is equally essential in the ethical use of AI in workforce decisions. Stakeholders—including employees, job applicants, and regulatory bodies—must have access to information about how AI systems function and the criteria used in decision-making processes. This includes providing clarity on the algorithms employed, the data sources utilized, and the rationale behind specific outcomes. Organizations can promote transparency by offering explanations for AI-driven decisions, such as why a candidate was not selected for a position or the factors influencing salary recommendations. By demystifying AI processes, organizations can build trust among employees and job seekers, fostering an environment where individuals feel respected and valued.

Furthermore, ethical frameworks for AI in workforce decisions should include mechanisms for accountability and redress. Organizations need to establish clear protocols for addressing grievances related to AI-driven decisions, allowing individuals to contest outcomes that they believe to be unfair or discriminatory. This can involve creating independent review boards or oversight committees to evaluate AI decisions and provide recourse for affected individuals.

Additionally, ongoing monitoring and auditing of AI systems are essential to ensure compliance with ethical standards and legal regulations. By committing to fairness, transparency, and accountability, organizations can ensure that AI is used ethically in workforce decisions, ultimately promoting a more equitable and inclusive work environment that values diversity and fosters employee engagement.

CHAPTER 14

ETHICAL IMPLICATIONS OF BIG DATA ANALYTICS

THE BENEFITS OF BIG DATA ANALYTICS FOR SOCIETY

Transforming Society with Big Data

The advent of big data has transformed the way organizations, governments, and individuals interact with information, offering numerous opportunities for positive societal outcomes. One of the most significant benefits of big data is its ability to drive innovation across a wide range of sectors, from healthcare and education to finance and transportation. In healthcare, for instance, big data analytics can help identify patterns in patient outcomes, enabling healthcare providers to deliver more personalized treatment plans and improve overall patient care. Similarly, in the education sector, data analytics can help institutions tailor their curriculum and instructional methods to better meet the diverse needs of students, ultimately enhancing learning outcomes and engagement.

By leveraging vast amounts of data, businesses can identify emerging trends, optimize operations, and enhance customer experiences, ultimately leading to more effective products and services. For example, retailers can analyze consumer purchasing behavior to develop targeted marketing strategies, while manufacturers can utilize predictive analytics to streamline supply chains and reduce costs.

Additionally, big data enables governments to make data-driven policy decisions, improving public services and fostering greater transparency and accountability in governance. By analyzing data on social issues such as crime rates or public health trends, policymakers can allocate resources more effectively, implement evidence-based solutions, and engage citizens in meaningful ways, ultimately promoting a more informed and participatory democracy.

Advancements in Healthcare and Agriculture

In healthcare, big data analytics plays a pivotal role in enhancing the quality of patient care through more precise diagnostics, personalized treatment plans, and proactive health management via predictive analytics. By systematically analyzing patient records, healthcare providers can identify patterns that may indicate the likelihood of disease outbreaks or the effectiveness of specific treatment protocols. This data-driven approach allows timely interventions, which can significantly improve patient outcomes. For instance, predictive analytics can help identify at-risk populations, enabling healthcare systems to implement preventive measures that reduce the incidence of diseases and lower overall healthcare costs.

In agriculture, big data is revolutionizing traditional farming practices by enhancing productivity through precision farming techniques. By employing data collected from various sensors—such as soil moisture levels, weather conditions, and crop health—farmers can make informed decisions regarding irrigation, fertilization, and pest management. This approach not only reduces waste and lowers costs but also improves crop yields and sustainability by optimizing resource use. As a result, such innovations contribute to food security, promote environmental stewardship, and lead to a higher quality of life for both farmers and consumers. Ultimately, the integration of big data across sectors not only drives efficiency and productivity but also fosters a more sustainable future for society as a whole.

Improvements in Public Services and Decision-Making

Big data serves as a transformative tool for improving public services and enhancing decision-making processes within governments. By utilizing big data analytics, governmental agencies can gain valuable insights that inform policies and initiatives aimed at optimizing urban planning and managing traffic congestion more effectively. For instance, transportation departments can harness data from traffic sensors, GPSes, and even social media to create smart city initiatives that proactively address traffic flow and public safety. Such data-driven strategies not only minimize congestion but also facilitate the development of infrastructure that meets the evolving needs of urban populations, ultimately contributing to a more efficient and livable environment.

In addition to urban management, big data plays a critical role in enhancing the delivery of public services, particularly in areas such as disaster response and resource allocation. During emergencies, real-time data from various sources—such as weather forecasts, social media alerts, and geographic information systems—can be analyzed to coordinate response efforts effectively and direct aid to the most affected regions. This capability allows a more agile and informed approach to disaster management, ensuring that resources are deployed where they are needed most.

By integrating big data into governance frameworks, governments can foster greater transparency and accountability, ultimately leading to improved outcomes for communities and individuals alike. These applications highlight how big data not only streamlines operations but also empowers governments to respond more adeptly to the challenges faced by their constituents.

Fostering Economic Growth and Business Innovation

Another key advantage of big data lies in its significant contribution to fostering economic growth and driving business innovation across various industries. Companies are increasingly harnessing data analytics to gain a deeper understanding of consumer behavior, which enables them to tailor their products and services more effectively. For instance, retailers utilize big data to predict consumer preferences, allowing them to personalize shopping experiences, optimize inventory levels, and enhance marketing strategies. This personalized approach not only boosts customer satisfaction and loyalty but also leads to increased sales and profitability. In addition, financial institutions leverage data-driven insights to detect fraudulent activity in real time, which not only reduces financial losses but also enhances consumer trust in digital transactions.

Moreover, the rise of startups leveraging big data analytics is reshaping the business landscape by creating new economic opportunities and addressing societal needs. These innovative companies use data to identify market gaps and develop solutions that cater to specific demands, thereby promoting entrepreneurship and job creation. For example, startups in the healthcare sector may analyze patient data to offer personalized wellness solutions, while those in the agriculture sector might use data to create precision farming technologies that improve food production efficiency. As these startups flourish, they contribute to economic resilience and diversity, reinforcing the idea that big data is a catalyst for overall economic prosperity. This dynamic environment fosters competition and encourages established companies to innovate, ultimately benefiting consumers and society as a whole.

BIG DATA USAGE RISKS AND MANAGEMENT

Risks

Despite the numerous benefits of big data, its use is fraught with risks that must be managed diligently to harness its potential without causing unintended harm. One of the most pressing concerns is privacy infringement, as the extensive collection of personal data often occurs without explicit consent from individuals. Organizations frequently gather more data than necessary for their operations, heightening the risk of misuse, data breaches, and unauthorized access.

The potential for sensitive information to be compromised raises significant ethical questions about data stewardship and individual rights. Moreover, as data breaches become more prevalent, public trust in organizations that handle large volumes of data may diminish, creating an environment of skepticism and concern regarding data privacy practices.

In addition to privacy issues, the risk of algorithmic bias poses a significant challenge in the realm of big data analytics. When the data used to train algorithms is biased or unrepresentative of the population, the resulting AI systems may inadvertently perpetuate or even amplify existing societal bias. For instance, if historical hiring data reflects past discriminatory practices, a recruitment AI trained on this data may continue to favor certain demographics while unfairly disadvantaging others.

Such outcomes can lead to unfair hiring practices and exacerbate inequality within the job market. Therefore, the ethical implications of big data necessitate a proactive approach to ensure that algorithms are transparent, data is collected responsibly, and measures are in place to identify and mitigate bias, ultimately promoting fairness and equity in the deployment of data-driven technologies.

Algorithmic Discrimination and Its Impact

Another significant ethical risk associated with big data and AI systems is algorithmic discrimination, which occurs when machine learning models are trained on biased datasets. Such bias can lead to unfair outcomes that disproportionately disadvantage certain groups based on characteristics such as race, gender, or socioeconomic status. For instance, if a financial institution uses historical data to train its loan approval algorithms, and that data reflects past discriminatory practices, the AI system may continue to deny loans to qualified applicants from marginalized communities. This situation not only reinforces existing inequality but also limits opportunities for individuals who are already at a disadvantage, thereby perpetuating a cycle of exclusion and economic disparity.

The implications of algorithmic discrimination extend beyond individual cases; they can create systemic issues that affect entire communities. In the criminal justice system, for example, predictive policing algorithms often rely on historical crime data, which may be inherently biased against certain neighborhoods or demographic groups. As a result, these algorithms may unfairly target specific communities, leading to over-policing and further entrenching social disparity.

The repercussions of such discrimination can be profound, as marginalized communities face heightened scrutiny and reduced trust in law enforcement. To mitigate these risks, it is essential for organizations to implement fairness audits, diversify training datasets, and continuously monitor the impact of AI systems to ensure that they operate equitably and do not reinforce harmful bias.

Lack of Transparency and Accountability

The lack of transparency and accountability in data-handling presents significant ethical risks, particularly as the complexity of algorithms and the prevalence of black-box models continue to rise. In critical areas such as credit scoring or employment screening, the opaque nature of these systems makes it challenging for individuals to comprehend how decisions that affect their lives are made. This ambiguity complicates the ability of individuals to contest decisions or seek redress when they believe they have been wronged. Without clear explanations for how data is utilized and how conclusions are drawn, affected parties may feel powerless to challenge unfair outcomes, leading to potential erosion of trust in the organizations employing these technologies.

Moreover, the lack of clarity surrounding data governance exacerbates the issue of accountability by obscuring who is responsible for data at various stages—from collection to processing and analysis. This uncertainty fosters an environment where ethical lapses can occur without detection, as there may be no designated party to oversee data integrity and ensure compliance with ethical standards. For instance, if data is mishandled or used inappropriately, it can be difficult to trace the source of the problem, making it nearly impossible to hold anyone accountable. Consequently, organizations may operate with insufficient oversight, allowing potential bias, errors, or unethical practices to persist unchecked. Establishing robust frameworks for data governance that emphasize transparency and accountability is crucial to mitigate these risks and foster a more ethical approach to data-handling.

Balancing Opportunities and Risks

In conclusion, while big data offers significant opportunities for societal advancement—such as improved healthcare outcomes, streamlined public services, and robust economic innovation—it also introduces inherent risks that cannot be overlooked, particularly regarding privacy and fairness. These challenges necessitate a comprehensive approach that prioritizes ethical standards and responsible data management. Organizations and governments must implement transparent practices that foster accountability and build public trust in data usage. Additionally, engaging stakeholders in discussions about data ethics can help ensure that diverse perspectives are considered in decision-making processes, ultimately leading to more equitable outcomes.

The key to maximizing the advantages of big data while mitigating its risks lies in establishing effective regulatory frameworks that safeguard individual rights without stifling innovation. By creating guidelines that govern data collection, usage, and sharing, policymakers can help ensure that organizations operate within a responsible and ethical framework. This balance is crucial in harnessing big data's potential to drive positive societal change while minimizing potential harm. As technology continues to evolve, a proactive stance on ethical governance will be essential in navigating the complexities of big data, ensuring it serves as a force for good in society.

ETHICAL RISKS: PRIVACY BREACHES AND MISUSE

Ethical Risks of Big Data

The use of big data and advanced technologies carries substantial ethical risks that can have far-reaching consequences for both individuals and society if not effectively managed. One of the most urgent concerns is the potential for privacy breaches, where sensitive personal information is exposed or accessed without proper authorization. These breaches can arise from various sources, including data leaks, hacking incidents, or even unintentional mismanagement of data by organizations.

When personal information is compromised, it not only violates individuals' privacy rights but also undermines public trust in institutions that handle data. The repercussions of such breaches can be profound, leading to financial loss, identity theft, and emotional distress for affected individuals, as well as broader societal implications, such as increased skepticism toward technology and data practices.

In addition to privacy breaches, the ethical landscape surrounding big data is complicated by issues related to consent and data ownership. Often, individuals are unaware of how their data is collected, used, or shared, leading to situations where consent is either implicit or inadequately informed. This lack of transparency can create a power imbalance, where individuals have little control over their own data, raising significant ethical questions about autonomy and agency.

Furthermore, the monetization of personal data can exacerbate inequality, as marginalized groups may be disproportionately affected by data misuse or exploitation. Addressing these ethical risks necessitates robust frameworks that emphasize transparency, informed consent, and individual rights, ensuring that the benefits of big data are realized without compromising fundamental ethical principles.

Privacy Breaches and Their Consequences

The vast quantities of data collected today often encompass highly personal details, including browsing histories, health records, and financial information. When such sensitive data is compromised, it can lead to serious repercussions for individuals, including identity theft, financial loss, and emotional distress. The implications of these breaches extend beyond the immediate harm to affected individuals; they can disrupt lives, create anxiety about future data security, and lead to a pervasive sense of vulnerability in an increasingly digital world. As individuals grapple with the fallout of such breaches, they may become more cautious about sharing personal information, which can stifle their engagement with digital services and hinder the overall growth of the digital economy.

The increased frequency of data breaches in recent years has underscored the vulnerability of personal information, particularly when organizations neglect to implement robust data security measures. High-profile incidents of data leaks and hacking attacks serve as stark reminders of the risks associated with inadequate protection of sensitive data. When organizations fail to safeguard the information entrusted to them, the consequences ripple outward, eroding public trust in both the organizations themselves and the technologies that underpin modern life.

The erosion of trust can have lasting effects, as individuals may become more hesitant to embrace new technologies or participate in data-sharing practices that are essential for innovation. To rebuild this trust, organizations must prioritize data security, transparency, and accountability, recognizing that their responsibilities extend beyond compliance to fostering a safe and secure digital environment for all users.

Data Misuse

Data misuse represents a significant ethical risk associated with the use of big data, as it involves employing data for purposes that extend beyond the original intent or agreement made by individuals. A prime example of this risk can be observed in how social media companies utilize personal data to influence political behavior or consumer preferences without obtaining explicit consent from users.

Such practices not only raise ethical concerns but can also lead to the manipulation of public opinion, thus undermining democratic processes and eroding individuals' autonomy. When individuals discover that their data is being used to shape their beliefs and choices without their knowledge or permission, it raises serious questions about agency, consent, and the ethical responsibilities of those who collect and analyze data.

Moreover, data misuse can manifest through unethical data-sharing practices between organizations, often conducted without the knowledge of the individuals whose data is being exchanged. This lack of transparency can result in situations where individuals feel powerless over their personal information, as they have little or no control over how their data is utilized or who has access to it. Such circumstances can lead to a profound loss of privacy, as individuals may find their personal data aggregated and analyzed in ways they never anticipated or agreed to. The absence of informed consent in these transactions can foster distrust not only toward the organizations involved but also toward the broader data ecosystem. To address these challenges, it is essential for organizations to establish clear guidelines and ethical standards governing data use, ensuring that individuals are informed, respected, and empowered regarding their personal information.

Addressing Ethical Risks

In conclusion, while big data and advanced analytics offer significant opportunities for growth and innovation across various sectors, they also introduce a range of ethical risks that cannot be overlooked. These risks, including privacy breaches, data misuse, algorithmic discrimination, and a lack of transparency, have the potential to undermine individual rights and erode public trust in organizations and technologies. As reliance on data-driven decision-making continues to increase, the consequences of these ethical challenges become even more pronounced, highlighting the need for proactive measures to address them.

To effectively mitigate these risks, organizations must adopt robust ethical guidelines that prioritize data protection and uphold accountability at every level of data-handling. This includes implementing comprehensive data protection measures to secure sensitive information, creating transparent processes that allow individuals to understand how their data is used, and establishing frameworks that ensure fairness in algorithmic decision-making.

By fostering a culture of ethical responsibility and prioritizing the rights of individuals, society can harness the benefits of big data while ensuring that technological advancements contribute positively to the public good. Ultimately, embracing ethical considerations will help build a sustainable technological landscape that supports innovation while safeguarding individual rights and maintaining public trust.

INFORMED CONSENT IN BIG DATA

The Ethical Imperatives of Informed Consent in Big Data

In the realm of big data, ensuring that individuals provide informed consent is essential for fostering trust and maintaining ethical standards in data collection and usage. This process is not merely a legal formality; rather, it serves as a foundational element for building and sustaining a positive relationship between organizations and users. To achieve this, organizations must focus on creating an environment where individuals feel empowered and informed about how their data will be used. This involves employing clear, accessible language in consent forms and providing users with comprehensive information about data practices, potential risks, and the benefits of data sharing. By prioritizing transparency in this way, organizations can help demystify the consent process and enable individuals to make knowledgeable choices regarding their personal information.

Given the complexity surrounding consent, organizations also need to implement effective techniques for consent management that emphasize user engagement and respect for individual autonomy. This can include interactive consent mechanisms, such as dynamic interfaces that allow users to easily adjust their privacy settings and preferences. Furthermore, ongoing communication is vital; organizations should update individuals about changes in data usage or policies and seek consent again, when necessary, thus creating an ongoing dialogue about data practices. By integrating user feedback into the consent management process, organizations can continuously refine their approaches to consent, ensuring they remain aligned with the evolving expectations and needs of users. Ultimately, these strategies will not only enhance user trust but also promote a culture of ethical data stewardship, which is crucial in today's data-driven landscape.

Navigating the Complexity of Consent in Big Data

In the era of big data, the concept of consent has evolved into a multi-faceted issue, laden with complexity and challenges that reflect the rapidly changing landscape of data usage. Traditional models of informed consent, which emphasize clear communication about what personal information is collected, how it will be used, and the potential risks involved, often fall short when applied to large-scale data collection practices.

With organizations now able to gather vast amounts of data from various sources, including social media, mobile applications, and IoT devices, individuals may find it increasingly difficult to fully comprehend the extent of data being collected and the implications of giving their consent. This ambiguity can lead to situations where consent is obtained through lengthy, technical privacy policies that most individuals may not read or understand, thereby undermining the foundational principle of informed consent.

Furthermore, the dynamic nature of data usage further complicates the issue of consent. Data collected for one purpose may be repurposed in ways that individuals never anticipated, raising ethical concerns about the scope of consent originally granted. For example, personal data initially collected for marketing purposes might later be used for targeted advertising or even shared with third-party entities without the individual's explicit knowledge. As a result, individuals often feel a loss of control over their personal information, leading to increased skepticism and reluctance to share data.

To navigate these challenges, there is a pressing need for more transparent and user-friendly consent mechanisms that empower individuals to make informed choices about their data, ensuring that consent remains a meaningful and respected aspect of data practices in the age of big data.

Challenges Due to the Scale of Data Collection

One of the primary challenges in the realm of consent arises from the unprecedented scale of data collection that organizations are now capable of achieving. In today's digital landscape, vast amounts of data are continuously gathered from various sources, including online interactions, IoT devices, social media platforms, and transactional histories. This automated and often seamless collection process frequently occurs without users' active engagement or even their awareness, creating a significant gap between what individuals believe they are consenting to and the actual extent of data usage.

Consequently, individuals often find themselves in a position where they must consent to complex data practices without fully understanding what data is being collected, how it will be used, and what potential risks are involved. This disconnect is particularly concerning as it undermines the essence of informed consent, which relies on individuals having a clear understanding of the implications of their agreement.

Additionally, the overwhelming volume of data can lead to cognitive overload, making it increasingly challenging for individuals to grasp the nuances of consent agreements. With lengthy and complex privacy policies that often accompany the collection of personal information, many users may feel disoriented or disengaged, leading them to skim over critical details or opt for acceptance without truly comprehending the terms. This phenomenon is further exacerbated by the rapidly changing nature of technology and data practices, which can render previously established consent agreements obsolete.

As organizations continue to evolve their data strategies, individuals may find themselves unknowingly agreeing to practices that deviate significantly from their initial understanding. To combat these challenges, there is an urgent need for clearer, more user-friendly consent mechanisms that enhance transparency and allow individuals to make informed decisions regarding their data, thereby restoring trust and agency in the data collection process.

Understanding the Scope of Data Usage and Consent Implications

The scope of data usage presents another significant hurdle in the consent landscape, particularly as organizations increasingly employ data in ways that extend far beyond the initial purpose for which it was collected. For instance, personal information gathered for a specific transaction—such as an online purchase—may later be repurposed for targeted advertising or market research, or even sold to third parties. This multi-purpose utilization complicates the consent process, as individuals may agree to the initial data collection without fully understanding or consenting to these subsequent uses. The potential for data to be repackaged and shared across various contexts raises ethical concerns, as individuals often lack insight into the evolving nature of their consent and how their information is leveraged.

Furthermore, the complexity of terms of service and privacy policies exacerbates the issue by creating barriers to understanding. These documents are frequently lengthy and laden with legal jargon, making it difficult for users to decipher how their data will be used and what rights they retain concerning their information. As a result, individuals may unknowingly relinquish their rights or consent to data practices that they do not support or fully understand. This opacity can foster a sense of helplessness and distrust, leading to a disconnection between organizations and the users they serve.

To address these challenges, organizations must prioritize transparency and user-friendly language in their consent agreements, enabling individuals to make informed decisions about their data and fostering a culture of respect for privacy and individual agency.

The Dynamic Nature of Data and the Need for Ongoing Consent

The dynamic nature of data further complicates the consent landscape, as data is inherently fluid and subject to change over time. As organizations gather and analyze data, new insights can emerge, revealing patterns and correlations that were not anticipated at the time of initial collection. This evolving landscape enables organizations to explore innovative applications for the data, potentially leading to uses that original data subjects did not foresee or consent to.

In this scenario, the challenge shifts from simply obtaining consent at the outset to maintaining valid consent throughout the data's lifecycle. Organizations must navigate the complexities of continuous consent, recognizing that individuals' understanding and willingness to consent may change as new information and uses are introduced.

The practicalities of maintaining continuous communication with users about their data usage can be daunting for organizations. Regularly updating users and seeking fresh consent for evolving data uses can be seen as burdensome, both operationally and in terms of user engagement. Many users may disengage from these communications, either due to notification fatigue or a lack of interest in the intricacies of data usage. This disengagement creates a further disconnect, making it challenging for organizations to ensure ethical data practices and uphold their responsibility to maintain transparency and accountability.

To overcome these hurdles, organizations must develop streamlined processes that balance the need for ongoing consent with user engagement strategies that keep individuals informed and empowered regarding their data.

Power Asymmetry in Data Collection

The asymmetry of power between data collectors and individuals significantly exacerbates the consent challenge. In many situations, consumers find themselves with little leverage or choice when it comes to agreeing to data collection practices. Often, access to essential services—such as social media platforms, online shopping, or banking—requires individuals to consent to extensive data collection that they may not fully comprehend or feel comfortable with.

This creates a power imbalance where individuals are effectively forced to agree to terms dictated by organizations, leaving them feeling coerced rather than empowered. As a result, individuals may find themselves in a position where they must relinquish control over their personal information to access services they deem necessary.

This dynamic raises profound ethical questions regarding the validity of consent and the responsibilities of organizations to ensure users are genuinely informed and capable of making autonomous choices regarding their data. When consent is obtained under duress or without true understanding, it undermines the very foundation of ethical data practices. Organizations must grapple with their role in creating an environment where consent is not just a formality but a meaningful process that respects individual autonomy. This involves not only providing clear and accessible information about data practices but also empowering individuals to negotiate the terms of consent.

Ultimately, it is crucial for organizations to acknowledge the ethical implications of the power dynamics at play and strive to create fairer practices that uphold users' rights and promote trust in the digital ecosystem.

Rethinking Consent Practices

In conclusion, the challenges associated with consent in big data are multifaceted and complex, arising from various interrelated issues, including the scale of data collection, the broad scope of data usage, the evolving nature of data, and the inherent power imbalance between individuals and organizations. To navigate these challenges effectively, there needs to be a comprehensive reevaluation of consent practices, ensuring they are not only robust and transparent but also genuinely informed. This involves a shift from one-size-fits-all consent forms to more tailored approaches that take into account the diverse contexts in which data is collected and used. Organizations must prioritize the development of consent mechanisms that are clear, concise, and user-friendly, allowing individuals to comprehend and exercise their rights regarding personal information.

Furthermore, fostering a culture of ethical data usage is paramount for organizations aiming to build trust and enhance their relationships with users. By actively promoting transparency and encouraging open dialogue about data practices, organizations can empower individuals to make informed choices about their data while respecting their preferences. This commitment to ethical practices not only safeguards individuals' rights but also paves the way for more responsible and sustainable data management.

Ultimately, by aligning their practices with ethical principles and prioritizing user empowerment, organizations can contribute to a digital landscape that respects privacy, fosters trust, and promotes positive societal outcomes.

TECHNIQUES FOR ETHICAL CONSENT MANAGEMENT IN DATA PRACTICES

Use Clear and Concise Communication

One effective approach is to utilize clear and concise language in consent forms and privacy policies. Traditional legalese often alienates users and obscures important details regarding how their data will be used. Instead, organizations should aim for simplicity, avoiding jargon and technical terms, and providing straightforward explanations of data collection practices. For instance, using bullet points to outline key points, such as the types of data collected, the purposes of data usage, and potential third-party sharing, can help individuals grasp the implications of their consent more easily.

Additionally, incorporating visual aids, such as infographics or flow-charts, can further enhance understanding by breaking down complex information into digestible formats. This clarity empowers users to make informed choices about their data and fosters a sense of agency in the consent process. Moreover, organizations can enhance transparency by including real-life examples or scenarios that illustrate how data will be utilized. By contextualizing the data usage, individuals can better relate to the information, leading to a more meaningful comprehension of their consent decisions.

Furthermore, providing avenues for users to ask questions or seek clarification about consent forms can significantly improve user engagement. Establishing a responsive support system—whether through chatbots, FAQs, or dedicated customer service teams—ensures that individuals feel supported in their decision-making processes. This proactive approach not only builds trust but also demonstrates an organization's commitment to respecting user rights and preferences, ultimately contributing to a more ethical framework for data collection and usage.

Adopt Dynamic Consent Mechanisms

Another vital technique is the implementation of dynamic consent mechanisms. Unlike traditional one-time consent requests, dynamic consent allows individuals to control their preferences regarding data usage over time. This flexibility can be facilitated through user-friendly interfaces that enable individuals to easily update their consent preferences as their circumstances or perceptions change.

For instance, a health app could allow users to adjust their consent settings, specifying which data they are comfortable sharing for research purposes while retaining the option to revoke access at any time. Such systems not only enhance user autonomy but also ensure that consent remains relevant and reflective of individuals' current views on their privacy and data usage. By adopting a dynamic approach, organizations demonstrate their commitment to respecting user preferences and maintaining an ongoing dialogue about data management practices.

Furthermore, dynamic consent mechanisms can foster a culture of transparency and trust between organizations and users. By providing users with the tools to modify their consent settings, organizations signal that they value individuals' autonomy and are willing to prioritize their privacy concerns. This ongoing engagement can also lead to more meaningful interactions, as users feel empowered to express their preferences and concerns.

Additionally, organizations can utilize these interactions to educate users about their data practices, thereby enhancing users' understanding of the implications of their consent. For example, notifications or reminders can inform users when data usage changes or when new features are introduced, allowing them to reassess their consent in light of new information. This proactive communication approach not only builds trust but also reinforces ethical practices in data-handling, ensuring that user consent is both informed and respected throughout the data lifecycle.

Contextualize Consent

Contextual consent is another effective technique that acknowledges the specific situations in which data is collected. By providing individuals with the ability to give or withdraw consent based on the context of each data request, organizations can better clarify users' comfort levels regarding data usage.

For instance, when users are prompted to consent to the collection of location data, organizations can offer clear contextual information about why this data is being requested and how it will enhance the user experience—such as enabling personalized recommendations based on their location. This approach not only informs individuals but also empowers them to make decisions that align with their comfort levels in specific scenarios, fostering a more user-centric data collection process.

Additionally, grounding consent in context enhances the overall user experience by making it more intuitive and relevant. When individuals understand the rationale behind data requests, they are more likely to perceive the organization as trustworthy and considerate of their privacy. This clarity can lead to increased willingness to engage with data-sharing practices, as users feel they have control over how their information is used. For example, an app that requests access to a user's camera for a specific feature can explain how this access is essential for functionality, such as enabling augmented reality experiences.

By contextualizing consent in such a manner, organizations can cultivate a positive relationship with users, ultimately promoting ethical data practices that respect individual preferences and enhance user satisfaction.

Enhance Consent Through Educational Initiatives

Organizations can significantly benefit from implementing educational initiatives designed to enhance user understanding of consent and data practices. By providing resources such as webinars, interactive tutorials, and informative articles, organizations empower individuals to make more informed decisions regarding their data.

For example, a series of online workshops could explain how data is collected, the reasons behind various data requests, and the implications of sharing personal information. By demystifying these concepts, users can gain clarity about their privacy rights and the potential benefits of data contribution. This proactive educational approach not only increases transparency but also builds trust, as users feel more equipped to navigate the complexities of consent in the digital age.

Engaging with users through educational initiatives reflects an ethical commitment to prioritizing their understanding and autonomy. When individuals are better informed about how their data is used and the associated risks, they are more likely to provide meaningful and genuine consent. This approach fosters a culture of informed consent where users actively participate in decisions about their data, rather than passively agreeing to opaque terms.

Moreover, as organizations invest in user education, they also demonstrate their dedication to ethical data practices, reinforcing their reputation as responsible stewards of personal information. Ultimately, such initiatives not only benefit individual users but also enhance organizational integrity, leading to stronger relationships built on trust and mutual respect.

Leverage Technology to Enhance Consent Management

Leveraging technology to streamline consent processes can significantly enhance the effectiveness of consent management. By implementing dedicated consent management platforms, organizations can provide users with a centralized location to oversee their data preferences across multiple services. These platforms can feature user-friendly interfaces and visual dashboards that clearly display consent status, options for data sharing, and a history of past consent, empowering individuals to take charge of their information.

Such transparency not only simplifies the consent process but also fosters user engagement, as individuals can easily adjust their preferences based on evolving comfort levels. This technological integration ensures that users remain informed and in control, ultimately leading to a more positive and empowering experience.

Additionally, by adopting advanced consent management technologies, organizations can reinforce their commitment to ethical data practices. These tools can be designed to automatically alert users about changes in data usage policies or new data collection practices, ensuring that consent remains informed and relevant over time. By facilitating continuous dialogue around data usage, organizations can build stronger relationships with their users, grounded in trust and transparency. Furthermore, as users gain confidence in their ability to manage their data, they are more likely to engage with organizations, leading to richer interactions and enhanced loyalty.

Ultimately, the incorporation of technology into consent management not only streamlines processes but also serves as a critical step toward fostering a culture of ethical responsibility and respect for individual privacy.

Build Trust Through Ethical Consent Practices

In conclusion, effective ethical consent management is critical for navigating the complexities of data collection and usage in the big data era. As organizations increasingly rely on vast amounts of personal data, the traditional models of consent are becoming insufficient. By implementing techniques such as clear and concise language in consent forms, dynamic and contextual consent mechanisms, and educational initiatives, organizations can enhance the informed consent process. These practices not only empower users to make informed decisions about their data but also ensure that their rights and preferences are respected. When individuals feel genuinely understood and valued, they are more likely to engage positively with organizations, fostering a collaborative environment that benefits both parties.

Ultimately, prioritizing transparency, user engagement, and respect for individual autonomy contributes to a more ethical and responsible approach to data management. Organizations that embrace these practices not only mitigate the risks associated with data misuse and breaches but also strengthen their reputations as trustworthy entities. By aligning organizational goals with the rights and expectations of individuals in a data-driven world, companies can cultivate a culture of ethical responsibility that promotes long-term sustainability. This alignment between ethical data practices and business objectives not only enhances user satisfaction but also serves as a competitive advantage in an increasingly data-conscious market, paving the way for a future where data is managed responsibly and ethically.

CHAPTER 15

DATA ETHICS IN BUSINESS CONTEXTS

CORPORATE DATA RESPONSIBILITY

Businesses' Role in Ethical Data Use

In today's data-driven world, businesses hold significant power and responsibility regarding how they manage and utilize the vast amounts of data at their disposal. The ethical use of data is crucial, as it impacts not only the individuals whose information is collected but also society as a whole. Companies must recognize that their practices shape public trust in technology and data-driven innovations. This goes beyond merely complying with legal regulations; businesses are tasked with cultivating an ethical culture that emphasizes accountability, transparency, and fairness in data-handling. By adopting ethical data practices, organizations can build strong relationships with consumers, foster brand loyalty, and enhance their reputation in the market.

The responsibility of businesses in ethical data use extends to actively advocating for consumer rights and societal well-being. This involves proactively identifying potential risks and bias in their data practices, engaging in transparent communication with stakeholders, and prioritizing user consent and privacy. For instance, businesses can implement robust data protection measures and regularly assess their data policies to ensure they align with ethical standards.

Additionally, organizations can take the lead in fostering industry-wide discussions about ethical data use and collaborate with regulators, consumers, and advocacy groups to develop best practices that benefit all parties involved. By embracing this broader corporate duty, businesses can not only protect the interests of consumers but also contribute to a more ethical and responsible data ecosystem, ultimately benefiting society as a whole.

Committing to Transparency

Responsibility begins with a commitment to transparency, where organizations openly communicate their data collection practices, the purposes behind them, and the potential risks involved. By providing clear and accessible information to customers, businesses can foster trust and empower individuals to make informed decisions about their data. For instance, companies can publish detailed privacy policies that outline not only what data is collected but also how it is used, shared, and protected.

Transparency also involves being forthcoming about any changes to data practices or policies, which can help maintain consumer trust even as technology and regulations evolve. Such proactive communication demonstrates a company's dedication to ethical data management and reassures customers that their rights and preferences are being respected.

Furthermore, this transparency is essential for establishing a positive relationship with consumers, who are increasingly concerned about how their personal information is being handled. As awareness of data privacy issues grows, individuals are more inclined to engage with businesses that prioritize ethical practices and demonstrate a commitment to safeguarding their information. By fostering an open dialogue about data usage, organizations can address consumer concerns, respond to inquiries, and create a collaborative atmosphere where individuals feel valued and heard. This engagement not only enhances customer satisfaction but also encourages loyalty, as consumers are likely to support brands that align with their values and prioritize ethical considerations. Ultimately, transparency serves as a cornerstone of responsible data practices, helping to build a more trustworthy and ethical data ecosystem.

Prioritizing Data Security

Businesses must prioritize data security as part of their ethical duty. This involves implementing robust security measures to safeguard personal data from breaches, misuse, and unauthorized access. The repercussions of data breaches can be devastating, leading to identity theft, financial loss, and irreparable damage to an organization's reputation.

Companies have a responsibility to invest in advanced security technologies, such as encryption, firewalls, and intrusion detection systems, to protect sensitive information from cyber threats.

Additionally, conducting regular audits and assessments can help identify vulnerabilities and ensure compliance with data protection regulations. Training employees on data protection practices is equally important, as human error remains a significant factor in data breaches. By equipping staff with the knowledge and skills needed to handle data responsibly, organizations can significantly reduce the risk of security incidents and reinforce their commitment to ethical data management.

Beyond technical safeguards, fostering a culture of ethical responsibility within the organization is crucial. This means encouraging employees at all levels to recognize the importance of ethical data practices and understand the implications of their actions in handling sensitive information. Leadership plays a vital role in setting the tone for this culture by establishing clear ethical guidelines and demonstrating a commitment to data integrity.

Regular discussions about data ethics, ongoing training, and opportunities for employees to voice concerns can further promote an environment where ethical considerations are prioritized alongside profitability. By instilling a sense of accountability and ethical awareness, businesses can not only enhance their data security measures but also build a strong foundation of trust with consumers, ultimately leading to sustainable success in a data-driven landscape.

Embracing Data Minimization

In addition to security and transparency, businesses should embrace the principle of data minimization, which advocates for collecting only the data necessary for specific purposes. This approach not only reduces ethical risks associated with data misuse but also demonstrates a commitment to respecting individual privacy. By being intentional about the data they collect, organizations can minimize their exposure to potential liability while enhancing customer trust. For instance, instead of collecting extensive personal information for a service that only requires minimal data, companies can streamline their data collection processes. This focused strategy can lead to improved compliance with privacy laws and foster positive customer relationships, as individuals appreciate organizations that prioritize their privacy.

Furthermore, data minimization aligns with regulatory frameworks such as the GDPR, which mandates organizations to limit data collection to what is necessary. By proactively adopting such practices, businesses can position themselves as ethical leaders in their respective industries, differentiating themselves from competitors who may prioritize short-term gains over responsible data management.

Adhering to data minimization not only helps organizations avoid potential legal repercussions but also enhances their reputation in the eyes of consumers who are increasingly conscious of their data rights. Ultimately, businesses that commit to data minimization can cultivate a culture of responsibility and integrity, setting a positive example for the industry and contributing to a more ethical data landscape.

Ensuring Fairness and Non-Discrimination

Another critical aspect of ethical data use is the need for fairness and non-discrimination in data analytics and decision-making processes. Businesses have a duty to ensure that their algorithms and data-driven decisions do not perpetuate bias or reinforce existing inequality. This requires a conscious effort to regularly evaluate and audit data models for fairness, accuracy, and inclusivity. For example, organizations can implement bias detection tools and perform impact assessments to identify any unintended discriminatory effects resulting from their algorithms.

By actively seeking to eliminate bias and incorporating diverse perspectives into data analysis, businesses can create systems that are more representative and reflective of the populations they serve. Such practices not only foster equitable outcomes but also demonstrate a commitment to social responsibility.

Moreover, the commitment to fairness enhances an organization's reputation and builds consumer trust. As society becomes increasingly aware of issues related to algorithmic bias and discrimination, consumers are more likely to support brands that prioritize ethical considerations in their data practices. By promoting inclusivity and ensuring that underrepresented groups are considered in data practices, organizations can respond to the growing expectations of consumers who demand transparency and accountability from the brands they engage with.

Ultimately, adopting a fairness-focused approach in data analytics not only mitigates potential legal risks but also positions organizations as leaders in ethical data use, positively contributing to societal well-being and fostering long-term loyalty among consumers.

Advocating for Ethical Data Practices

Finally, businesses play an essential role in advocating for ethical data practices beyond their internal operations. This involves actively engaging with policymakers, industry associations, and other stakeholders to promote frameworks and standards that prioritize ethical data use. By participating in discussions surrounding data governance and privacy regulations, organizations can help shape policies that not only protect individual rights but also foster innovation and economic growth. For instance, businesses can collaborate with regulatory bodies to develop guidelines that strike a balance between encouraging technological advancement and ensuring consumer protection. This proactive engagement reflects a commitment to ethical leadership, positioning businesses as responsible stewards of data within their communities.

Furthermore, by advocating for ethical practices, organizations can contribute to building a broader culture of responsibility and trust in the digital landscape. When businesses take the initiative to promote best practices and share knowledge with peers, they can create a ripple effect that encourages others to follow suit. This collaborative approach fosters an environment where ethical considerations are woven into the fabric of data management across industries.

Additionally, by championing ethical data use, companies can enhance their reputation, attract consumers who value responsible practices, and ultimately drive positive change in society. This holistic commitment not only benefits individual organizations but also contributes to a more equitable and trustworthy digital ecosystem for everyone.

Ethical Data Responsibility for Businesses

In conclusion, businesses play a vital role in ethical data use, which encompasses transparency, security, data minimization, fairness, and advocacy. By recognizing their corporate duty to manage data responsibly, organizations can foster trust with consumers and mitigate risks associated with data breaches and misuse. When companies are open about their data collection practices, prioritize the security of sensitive information, and limit data collection to what is strictly necessary, they not only protect their customers but also build a strong foundation of credibility. This ethical commitment can differentiate a company in a competitive marketplace, enhancing customer loyalty and creating lasting relationships built on trust and respect.

Moreover, in an age where data is a critical asset, ethical data practices are essential for sustainable business success in the long run. Companies that embed ethical considerations into their data management strategies are better positioned to navigate the complexities of regulatory frameworks and societal expectations. As consumers become increasingly aware of their rights and the implications of data usage, they are likely to gravitate toward brands that prioritize ethical practices.

Ultimately, ethical data use transcends mere legal obligation; it embodies a fundamental aspect of corporate responsibility that can drive meaningful change in the digital age. By leading the charge in responsible data management, businesses can not only contribute to a more equitable society but also enhance their own operational resilience and long-term viability.

ETHICAL AND UNETHICAL PRACTICES: INDUSTRY CASE STUDIES

The landscape of data ethics is illuminated by various real-world examples, showcasing both ethical and unethical practices across different industries. These case studies serve as valuable lessons for organizations aiming to navigate the complex realm of data management, highlighting the consequences of their actions on individuals and society.

Ethical Practices

One prominent example of ethical data use comes from Salesforce, a cloud-based software company known for its customer relationship management solutions. Salesforce has implemented a strong commitment to ethical data practices, focusing on transparency and customer empowerment. The company actively informs its users about the data it collects and how it will be used, ensuring that customers are aware of their rights regarding data privacy. Salesforce's *Privacy by Design* framework ensures that data privacy considerations are integrated into the development of their products and services from the outset, rather than as an afterthought. Furthermore, Salesforce provides its customers with tools to manage their data preferences easily, allowing individuals to make informed decisions about their data. This approach not only builds trust but also enhances customer loyalty, as users appreciate the company's commitment to safeguarding their information.

Another example of ethical data practices is seen in the healthcare sector, particularly with Mayo Clinic. The organization has adopted stringent data governance policies that prioritize patient privacy and data security. Mayo Clinic employs advanced encryption techniques to protect patient records and strictly adheres to regulations such as the Health Insurance Portability and Accountability Act (HIPAA) to ensure that patient information remains confidential. Additionally, the clinic actively involves patients in their healthcare decisions by providing transparent information about how their data will be used in research and treatment processes. This practice fosters trust and reinforces the ethical obligation of healthcare providers to prioritize patient welfare while advancing medical knowledge.

Unethical Practices

Conversely, there have been numerous instances of unethical data practices that highlight the potential harms of inadequate data governance. One of the most notorious examples is the Cambridge Analytica scandal. In this case, the political consulting firm obtained personal data from millions of Facebook users without their consent, leveraging this information to create highly targeted political advertising during the 2016 United States presidential election. The unethical practices surrounding data harvesting, including the lack of informed consent and transparency, led to widespread outrage and raised critical questions about data privacy and the responsibilities of social media platforms. The fallout from this scandal resulted in increased scrutiny of data practices in the tech industry and prompted calls for more stringent regulations regarding user data protection.

Another example of unethical data practices can be seen in the case of Equifax, one of the largest credit reporting agencies. In 2017, Equifax suffered a massive data breach that exposed the personal information of approximately 147 million individuals, including Social Security numbers, addresses, and credit card details. The breach occurred due to the company's failure to apply necessary security patches to its systems, demonstrating a lack of accountability and negligence in safeguarding sensitive consumer data. Following the breach, Equifax faced a significant backlash for its inadequate response, including delays in notifying affected individuals and a lack of transparency regarding the extent of the breach. This incident underscores the critical importance of data security and the ethical responsibility of organizations to protect consumer information from harm.

Lessons Learned

These case studies illustrate the stark contrast between ethical and unethical data practices, emphasizing the need for organizations to prioritize ethical considerations in their data management strategies. Ethical practices, as demonstrated by Salesforce and Mayo Clinic, can lead to enhanced trust, customer loyalty, and a positive reputation, ultimately contributing to long-term success. Conversely, unethical practices, such as those seen in the Cambridge Analytica scandal and Equifax breach, can result in significant harm to individuals, reputational damage, and regulatory scrutiny.

As businesses navigate the complexities of data ethics, they must draw lessons from these examples to shape their own data practices. Implementing transparent policies, engaging customers in data governance, and prioritizing data security are essential steps toward fostering an ethical data culture. By doing so, organizations can build a foundation of trust with their customers and contribute positively to the evolving landscape of data management in an increasingly digital world. Ultimately, the responsibility lies with organizations to ensure that they not only comply with legal requirements but also uphold ethical standards that protect individual rights and promote social good.

BALANCING PROFITABILITY WITH ETHICAL PRACTICE

Navigating Ethical Dilemmas

In today's competitive business landscape, organizations are increasingly confronted with the challenge of navigating ethical dilemmas that arise from the tension between profitability and ethical considerations. The relentless drive for financial success can often clash with the imperative to uphold ethical standards, leading companies to grapple with decisions that can significantly impact various stakeholders, including customers, employees, and the broader community. For instance, the temptation to cut corners on product safety or to exploit labor can yield immediate financial benefits but risks severe reputational damage and long-term consequences. Therefore, organizations must recognize that their choices carry weight beyond the balance sheet; they influence public perception, employee morale, and customer loyalty, ultimately shaping the sustainability of their business model.

Striking a balance between these competing priorities requires a comprehensive understanding of the ethical implications of business practices, alongside a steadfast commitment to sustainable decision-making that prioritizes long-term value over short-term gains. This entails integrating ethical considerations into the core business strategy, ensuring that decisions are not solely driven by financial metrics but also by their potential social and environmental impacts. Companies can benefit from adopting frameworks that encourage ethical reflection and stakeholder engagement in their decision-making processes, thus promoting a culture of accountability and transparency. By aligning their operations with ethical principles, organizations can build a resilient foundation that fosters trust and loyalty among consumers and stakeholders, ultimately contributing to their enduring success in the marketplace.

Understanding the Profitability-Ethics Dichotomy

At its core, the profitability-ethics dichotomy is rooted in the belief that businesses exist primarily to generate profit for their shareholders. This perspective can lead organizations to prioritize financial performance at the expense of ethical considerations, often resulting in practices that may exploit consumer data, disregard employee well-being, or harm the environment. For instance, a tech company may be tempted to monetize user data without obtaining proper consent or to employ aggressive marketing tactics that mislead consumers. While these practices may yield short-term financial benefits, they can also erode consumer trust and lead to reputational damage, regulatory penalties, and long-term sustainability challenges.

Conversely, organizations that prioritize ethical considerations can cultivate a positive reputation and foster loyalty among customers and employees. For example, companies that demonstrate a commitment to environmental sustainability by implementing eco-friendly practices may initially incur higher costs. Such investments do, however, often lead to increased brand loyalty, enhanced customer satisfaction, and long-term financial gains. Ethical practices can also attract top talent, as employees are increasingly seeking workplaces that align with their values. Thus, the pursuit of profitability does not have to come at the expense of ethics; rather, organizations can achieve a competitive advantage by integrating ethical considerations into their business models.

Effective Strategies for Balancing Profit and Ethics

To successfully navigate the complexities of ethical dilemmas, organizations can adopt several strategies that promote a balance between profitability and ethical considerations. One effective approach is to cultivate a strong corporate culture centered on ethical values. By establishing a clear set of ethical guidelines and expectations, organizations can empower employees to make decisions that align with the company's values. Leadership plays a crucial role in modeling ethical behavior and fostering an environment where employees feel comfortable raising ethical concerns. Regular training and discussions around ethical dilemmas can also help employees navigate challenging situations and reinforce the organization's commitment to ethical conduct.

Another key strategy involves incorporating stakeholder perspectives into decision-making processes. By actively engaging with stakeholders, including customers, employees, suppliers, and the community, organizations can gain insights into the ethical implications of their practices. This engagement not only helps identify potential ethical dilemmas but also fosters a sense of shared responsibility and accountability. For instance, businesses can solicit feedback from customers regarding data privacy practices, allowing them to tailor their approaches in a manner that respects consumer rights while still achieving business objectives. By prioritizing stakeholder interests, organizations can create a win-win scenario that supports both profitability and ethical responsibility.

Businesses can also leverage technology and data analytics to enhance ethical decision-making. By implementing advanced analytics tools, organizations can gain a deeper understanding of consumer behavior and preferences while ensuring compliance with data protection regulations. This data-driven approach enables businesses to develop targeted marketing strategies that respect consumer privacy and build trust. Furthermore, technology can facilitate transparency in supply chains, allowing organizations to identify and address ethical concerns related to sourcing and production processes. By utilizing technology as a tool for ethical decision-making, businesses can navigate potential dilemmas more effectively and promote responsible practices that contribute to long-term success.

Balancing Ethics and Profits

Navigating ethical dilemmas in business is a complex but essential endeavor that requires organizations to balance profitability with ethical considerations. While the pressure to maximize profits can lead to unethical practices, companies that prioritize ethics can cultivate trust, loyalty, and long-term sustainability. By fostering a strong corporate culture centered on ethical values, incorporating stakeholder perspectives into decision-making, and leveraging technology to enhance transparency, organizations can successfully navigate the challenges of ethical dilemmas.

Ultimately, the ability to align profitability with ethical considerations not only strengthens a company's reputation but also contributes to a more responsible and sustainable business landscape. As consumers and stakeholders increasingly demand ethical accountability, organizations that prioritize ethics will be better positioned to thrive in the ever-evolving market.

CORPORATE SOCIAL RESPONSIBILITY: AN ETHICAL APPROACH

Corporate social responsibility (CSR) represents a company's commitment to conducting its business in an ethical manner, considering the social, environmental, and economic impacts of its operations. In recent years, numerous organizations have embraced CSR, demonstrating a strong commitment to ethical practices that extend beyond profit maximization. These instances showcase how prioritizing ethics not only benefits society but also contributes to long-term business success.

Patagonia: Environmental Stewardship

Patagonia, the outdoor apparel company, is a leading example of a brand that has embedded ethics into its core operations. The company is renowned for its environmental stewardship and commitment to sustainability. Patagonia's mission statement—"We're in business to save our home planet"—reflects its dedication to addressing environmental issues. The company takes an active stance against fast fashion, encouraging customers to buy less and repair their gear instead. In 2016, Patagonia even ran an advertisement stating, "Don't buy this jacket," urging consumers to reconsider their purchasing habits and promoting sustainable consumption.

Furthermore, Patagonia allocates a percentage of its profits to environmental causes through its *1% for the Planet* initiative, supporting grassroots organizations working on environmental issues. This commitment not only demonstrates ethical leadership but also fosters a loyal customer base that values the company's dedication to protecting the planet. By prioritizing environmental ethics, Patagonia has positioned itself as a market leader, proving that ethical business practices can coexist with financial success.

Ben & Jerry's: Social Justice Advocacy

Ben & Jerry's, the popular ice cream brand, is another exemplary case of a company prioritizing ethics through its commitment to social justice. The founders, Ben Cohen and Jerry Greenfield, have a long history of advocating for social issues, from climate change to racial equality. The company's approach to CSR is deeply rooted in its values, emphasizing the importance of human rights and social justice.

One notable instance of Ben & Jerry's commitment to ethics is its response to the Black Lives Matter movement. In 2020, the company released a statement affirming its support for racial justice, calling for systemic changes to address racial inequality in the United States. Ben & Jerry's not only spoke out against racial injustice but also used its platform to educate consumers on these issues, encouraging them to engage in activism. The company even introduced flavors such as "Pecan Resist" to support organizations fighting for social justice. This commitment to ethical advocacy has not only enhanced the brand's reputation but has also engaged consumers who share similar values, creating a strong emotional connection between the company and its customers.

Microsoft: Commitment to Accessibility

Microsoft has consistently demonstrated its commitment to CSR by prioritizing accessibility and inclusivity in technology. The company recognizes that technology should be available to everyone, regardless of their physical or cognitive abilities. In 2018, Microsoft introduced the *Xbox Adaptive Controller*, designed specifically for gamers with limited mobility. This innovative product reflects the company's commitment to ensuring that gaming is an inclusive experience for all individuals.

Moreover, Microsoft has established accessibility as a core principle in its product development process. The company conducts regular audits of its products to identify barriers faced by users with disabilities and actively seeks feedback from the disabled community. Through initiatives such as the *AI for Accessibility* program, Microsoft is leveraging AI to create solutions that enhance accessibility in various aspects of life, including education and employment. By prioritizing ethical considerations in product development, Microsoft not only fulfills its CSR but also positions itself as a leader in the tech industry, demonstrating that ethical practices can drive innovation.

Unilever: Sustainable Sourcing and Community Impact

Unilever, the multinational consumer goods company, has made significant strides in incorporating CSR into its business model. The company's *Sustainable Living Plan* aims to reduce its environmental footprint while enhancing the livelihoods of people across its supply chain. Unilever has committed to sourcing 100% of its agricultural raw materials sustainably and has made substantial investments in community development programs.

One notable example is Unilever's work with smallholder farmers. The company has established partnerships to improve agricultural practices, providing farmers with training, resources, and access to markets. These initiatives not only support local economies but also promote sustainable farming practices that benefit the environment. Unilever's commitment to ethical sourcing and community engagement has resulted in positive social impacts, demonstrating that businesses can thrive while contributing to societal well-being.

The Impact of Ethical Practices on Business Success

These examples illustrate how prioritizing ethics through CSR can lead to positive outcomes for both businesses and society. Companies such as Patagonia, Ben & Jerry's, Microsoft, and Unilever demonstrate that ethical practices are not only compatible with profitability but can also enhance brand reputation and customer loyalty. As consumers increasingly demand transparency and accountability from businesses, the importance of CSR will only continue to grow. Organizations that embrace ethical principles in their operations will not only fulfill their moral obligations but will also position themselves for long-term success in an ever-evolving marketplace. Ultimately, prioritizing ethics in business is not just a trend; it is a fundamental aspect of responsible corporate citizenship that can drive meaningful change in society.

CHAPTER 16

REGULATORY FRAMEWORKS AND COMPLIANCE

KEY DATA REGULATIONS

In an increasingly data-driven world, the regulation of personal data has become a critical concern for governments, organizations, and individuals alike. As companies collect, store, and utilize vast amounts of personal information, regulations have been introduced globally to protect consumer privacy and ensure ethical data-handling. This overview discusses two of the most significant data protection regulations—the GDPR and the CCPA—along with other major data laws that influence data governance practices worldwide.

GENERAL DATA PROTECTION REGULATION

The GDPR is a comprehensive data protection law enacted by the EU in 2018. Designed to enhance individuals' control over their personal data, the GDPR represents a paradigm shift in how organizations approach data privacy. It applies to any organization that processes the personal data of EU residents, regardless of where the organization is located, thus establishing a broad jurisdictional reach.

One of the cornerstone principles of the GDPR is data subject consent. Organizations must obtain explicit and informed consent from individuals before collecting or processing their personal data. Moreover, individuals have the right to withdraw consent at any time, highlighting the importance of user control over personal information. The GDPR also establishes several key rights for individuals, including the right to access their data, the right to rectification, the right to erasure (the "right to be forgotten"), and the right to data portability, which allows individuals to transfer their data between service providers easily.

Another significant aspect of the GDPR is its emphasis on data minimization and accountability. Organizations are required to collect only the data necessary for specified purposes and are held accountable for compliance. Data breaches must be reported to relevant authorities within 72 hours, and organizations may face significant penalties for non-compliance, with fines reaching up to €20 million or 4% of annual global turnover, whichever is higher. The GDPR has set a global standard for data protection, influencing similar regulations worldwide and prompting organizations to adopt more robust data governance practices.

CALIFORNIA CONSUMER PRIVACY ACT

The CCPA is a landmark privacy law that went into effect in 2020, marking a significant advancement in consumer data rights in the United States. The CCPA applies to businesses that collect personal data from California residents and meet specific revenue thresholds or engage in certain data practices. Like the GDPR, the CCPA grants consumers several rights concerning their personal information, emphasizing transparency and user control.

Under the CCPA, consumers have the right to know what personal data is being collected about them and how it is being used and shared. They can request the deletion of their personal information and opt out of the sale of their data to third parties. Moreover, businesses must provide clear notices about their data collection practices and may not discriminate against consumers who exercise their rights under the law.

While the CCPA shares similarities with the GDPR, it also includes provisions specific to the unique legal landscape in the United States. For instance, the CCPA has a broader definition of personal data and includes certain exemptions for businesses in specific sectors. Additionally, the CCPA allows consumers to pursue legal action in the event of a data breach, enabling individuals to seek statutory damages. In response to growing concerns about data privacy, the CCPA has served as a model for similar state-level legislation and has spurred discussions about the need for a comprehensive federal data privacy law in the United States.

OTHER MAJOR DATA LAWS

In addition to the GDPR and CCPA, several other regulations have emerged globally to address data privacy and protection.

Children's Online Privacy Protection Act (COPPA)

COPPA is a United States federal law that was enacted in 1998 to protect the privacy of children under the age of 13 online. COPPA requires Web sites and online services directed at children, or that knowingly collect personal information from children, to obtain verifiable parental consent before collecting, using, or disclosing such information. Additionally, operators of these Web sites must provide a clear and comprehensive privacy policy that outlines their information practices, including what data is collected, how it is used, and whether it is shared with third parties. The law also grants parents the right to review their child's personal information, request its deletion, and refuse further collection or use of their child's data. To ensure the confidentiality, security, and integrity of the personal information they collect, operators are required to take reasonable steps to protect this data.

HEALTH INSURANCE PORTABILITY AND ACCOUNTABILITY ACT

HIPAA is a United States federal law that regulates the handling of protected health information (PHI) by healthcare providers, health plans, and their business associates. Enacted in 1996, HIPAA establishes comprehensive standards aimed at protecting the privacy and security of PHI, which includes any individually identifiable health information, such as medical records, treatment histories, and billing information. By implementing these regulations, HIPAA ensures that individuals' medical records are safeguarded against unauthorized access or disclosure, fostering trust in the healthcare system. As a result, healthcare organizations are required to adhere to strict protocols for managing PHI, which ultimately enhances the overall protection of patient rights and confidentiality.

Personal Information Protection and Electronic Documents Act (PIPEDA)

This Canadian law governs the collection, use, and disclosure of personal information by private sector organizations. It provides individuals with rights regarding their personal data and imposes obligations on organizations to obtain consent and ensure data security.

Brazilian General Data Protection Law (LGPD)

Enacted in 2020, the LGPD closely mirrors the GDPR and aims to protect the personal data of Brazilian citizens. It establishes principles for data processing, outlines individuals' rights, and imposes penalties for non-compliance, reflecting Brazil's commitment to data privacy.

Data Protection Act 2018

This UK law supplements the GDPR, providing additional provisions related to data protection in the UK context. It sets out the framework for data processing and the rights of individuals while ensuring compliance with EU standards.

Ensuring Ethical Data-handling

As the landscape of data privacy continues to evolve, regulations such as the GDPR and CCPA play a crucial role in shaping how organizations handle personal data. These laws empower individuals, ensuring they have control over their information and fostering transparency in data practices. In addition, other data protection laws worldwide underscore the global consensus on the importance of ethical data-handling. As organizations navigate this complex regulatory environment, adhering to these regulations not only helps mitigate legal risks but also builds trust with consumers, ultimately contributing to a more responsible and sustainable data economy.

REGULATIONS AND ETHICAL DATA USE

Transforming Corporate Behavior

The introduction of data protection regulations, such as the GDPR and CCPA, has transformed how organizations approach data usage, shifting from mere compliance to fostering ethical practices. These frameworks emphasize transparency, consent, and accountability, encouraging responsible data management that respects privacy rights. As businesses reevaluate their data strategies, many now prioritize ethical considerations, fostering trust and enhancing their reputation. This shift reflects a broader cultural change where ethical data use is integral to corporate responsibility and long-term success. Companies that embrace these values not only meet legal standards but also position themselves as leaders in ethical data stewardship.

Driving Ethical Practices

Regulations such as the GDPR and CCPA push organizations to adopt ethical data practices beyond compliance. Mandating transparency, consent, and accountability, these laws drive companies to reevaluate how they collect, use, and disclose personal data. For example, the GDPR's requirement for explicit consent has led businesses to ensure clarity around data collection processes. By doing so, organizations foster trust and loyalty among customers, aligning their strategies with ethical data management principles.

These regulations also promote data minimization, requiring companies to collect only the data necessary for specific purposes. This reduces risks such as data breaches while aligning corporate behavior with ethical standards. By prioritizing responsible data practices, companies can not only enhance their reputation but also attract socially conscious consumers, contributing to their long-term success.

Enhancing Accountability and Responsibility

A key feature of regulations such as the GDPR is their strong emphasis on accountability. The threat of substantial financial penalties for non-compliance, such as fines of up to €20 million or 4% of global turnover, incentivizes organizations to prioritize ethical data use. In response, many companies have appointed data protection officers (DPOs) and established compliance teams to oversee data practices, fostering a culture of responsibility.

Additionally, organizations are adopting comprehensive data governance policies. This often includes conducting data protection impact assessments (DPIAs) to identify risks in data processing activities. By proactively addressing these risks, companies not only comply with regulations but also demonstrate their commitment to ethical data stewardship.

Fostering Technological Innovations

Regulatory frameworks are also driving innovation in data governance technologies. Organizations are investing in privacy-enhancing technologies (PETs), such as data anonymization techniques and secure storage solutions, to comply with regulations while minimizing risks to privacy. This push for innovation promotes ethical data use by integrating these considerations into technology development.

Moreover, the demand for regulatory compliance solutions has led to the rise of tools that help manage consent, automate reporting, and streamline compliance processes. This allows businesses to focus on leveraging data ethically while maintaining regulatory adherence.

Cultural Shift Toward Ethical Data Use

The advent of data protection regulations has contributed to a broader cultural shift within organizations. As data privacy becomes a significant public concern, ethical data practices are evolving from a regulatory obligation into a core element of corporate identity. This shift aligns with the growing focus on CSR, as companies seek to integrate societal values into their strategies.

By embracing transparency, accountability, and user-centric approaches, organizations can build stronger customer relationships. This ethical commitment fosters brand loyalty, positioning businesses as trusted entities that protect consumer data and privacy.

Catalysts for Ethical Change

The impact of regulations such as the GDPR and CCPA extends beyond legal compliance; they have catalyzed a transformation in corporate behavior, driving responsible data governance and ethical practices. By emphasizing transparency, accountability, and innovation, these frameworks have paved the way for a culture that prioritizes ethical data use. As organizations adapt to this evolving landscape, they not only reduce legal risks but also set themselves apart as leaders in responsible data management. In an age where privacy is a top consumer concern, ethical data practices are becoming a key differentiator in the competitive marketplace.

COMPLIANCE STRATEGIES

Regulatory Compliance Best Practices

In an era marked by rapid technological advancements and increasing scrutiny over data privacy, organizations must prioritize regulatory compliance as a fundamental aspect of their operations. Compliance with regulations such as the GDPR, CCPA, and other data protection laws not only mitigates legal risks but also fosters trust among customers and stakeholders. To effectively align with these regulations, organizations should adopt best practices that encompass various aspects of their data management strategies. The following sections discuss several key practices that can help organizations ensure regulatory compliance while promoting ethical data use.

Conduct Comprehensive Data Audits

One of the first steps toward regulatory compliance is conducting a thorough data audit. Organizations should assess what types of personal data they collect, how it is processed, stored, and shared, and for what purposes. This audit should also include an evaluation of third-party vendors and partners who may have access to sensitive data. By understanding their data landscape, organizations can identify potential compliance gaps and risks associated with data processing activities.

In addition to identifying existing data, organizations should classify data based on sensitivity and compliance requirements. This classification can help prioritize data protection efforts and inform the development of data governance policies. For instance, sensitive data may require more stringent security measures and handling protocols compared to non-sensitive information. Regular audits should be a part of an organization's ongoing compliance strategy, ensuring that data practices are continuously aligned with evolving regulations.

Implement Robust Data Governance Policies

Establishing strong data governance policies is crucial for regulatory compliance. These policies should outline the organization's approach to data collection, processing, storage, and sharing, ensuring that all practices align with applicable regulations. Key components of effective data governance policies are described in the following sub-sections.

Data Minimization

Organizations should adopt the principle of data minimization, collecting only the data necessary for specific purposes. This practice reduces risks associated with data breaches and ensures compliance with regulations that mandate limited data collection.

Access Controls

Implementing strict access controls is essential for protecting personal data. Organizations should define user roles and permissions, ensuring that only authorized personnel have access to sensitive information. Regularly reviewing access permissions helps maintain a secure data environment.

Data Retention Policies

Establishing clear data retention policies ensures that organizations do not retain personal data longer than necessary. These policies should specify how long different types of data will be stored and the processes for securely deleting data that is no longer needed.

Invest in Employee Training and Awareness

Compliance is not solely the responsibility of the compliance team; it requires the active participation of all employees within the organization. Investing in regular training and awareness programs helps employees understand their roles in maintaining compliance with data protection regulations. The content to be covered in these training sessions is described in the following sub-sections.

Data Protection Principles

Employees should become familiar with key data protection principles, such as the importance of obtaining informed consent, safeguarding personal information, and reporting potential breaches.

Incident Response Procedures

Training should include guidelines on how to respond to data breaches or incidents. Employees should know the proper reporting channels and actions to take to mitigate risks and comply with notification requirements.

Updates on Regulatory Changes

Regulations are subject to change, and organizations must keep their employees informed about any updates or new compliance requirements. Regular communication helps maintain a culture of compliance throughout the organization.

Utilize Technology Solutions for Compliance

Leveraging technology can significantly enhance an organization's ability to comply with regulations. Various tools and software solutions are available to assist organizations in managing compliance efforts effectively. Key technological solutions are described in the following sub-sections.

Data Management Platforms

These platforms can help organizations streamline data collection, processing, and reporting, ensuring that practices align with regulatory requirements. Features such as data mapping and tracking can enhance transparency and accountability.

Consent Management Solutions

Implementing consent management solutions enables organizations to obtain and manage user consent more effectively. These tools help track consent preferences and ensure compliance with regulations that mandate explicit consent for data processing.

Monitoring and Reporting Tools

Technology can aid in monitoring data usage and generating reports to demonstrate compliance. Automated reporting tools can help organizations maintain records of data processing activities, which is essential for regulatory compliance audits.

Establish a Culture of Compliance and Ethics

Finally, organizations should strive to establish a culture of compliance and ethics at all levels. This culture should be supported by leadership, with senior management demonstrating a commitment to regulatory compliance and ethical data practices. Regularly communicating the importance of compliance, recognizing employees who contribute to ethical data use, and fostering an environment of accountability can enhance compliance efforts.

Organizations can also consider appointing a chief compliance officer or data protection officer to oversee compliance initiatives and ensure alignment with regulatory requirements. These individuals can serve as points of contact for compliance-related inquiries and lead efforts to integrate ethical considerations into business practices.

Navigating Data Compliance

Aligning with data protection regulations is essential for organizations operating in today's data-centric landscape. By implementing best practices such as conducting comprehensive data audits, establishing robust data governance policies, investing in employee training, utilizing technology solutions, and fostering a culture of compliance, organizations can navigate the complex regulatory environment effectively. As data privacy concerns continue to rise, organizations that prioritize compliance not only mitigate legal risks but also build trust and loyalty among consumers, ultimately contributing to long-term business success.

COMPLIANCE CHALLENGES

Navigating the Complexities of Data Compliance

As organizations strive to navigate the complex landscape of data protection regulations, they often encounter a myriad of challenges that hinder their ability to achieve compliance. The implementation of regulations such as the GDPR and CCPA requires significant adjustments to business operations, data management practices, and corporate culture. Understanding these challenges is crucial for organizations aiming to create effective compliance strategies. This discussion outlines common difficulties faced by organizations in meeting compliance requirements.

The Complexity and Ambiguity of Regulations

One of the most significant challenges that organizations face is the complexity and ambiguity inherent in data protection regulations. Laws such as the GDPR and CCPA are extensive, comprising numerous provisions and stipulations that can be difficult to interpret and apply consistently across various organizational contexts. For example, the definition of personal data under the GDPR is broad, encompassing a wide range of information that can identify an individual. This ambiguity can lead to confusion regarding what constitutes personal data, complicating compliance efforts.

Moreover, regulations may vary significantly between jurisdictions, particularly for organizations operating internationally. Different countries may have distinct requirements, leading to complications in aligning data practices with local laws. This inconsistency can overwhelm organizations, particularly small businesses that lack the resources to conduct thorough legal analysis and stay up to date on changing regulations. Consequently, many organizations struggle to implement uniform compliance measures across different regions.

Resource Constraints

Meeting compliance requirements often demands considerable time, financial investment, and human resources. Many organizations, especially small and medium-sized enterprises (SMEs), may lack the necessary resources to implement comprehensive compliance programs. Hiring dedicated DPOs, legal counsel, and compliance specialists can be financially burdensome, leading to insufficient staffing for compliance-related initiatives.

Furthermore, the need for ongoing training and education for employees adds another layer of complexity. Organizations must allocate resources for regular training sessions, which may divert attention from other critical business functions. Inadequate resource allocation can result in compliance gaps, increasing the risk of regulatory breaches and associated penalties. Consequently, organizations may find it challenging to balance compliance efforts with their day-to-day operations and strategic goals.

Integration of Compliance into Existing Systems

Integrating compliance requirements into existing business systems and processes presents another significant challenge. Organizations often operate with legacy systems that may not be designed to support data protection regulations effectively. For example, outdated customer relationship management systems may not have the capabilities to manage consent preferences or track data processing activities as required by regulations.

This integration challenge may require organizations to invest in new technologies and tools, which can be both time-consuming and costly. Additionally, the process of migrating data from legacy systems to new platforms can create potential vulnerabilities if not handled correctly. Data breaches during this transition period can lead to regulatory penalties and erode consumer trust, making organizations hesitant to pursue necessary upgrades.

Cultural Resistance to Change

Another obstacle organizations face in achieving compliance is cultural resistance to change. Implementing new data protection policies and practices often requires a shift in organizational culture and employee mindset. Employees accustomed to certain data-handling practices may be resistant to adopting new protocols, viewing them as unnecessary or burdensome. This resistance can hinder the effective rollout of compliance initiatives and create silos of non-compliance within the organization.

To overcome this challenge, organizations must prioritize communication and engagement with employees. Leadership should actively promote the importance of compliance, illustrating how it aligns with broader organizational goals and consumer trust. Fostering a culture of compliance requires ongoing efforts to educate employees about their roles in safeguarding personal data and the potential consequences of non-compliance.

Balancing Business Objectives with Compliance Needs

Striking a balance between achieving business objectives and meeting compliance requirements can be challenging for organizations. In a competitive marketplace, organizations may prioritize growth and profitability over compliance, viewing regulatory obligations as obstacles to agility. This mindset can lead to non-compliance, resulting in legal repercussions and damage to reputation.

To address this challenge, organizations must adopt a holistic approach that incorporates compliance into their strategic planning. This involves recognizing compliance not as a hindrance but as a fundamental component of responsible business practice. By integrating compliance considerations into product development, marketing strategies, and customer engagement, organizations can create a culture that values ethical data use while driving business success.

Navigating Compliance Challenges

Meeting compliance with data protection regulations presents a range of challenges for organizations. From the complexity and ambiguity of regulations to resource constraints, integration issues, cultural resistance, and the need to balance business objectives, organizations must navigate a multifaceted landscape. By recognizing these challenges, organizations can proactively develop strategies to enhance their compliance efforts. This may involve investing in technology solutions, fostering a culture of compliance, providing ongoing employee training, and integrating compliance considerations into their overall business strategy. Ultimately, a commitment to compliance not only mitigates legal risks but also fosters trust and loyalty among consumers, contributing to long-term organizational success.

CHAPTER 17

THE FUTURE OF DATA ETHICS

EMERGING TRENDS IN DATA ETHICS

The Impact of Emerging Technologies on Data Ethics

The rapid advancement of emerging technologies, particularly AI and quantum computing, is reshaping various industries and fundamentally altering how data is collected, processed, and utilized. As organizations increasingly leverage these technologies for their operational advantages, the implications for data ethics become more pronounced. Emerging technologies introduce unique challenges and opportunities that require a reevaluation of ethical principles and frameworks governing data usage. This section explores the impact of these technologies on data ethics and the critical considerations organizations must address to navigate this evolving landscape responsibly.

The Ethical Impact of AI

AI has emerged as a transformative force across sectors, from healthcare to finance, offering unparalleled capabilities for data analysis and decision-making. The deployment of AI systems raises significant ethical concerns, particularly in areas such as bias, transparency, and accountability. One of the most pressing issues is algorithmic bias, where AI models may inadvertently perpetuate or exacerbate existing societal bias. For instance, facial recognition technologies have been shown to misidentify individuals from marginalized communities at disproportionately higher rates, leading to serious consequences such as wrongful arrests or denied opportunities.

This bias often stems from the data used to train AI models, which may reflect historical prejudices and systemic inequality. As organizations harness AI for decision-making, they must prioritize the ethical responsibility of ensuring fairness and equity in their algorithms. This entails not only scrutinizing the datasets used for training but also implementing robust bias mitigation strategies throughout the AI development lifecycle. Transparency is also vital in AI ethics; organizations should be clear about how AI systems make decisions and the data they rely upon. Engaging in open dialogue with stakeholders, including affected communities, can help organizations build trust and accountability in their AI practices.

Quantum Computing: New Frontiers and Ethical Implications

Quantum computing represents a significant leap in computational capabilities, promising to solve complex problems beyond the reach of classical computers. While the potential benefits of quantum computing are immense, such as advancements in drug discovery and optimization of supply chains, it also poses ethical challenges related to data security and privacy. Quantum computers could potentially break encryption methods currently used to secure sensitive data, rendering many data protection measures obsolete. This capability raises alarms about the vulnerability of personal information, financial records, and classified data, necessitating a proactive approach to data ethics and security.

As quantum computing technologies mature, organizations must consider the ethical implications of their use. This includes investing in post-quantum cryptography—new encryption methods designed to withstand the capabilities of quantum computers.

Furthermore, organizations need to evaluate the societal impact of deploying quantum computing solutions, especially in terms of access and fairness. The unequal availability of quantum technologies could exacerbate existing disparity, as organizations with greater resources may leverage quantum computing to gain competitive advantages, leaving smaller players behind. Ensuring equitable access to these technologies and their benefits will be a critical ethical consideration as the field evolves.

The Interplay Between AI and Quantum Computing

The convergence of AI and quantum computing introduces a new dimension to data ethics. Quantum machine learning—an interdisciplinary field combining quantum computing with AI—holds the promise of unlocking new insights from vast datasets at unprecedented speeds. This synergy, however, raises ethical questions regarding the implications of hyper-efficient data processing capabilities. The potential to analyze sensitive data rapidly could lead to privacy infringements, as individuals may find it increasingly challenging to control how their data is used and shared.

Moreover, as AI systems become more powerful through quantum computing advancements, the potential for misuse increases. Organizations must grapple with the ethical implications of deploying powerful AI systems that can manipulate data in ways that could infringe on individual rights or contribute to harmful outcomes. This necessitates the development of ethical frameworks and guidelines that govern the responsible use of these technologies, ensuring that they enhance rather than undermine societal values.

Establishing Ethical Frameworks for Emerging Technologies

As emerging technologies continue to evolve, organizations must proactively establish ethical frameworks that guide their use. These frameworks should prioritize core ethical principles such as transparency, accountability, fairness, and privacy. Organizations can engage in collaborative efforts with industry peers, policymakers, and civil society organizations to develop comprehensive ethical guidelines that address the unique challenges posed by AI and quantum computing.

Additionally, ongoing ethical training and awareness programs for employees are crucial. Organizations must cultivate a culture that emphasizes ethical considerations in technology development and deployment. By fostering an environment where ethical discussions are encouraged, organizations can better anticipate and mitigate the risks associated with emerging technologies.

Conclusion: Ethics in Emerging Technologies

The impact of emerging technologies such as AI and quantum computing on data ethics is profound and multifaceted. While these technologies provide remarkable opportunities for innovation and efficiency, they also pose significant ethical challenges that organizations must address. By prioritizing ethical considerations such as bias mitigation, transparency, and equitable access, organizations can harness the potential of these technologies responsibly. Establishing robust ethical frameworks and fostering a culture of ethical awareness will be essential as organizations navigate the complexities of this evolving landscape. Ultimately, the successful integration of emerging technologies into society will depend on a commitment to ethical principles that protect individual rights and promote the greater good.

FUTURE ETHICAL DILEMMAS IN DATA ETHICS

As society becomes increasingly reliant on data-driven technologies and analytics, new ethical dilemmas are emerging that challenge traditional frameworks of data ethics. The rapid pace of technological innovation introduces complexity that necessitates a reevaluation of ethical considerations surrounding data collection, usage, and sharing. This exploration of potential future challenges in data ethics highlights several key areas that organizations, policymakers, and society as a whole must address to navigate the evolving landscape responsibly.

The Rise of Autonomous Systems

One of the most significant ethical dilemmas on the horizon stems from the development and deployment of autonomous systems, such as self-driving vehicles and drones. These technologies promise to revolutionize industries, enhance efficiency, and improve safety, but they also raise critical ethical questions about accountability, decision-making, and the potential for harm. For instance, in situations where autonomous vehicles must make decisions in life-threatening scenarios, ethical frameworks will be required to determine how these systems should prioritize human lives.

Moreover, the issue of accountability becomes paramount: if an autonomous vehicle is involved in an accident, who is responsible—the manufacturer, the software developer, or the owner? Current legal and regulatory frameworks may not adequately address these questions, leading to a potential crisis of accountability. As organizations develop and implement autonomous systems, they must establish clear ethical guidelines that govern their design, deployment, and oversight. This includes engaging in transparent dialogue with stakeholders, including policymakers and the public, to build trust and address concerns related to safety, liability, and ethical decision-making.

Surveillance and Data Privacy

As surveillance technologies, such as facial recognition and geolocation tracking, become more pervasive, the ethical implications of these practices will continue to expand. While these technologies can enhance security and efficiency, they also pose significant risks to individual privacy and civil liberties. The potential for widespread surveillance by governments and corporations raises concerns about the erosion of privacy rights and the chilling effects on free expression and dissent.

The ethical dilemmas associated with surveillance technologies are further complicated by the rise of data aggregation and analytics capabilities. Organizations can now collect vast amounts of data on individuals, often without their explicit consent or knowledge. This raises fundamental questions about the ethics of consent and the extent to which individuals can exercise control over their data. As surveillance technologies evolve, society must grapple with how to balance the benefits of enhanced security with the rights to privacy and autonomy. Developing robust ethical guidelines and regulatory frameworks that govern the use of surveillance technologies will be critical in addressing these challenges.

Manipulation Through Data and AI

Another emerging ethical dilemma revolves around the potential for manipulation through data and AI. As organizations increasingly leverage advanced analytics and AI-driven algorithms to influence consumer behavior, political opinions, and social dynamics, ethical concerns regarding manipulation and exploitation are magnified. For example, targeted advertising and personalized content delivery can reinforce existing bias and create echo chambers, leading to societal polarization and misinformation.

The ethical challenge lies in determining the boundaries of acceptable influence and manipulation. While organizations may argue that targeted marketing and content personalization enhance user experience, they must also consider the potential harm of exploiting vulnerabilities in human psychology. The responsible use of data and AI requires organizations to prioritize transparency and fairness in their practices, ensuring that individuals are informed about how their data is used and the implications of algorithmic decision-making.

Data Ownership and Control

The question of data ownership and control is set to become increasingly contentious in the coming years. As individuals generate more data through their interactions with digital platforms, the debate over who owns this data intensifies. Traditionally, organizations have claimed ownership over user data collected through their services, often leading to an imbalance in power and control. Individuals are increasingly demanding greater autonomy and control over their data, raising ethical questions about data ownership rights.

This shift necessitates a reevaluation of existing frameworks surrounding data ownership and consent. Organizations must recognize individuals as stakeholders in the data ecosystem, respecting their rights to access, control, and manage their personal information. Developing ethical practices around data ownership, such as clear consent mechanisms and transparent data-sharing policies, will be crucial in fostering trust between organizations and individuals.

Environmental Considerations in Data Ethics

The environmental impact of data generation and storage presents an emerging ethical dilemma that requires attention. As the demand for data storage and processing grows, so does the energy consumption associated with data centers and cloud computing. The carbon footprint of data technologies raises questions about the sustainability of current data practices and the ethical implications of contributing to climate change.

Organizations must consider the environmental consequences of their data practices and explore sustainable alternatives. This includes investing in energy-efficient technologies, adopting green data centers, and promoting practices that reduce data redundancy and waste. By integrating environmental considerations into their data ethics frameworks, organizations can align their practices with broader societal goals of sustainability and responsibility.

Concluding Reflections

As emerging technologies continue to shape the landscape of data ethics, the potential for new ethical dilemmas is significant. Addressing the challenges posed by autonomous systems, surveillance technologies, manipulation through data and AI, data ownership, and environmental considerations will require collaborative efforts among organizations, policymakers, and society. By proactively engaging with these ethical dilemmas and establishing robust ethical frameworks, stakeholders can navigate the complexities of the evolving data landscape responsibly. Ultimately, fostering a culture of ethical responsibility in data practices will be essential for building trust, protecting individual rights, and promoting the greater good in an increasingly data-driven world.

BUILDING ETHICAL DATA CULTURES

Empowering Ethical Data Practices Through Education

In an increasingly data-driven world, the importance of education and awareness in promoting ethical data practices cannot be overstated. As organizations and individuals harness the power of data for decision-making, the potential for ethical breaches and misuse rises. Education plays a pivotal role in equipping stakeholders with the knowledge, skills, and ethical frameworks necessary to navigate the complexities of data ethics. This discussion explores how education and awareness initiatives can foster ethical data practices across various sectors, ultimately contributing to a more responsible data ecosystem.

Cultivating Awareness of Data Ethics

The first step in promoting ethical data practices is raising awareness about the implications of data collection, usage, and sharing. Many individuals and organizations may not fully understand the ethical considerations surrounding data, particularly in terms of privacy, consent, and accountability. Educational programs that focus on data ethics can help demystify these concepts, providing stakeholders with a foundational understanding of why ethical data practices matter.

By highlighting real-world examples of ethical breaches and their consequences, educational initiatives can illustrate the potential risks associated with poor data practices. For instance, case studies highlighting the impact of data breaches on individuals and organizations can serve as powerful teaching tools. These case studies can emphasize the importance of safeguarding personal information and respecting user consent, thereby fostering a culture of accountability.

Furthermore, raising awareness about the ethical implications of emerging technologies, such as AI and big data analytics, can prepare individuals to navigate the challenges associated with these innovations responsibly.

Embedding Data Ethics Across Educational Curricula

To effectively promote ethical data practices, educational institutions must integrate data ethics into their curricula across various disciplines. This integration ensures that students, regardless of their field of study, are exposed to ethical considerations relevant to data usage. For instance, business programs can incorporate data ethics into their courses on marketing, operations, and data analytics, teaching students how to make responsible decisions in their future careers. Similarly, computer science and engineering programs can emphasize the ethical design and deployment of technology, ensuring that future developers and engineers prioritize ethical considerations in their work.

Beyond formal education, organizations can also implement training programs for employees to enhance their understanding of ethical data practices. These programs should cover topics such as data privacy laws, ethical decision-making frameworks, and best practices for data-handling. By providing ongoing education and training, organizations can cultivate a workforce that is not only skilled in technical competencies but also committed to ethical behavior in their data practices.

Fostering Critical Thinking for Ethical Decision-Making

Education plays a critical role in promoting critical thinking and ethical decision-making among individuals who handle data. As data professionals encounter complex ethical dilemmas, they must possess the ability to analyze situations critically and make informed decisions that align with ethical principles. Educational initiatives should focus on developing these skills through interactive learning experiences, case discussions, and ethical scenario analysis.

Encouraging students and professionals to engage in discussions about ethical dilemmas and potential solutions fosters a culture of reflection and accountability. Additionally, incorporating interdisciplinary perspectives into education can enrich the discourse on data ethics. For example, insights from philosophy, sociology, and law can provide valuable context for understanding the ethical implications of data practices in various settings.

Cultivating a Culture of Ethical Responsibility

Ultimately, education and awareness initiatives contribute to building a culture of ethical responsibility within organizations and society at large. When stakeholders understand the importance of ethical data practices, they are more likely to prioritize them in their decision-making processes. This cultural shift can lead to a positive feedback loop, where ethical behavior becomes ingrained in organizational values and practices.

Moreover, educational institutions and organizations can collaborate to establish partnerships that promote ethical data practices beyond the classroom. Initiatives such as community outreach programs, workshops, and public awareness campaigns can extend the reach of educational efforts, ensuring that ethical data practices resonate with a broader audience.

Engaging stakeholders from various sectors—including government, academia, and industry—can facilitate a collective approach to addressing data ethics challenges and fostering responsible practices.

Key Takeaways for Ethical Data Practices

In conclusion, education and awareness play a crucial role in promoting ethical data practices in today's data-centric world. By raising awareness about data ethics, integrating ethical considerations into curricula, fostering critical thinking and ethical decision-making, and building a culture of ethical responsibility, educational initiatives can significantly contribute to a more ethical data ecosystem. As organizations and individuals navigate the complexities of data usage, a commitment to education and awareness will be essential in ensuring that ethical principles guide data practices. Ultimately, investing in education around data ethics not only benefits individuals and organizations but also strengthens societal trust in the responsible use of data.

ESTABLISHING ETHICAL FRAMEWORKS FOR RESPONSIBLE DATA PRACTICES

As the world becomes increasingly data-driven, the necessity for robust ethical frameworks to guide data practices has never been more pressing. The rapid advancement of technology, coupled with the exponential growth of data collection and usage, presents new ethical challenges that existing frameworks often struggle to address. Developing comprehensive ethical guidelines is crucial not only for compliance with regulations but also for fostering public trust and ensuring that data is used responsibly. This discussion delves into the components of effective ethical frameworks, the process of developing them, and their importance in enhancing adherence to data ethics.

Key Components of an Ethical Framework

An effective ethical framework for data practices should encompass several key components. First and foremost, it must define core ethical principles, such as transparency, accountability, privacy, and fairness. These principles serve as guiding tenets that organizations can refer to when making data-related decisions. For instance, transparency involves openly communicating data practices to stakeholders, while accountability ensures that individuals and organizations are held responsible for their actions regarding data usage.

Moreover, an ethical framework should include practical guidelines for implementing these principles in everyday operations. This may involve establishing clear protocols for data collection, processing, and sharing, as well as outlining procedures for obtaining informed consent from data subjects. Furthermore, organizations should define the roles and responsibilities of employees at various levels to ensure that ethical considerations are integrated into all aspects of data management.

Another vital component is the establishment of mechanisms for ethical oversight. This could take the form of an ethics committee or a dedicated data governance board responsible for reviewing data practices and ensuring adherence to the established ethical framework. Regular audits and assessments can help identify potential ethical breaches and facilitate continuous improvement in data practices.

Collaborating with Stakeholders in Framework Development

The development of ethical frameworks should be a collaborative effort that involves diverse stakeholders, including industry experts, policymakers, academia, and the communities impacted by data practices. Engaging stakeholders ensures that a wide range of perspectives and values are considered, ultimately leading to more comprehensive and effective guidelines.

Workshops, focus groups, and public consultations can provide platforms for dialogue among stakeholders, allowing them to share their insights and experiences regarding data ethics. By incorporating feedback from various groups, organizations can create ethical frameworks that address real-world concerns and reflect the values of the communities they serve.

Furthermore, involving stakeholders in the framework development process fosters a sense of ownership and commitment to ethical practices. When individuals and organizations feel that their voices are heard and their concerns are addressed, they are more likely to adhere to the established guidelines. This participatory approach can help build trust and strengthen relationships between organizations and their stakeholders, reinforcing the importance of ethical behavior in data practices.

Building Flexible and Dynamic Ethical Frameworks

Given the rapid pace of technological advancements, ethical frameworks must be adaptable and dynamic to remain relevant. Organizations should regularly review and update their guidelines to reflect emerging ethical challenges and changing societal norms. This ongoing process ensures that the framework evolves in tandem with advancements in data technologies and practices.

Organizations should also foster a culture of continuous learning and improvement regarding data ethics. Providing ongoing training and resources for employees can help them stay informed about ethical considerations and emerging best practices. Encouraging open discussions about ethical dilemmas and potential solutions within the organization can further enhance adherence to ethical frameworks.

Effective Implementation and Communication of the Ethical Framework

Once developed, it is crucial to implement the ethical framework effectively throughout the organization. This involves not only disseminating the guidelines to all employees but also integrating them into existing policies and practices. Organizations should ensure that ethical considerations are embedded in decision-making processes, from data collection to analysis and reporting.

Communication is key to fostering an ethical culture. Organizations should regularly communicate the importance of ethical data practices to all stakeholders, including employees, customers, and partners. Transparency in how data is managed and the steps taken to uphold ethical standards can build trust and confidence in an organization's commitment to ethical behavior.

Additionally, organizations should provide avenues for reporting ethical concerns or violations without fear of retaliation. Establishing a whistleblower policy and ensuring that employees feel safe voicing their concerns can strengthen adherence to the ethical framework and promote accountability.

Key Insights on Ethical Frameworks

In conclusion, developing ethical frameworks is essential for enhancing adherence to data ethics in a rapidly evolving technological landscape. By defining core ethical principles, engaging diverse stakeholders, creating adaptable guidelines, and implementing effective communication strategies, organizations can foster a culture of ethical responsibility in data practices. As the challenges associated with data collection and usage continue to grow, robust ethical frameworks will be vital in guiding organizations toward responsible and ethical data practices. Ultimately, a commitment to ethical guidelines not only benefits organizations but also safeguards individual rights, promotes public trust, and contributes to the responsible advancement of technology in society.

CASE STUDIES

CRIMINAL JUSTICE AND LAW ENFORCEMENT

COMPAS Recidivism Algorithm

The Correctional Offender Management Profiling for Alternative Sanctions (COMPAS) algorithm was developed to support judges in evaluating the risk of a defendant reoffending, with the aim of improving decision-making in sentencing and parole hearings. This tool assigns a risk score based on factors such as criminal history and personal background, intending to bring consistency and objectivity to the judicial process. A 2016 ProPublica investigation, however, revealed serious racial bias within the algorithm, with black defendants disproportionately receiving higher risk scores than white defendants, regardless of their likelihood to reoffend.

The ProPublica study highlighted a concerning trend: black defendants were almost twice as likely to be classified as high-risk for future crimes despite not reoffending, while white defendants were more often mislabeled as low-risk despite having higher reoffense rates. This imbalance mirrored racial disparities present within the broader criminal justice system, where black and minority individuals already face systemic disadvantages. Rather than neutralizing these disparities, the COMPAS algorithm unintentionally amplified them, embedding historical bias within its risk assessments.

A core issue with COMPAS was the data it was trained on, which reflected long-standing racial inequities in the criminal justice system.

Since black individuals have historically been arrested and incarcerated at disproportionately higher rates due to systemic racism, any AI trained on such data inherits and perpetuates this bias. Additionally, COMPAS's proprietary nature limits transparency, preventing defendants from understanding or challenging the criteria that generate their risk scores, which raises significant ethical and procedural concerns.

The use of COMPAS in courts has sparked extensive debate regarding AI's role in high-stakes judicial decisions. While proponents argue that tools such as COMPAS can reduce human subjectivity, critics contend that they risk reinforcing existing bias, especially without sufficient oversight. Several advocacy groups have called for reforms, including enhancing transparency, implementing fairness constraints, and reevaluating AI's function in the criminal justice system to prevent discrimination. Due to the scrutiny around COMPAS, some states have reconsidered their reliance on AI-based risk assessment tools.

The ethical implications of using AI in legal systems continue to shape discussions on AI governance, where mistakes have profound, life-altering consequences. The COMPAS case has become a pivotal example of the need for ethical frameworks in AI, emphasizing that without addressing inherent bias, such systems may unintentionally undermine the very principles of justice they aim to uphold.

Machine Bias: Case Study of Brisha Borden

Machine bias refers to the prejudiced outcomes produced by algorithms and AI systems, often arising from biased training data or flawed design assumptions. This issue significantly impacts law enforcement, where predictive policing software is used across the United States to forecast criminal activity and identify potential offenders. Such algorithms typically rely on historical crime data, which perpetuates societal bias and disproportionately affects marginalized communities, especially black individuals.

The case of Brisha Borden in Florida exemplifies machine bias. In 2014, Borden, an 18-year-old black woman, was arrested based on predictive policing software that flagged her as a potential offender. The algorithm utilized data from past arrests and neighborhood crime statistics, which often reflect systemic inequality. Following her arrest, Borden faced severe repercussions, including being rejected for jobs at McDonald's and a local dollar store, highlighting the lasting impact of algorithmic predictions on individuals' lives.

Predictive policing tools, such as Geolitica and HunchLab, analyze extensive data to forecast crime locations and potential offenders, but these algorithms frequently rely on biased datasets that overrepresent crimes in predominantly black neighborhoods. This results in over-policing, leading to increased arrest rates for black individuals, which further reinforces the cycle of bias in these communities. Such systemic issues reveal the flaws in using historical data to predict future offenses without addressing the underlying societal factors.

Research indicates that predictive policing algorithms can exhibit racial bias, increasing surveillance and intervention in black communities. Studies, such as those from the AI Now Institute, show that algorithms trained on biased data often target areas with a history of over-policing, correlating with high arrest rates for minor offenses. This disproportionate focus undermines the legitimacy of the justice system and fosters distrust between marginalized communities and law enforcement.

To combat machine bias in predictive policing, a multifaceted approach is essential. This includes critically evaluating the data used to train algorithms, ensuring it does not reflect historical bias, and promoting transparency in decision-making processes. Engaging with affected communities is crucial for developing equitable policing practices that prioritize public safety while safeguarding civil rights. Ultimately, addressing machine bias is vital for fostering a more just and equitable society.

Accused by an Algorithm

Robert Julian-Borchak Williams's experience reveals the troubling realities of FRT in law enforcement. In January 2020, Williams was arrested at his home in front of his family based on a supposed match from a facial recognition system. Held for over 30 hours, he was later released when it became clear that he had been misidentified. Williams's case is notable as one of the first documented wrongful arrests based on FRT errors, and it has sparked significant concerns about FRT's potential to misidentify individuals, especially people of color.

Studies have shown that FRT algorithms often perform worse on non-caucasian faces due to limited diversity in the datasets on which these systems are trained. Research by MIT and the National Institute of Standards and Technology (NIST) found that false positive rates for African American and Asian faces were ten to one hundred times higher than for white faces. Although companies such as Amazon, Microsoft, and IBM have paused their FRT offerings for law enforcement, facial recognition systems continue to be widely used by police departments, highlighting the need for rigorous testing and bias mitigation.

In Williams's case, the flawed identification highlights a more systemic issue where FRT output was over-relied upon without corroborative evidence. The Detroit police obtained a low-quality surveillance image, matched it to Williams's driver's license photo, and accepted this match as probable cause, despite warnings that FRT should only be an investigative lead, not sole proof. The process also missed an opportunity to obtain additional evidence, such as eyewitness verification or Williams's phone location, that could have prevented the wrongful arrest.

Beyond algorithmic flaws, the human element also exacerbates FRT's issues. When FRT outputs are interpreted without proper checks or are influenced by human bias, they can lead to severe consequences. Different agencies may interpret the same FRT results with varying thresholds or confidence levels, potentially leading to unjust arrests. Experts suggest that these differences, known as *institutional shifts*, show that systems are often applied inconsistently, making it necessary to develop a unified framework for FRT usage.

For FRT to be reliable, experts recommend implementing robust testing protocols that focus on transparency, independent evaluations, and regular algorithm recertifications. Such measures would help account for *domain shifts*, where performance varies significantly between controlled and real-world settings. Policymakers and agencies should set higher accuracy benchmarks and ensure regular audits, with mandatory protocols to minimize bias. These steps are essential to preventing wrongful arrests and ensuring FRT operates within a framework that prioritizes fairness and human rights.

AUTONOMOUS DRIVING

Uber Self-Driving Car Fatality

In 2018, an autonomous Uber vehicle operating in Tempe, Arizona, struck and killed a pedestrian, marking the first fatality involving a self-driving car. The incident triggered a wave of concern over the safety and reliability of autonomous vehicle technology. Investigations revealed that the car's AI system failed to correctly identify the pedestrian, Elaine Herzberg, who was crossing the street at night with a bicycle. Although the system detected an object, it could not classify it as a human in time to take evasive action.

The failure was attributed to several factors, including the vehicle's sensors and software, which struggled with situational awareness and obstacle identification. Additionally, the backup safety driver, who was supposed to intervene in case of an emergency, was found to be distracted at the time of the crash. Uber promptly suspended its self-driving car program in Arizona and made substantial changes to its testing procedures. The company ultimately withdrew entirely from the autonomous vehicle industry.

This tragedy underscored the ethical and technical challenges of deploying AI in real-world scenarios where human lives are at stake. Autonomous vehicle developers face the daunting task of creating systems that can reliably operate in complex, unpredictable environments. The Uber fatality also reignited debates about the role of human oversight in AI-driven systems and whether such technology is ready for widespread use.

The Uber case serves as a reminder that AI technologies, particularly those with life-or-death implications, require rigorous testing, regulation, and safety protocols. The incident has had a lasting impact on the self-driving car industry, prompting both regulators and companies to adopt more cautious approaches to autonomous vehicle deployment.

Tesla Autopilot Crashes

Tesla's Autopilot system, a driver-assistance feature, has sparked considerable debate due to its involvement in multiple high-profile crashes, some of which were fatal. Initially introduced to assist with tasks such as steering and braking, Autopilot is not intended as a fully autonomous system, but its branding and marketing have led some drivers to mistakenly trust it as such. Notable incidents, including a 2018 crash in which a Tesla Model X collided with a highway barrier, have revealed that Autopilot can fail to detect certain obstacles, creating dangerous situations when drivers over-rely on it.

One major concern involves the system's performance limitations in complex scenarios, such as when a tractor-trailer crossed the road in front of a Tesla in 2016, leading to a fatal accident. The system's sensors and cameras, while effective in controlled settings, have limitations in unpredictable environments, where they may fail to interpret real-world hazards accurately. This gap between Autopilot's capabilities and real-world demands has raised questions about whether autonomous technology is ready for widespread use, especially in situations where human judgment is still essential.

Tesla's branding of Autopilot has also drawn criticism for potentially creating overconfidence in the system's capabilities. Though drivers are required to stay alert and take control, when necessary, the "Autopilot" label has led some users to misinterpret its abilities, which has sometimes had fatal consequences. This has ignited discussions on corporate responsibility, particularly around how companies should communicate the limitations of AI-driven technologies that have life-or-death implications.

These incidents have prompted regulatory bodies in several countries to investigate Tesla's marketing practices and the safety of Autopilot. While Tesla continues to update its software and has introduced features such as Full Self-Driving (FSD), regulators and safety advocates argue that these updates alone may not fully address the ethical and safety challenges inherent in autonomous driving systems. The scrutiny highlights the importance of robust regulations and transparency when deploying such high-stakes technologies.

Tesla's Autopilot controversy underscores the broader ethical responsibility companies face in the deployment of AI systems. While autonomous vehicle technology holds great potential to reduce accidents caused by human error, its premature release in real-world environments can have serious consequences. The case highlights the need for stringent testing, safety regulations, and clear public communication about AI limitations to protect users and advance responsible innovation in autonomous technology.

PREDICTIVE ANALYTICS

Predictive Analytics Can Be the Problem

The Robert McDaniel case highlights the controversial use of predictive analytics by the Chicago Police Department (CPD) through its Strategic Subject List (SSL). This predictive analytics algorithm was designed to identify individuals likely to be involved in shootings, either as perpetrators or victims. The data-driven approach was based on various factors, including an individual's associations with known shooters and their geographical proximity to incidents of gun violence.

In 2013, McDaniel was approached by police officers who informed him that he was among the top 0.1% of individuals likely to be involved in a shooting, though they did not specify whether he would be a perpetrator or a victim. This startling interaction significantly impacted his life, marking the beginning of a troubling sequence of events. Despite having no prior criminal record, the label placed on him by the algorithm and the police's subsequent surveillance led to increased scrutiny and tension in his daily life.

Furthermore, the use of predictive analytics in policing often results in a self-fulfilling prophecy, where individuals flagged by such systems may face heightened police presence and intervention, potentially increasing the likelihood of encounters with law enforcement. In McDaniel's case, the ongoing police attention and frequent visits from officers looked suspicious to those in his neighborhood. This not only affected his mental well-being but also influenced how he was treated within his community. He ultimately ended up being shot twice by individuals who believed he was a police informant.

This case exemplifies the broader issues associated with predictive policing technologies, particularly the risks of perpetuating systemic bias. Algorithms are frequently built on historical crime data, which can reflect and reinforce existing inequality, disproportionately targeting communities of color. In McDaniel's situation, the algorithm's reliance on historical data labeled his neighborhood as high-risk, leading to increased policing that further entrenched the cycle of surveillance and suspicion.

Ultimately, while the CPD discontinued the program in 2019, the implications of such predictive policing tools continue to raise ethical concerns. Cases such as McDaniel's underscore the need for greater scrutiny and accountability regarding the use of algorithms in law enforcement to avoid stigmatizing individuals and communities based solely on predictive assessments. This ongoing debate emphasizes the importance of ensuring that technological solutions do not exacerbate social injustice, highlighting the need for community involvement in developing fairer policing practices.

Zillow's Algorithm for Predicting Market Trends

Zillow, a major online real estate marketplace, relied heavily on its Zestimate algorithm, which provided estimates of home values based on a variety of data points such as comparable sales, tax assessments, and property features. In 2021, the company's reliance on this AI-driven tool for its home-buying program, Zillow Offers, led to significant financial losses.

The Zestimate algorithm began overvaluing properties in many regions, leading Zillow to purchase homes at inflated prices. When the real estate market cooled and home prices didn't rise as expected, Zillow found itself with a surplus of overvalued homes that it could not sell for a profit. As a result, the company had to shut down its home-buying program and lay off approximately 25% of its workforce. Zillow lost hundreds of millions of dollars in the process.

The failure of the Zestimate algorithm to accurately predict market trends and home values exposed the risks of over-reliance on AI in high-stakes business decisions. While the algorithm worked well as a general tool for estimating home values, it struggled with the complexities of fluctuating markets and local variations, leading to costly errors.

This case underscores the importance of human oversight in AI-driven decision-making processes, especially in industries where market conditions can change rapidly. It also serves as a cautionary tale about the limits of AI predictions in complex, real-world scenarios.

GENDER DISCRIMINATION

Amazon's AI Recruitment Tool

Amazon's attempt to automate its hiring process with an AI-powered tool became a notable example of biased algorithm development in the tech industry. The tool was designed to evaluate and rank job candidates based on resume data, intending to streamline recruitment. Unfortunately, the AI was trained on resumes submitted over the previous decade—a period when the tech industry, and Amazon itself, was predominantly male. This led the algorithm to favor certain resume patterns typical of male candidates and to penalize terms such as "women's," reflecting the gender bias inherent in the data.

The system inadvertently reinforced gender disparity, penalizing resumes that mentioned women's organizations or activities often associated with female candidates. The algorithm prioritized resumes featuring technical terms or job titles common in male-dominated profiles, leading to a hiring pipeline skewed against qualified female candidates. This unintended bias illustrated how AI, when trained on historical data reflecting existing inequality, can perpetuate disparity rather than provide a neutral assessment.

Amazon identified the issue after internal reviews flagged biased recommendations, leading the company to abandon the project before it could impact actual hiring decisions. This case became a cautionary example of the risks of training AI on historical data, particularly in areas such as hiring, where diversity and fairness are paramount. Despite its intention to reduce human bias, the tool ultimately reinforced gender stereotypes, exposing the potential pitfalls of algorithmic decision-making in employment.

The Amazon AI hiring case had broader implications for the tech industry, underscoring the importance of transparency and ethical oversight in AI-driven decision-making. A key issue was the algorithm's black-box nature, which meant that its decision-making criteria were neither visible to applicants nor easily interpretable by Amazon's own staff. This lack of transparency highlighted a critical challenge: ensuring that AI-driven decisions in sensitive areas, such as employment, are fair, explainable, and contestable by those affected.

Amazon scrapped the AI hiring tool after recognizing the difficulty of creating unbiased AI in hiring. The case has since served as a cautionary tale for other companies pursuing AI-based recruitment solutions, emphasizing the importance of rigorous bias testing, ongoing oversight, and diverse datasets to foster fairness. It underscores the need for ethical AI practices and fairness audits to ensure that such systems promote equity rather than reinforcing historical bias in the workplace.

Apple Card Credit Limit Discrimination

In 2019, Apple's newly launched credit card, issued by Goldman Sachs, faced criticism over allegations of gender bias in its credit limit decisions. Several users reported that women were consistently offered lower credit limits than men, even when they had higher credit scores or better financial profiles. This issue drew significant public attention after tech entrepreneur David Heinemeier Hansson tweeted that his wife received a credit limit 20 times lower than his, despite her superior credit score. Apple co-founder Steve Wozniak later shared a similar experience, reinforcing concerns about potential algorithmic bias.

The incident underscored the challenges of AI in financial services, where credit-scoring algorithms are often trained on historical data that may carry embedded gender bias. Although Goldman Sachs denied intentional bias, the lack of transparency in the credit assessment process raised questions about the algorithm's fairness. Customers were not given clear explanations for the assigned credit limits, making it difficult to understand or challenge the rationale behind the decisions. This lack of transparency is a recurring issue with AI systems, especially in sensitive areas such as finance, where decisions can significantly impact individuals' financial opportunities.

The Apple Card controversy highlighted the risks of using AI for high-stakes financial decisions without proper safeguards. Credit scoring algorithms that rely on historical data can inadvertently reflect and perpetuate societal inequality, leading to discriminatory outcomes. In this case, the AI-driven credit model seemed to systematically favor male applicants over female ones, suggesting potential flaws in the data used to train the model or the criteria employed in evaluating creditworthiness.

Following the backlash, the New York Department of Financial Services (NYDFS) launched an investigation into potential gender discrimination. Goldman Sachs responded by reevaluating the credit limits for affected customers but continued to deny that gender played a role in the algorithm's decision-making. The incident has since prompted calls for regulatory oversight and fairness audits of AI in financial services to prevent automated systems from amplifying existing inequality.

The Apple Card case serves as a cautionary tale of the importance of fairness and transparency in AI systems, especially when used in critical areas such as finance. It emphasizes the need for companies to rigorously test AI-driven models for potential bias and to ensure that their decisions are explainable and accountable. Ultimately, this controversy illustrates that while AI has the power to transform industries, it also holds the potential to reinforce inequity if not carefully designed, monitored, and regulated.

EMPLOYMENT

Hiring by an Algorithm

Face-scanning software has increasingly been integrated into hiring processes, offering companies innovative tools to evaluate job candidates. One prominent application of this technology is HireVue, which utilizes AI to analyze candidates' facial expressions, tone of voice, and body language during video interviews. By assessing these non-verbal cues, HireVue aims to predict a candidate's potential fit for a role and their likelihood of success within a company. This approach enables organizations to streamline their recruitment efforts, reduce bias in initial screenings, and identify talent more efficiently.

HireVue's algorithm is designed to recognize patterns associated with successful job performance, allowing it to provide insights that may not be evident through traditional interview methods. For example, a candidate's enthusiasm, confidence, and engagement level can be quantitatively measured, providing recruiters with a data-driven basis for their decisions. This reliance on technology can also lead to concerns about fairness and discrimination, as bias embedded in the training data may inadvertently skew results against certain demographic groups.

Moreover, the integration of face-scanning software such as HireVue in hiring processes raises important ethical questions about informed consent and candidate privacy. Many job seekers are often unaware of the extent to which their facial data may be analyzed and used in hiring decisions. This lack of transparency can lead to feelings of unease and mistrust among candidates, particularly for those from marginalized groups who may be disproportionately affected by biased algorithms. Companies using such technology are increasingly urged to prioritize clear communication regarding data collection practices, ensuring candidates understand how their data will be used, stored, and protected.

While the use of HireVue and similar applications can enhance efficiency in recruitment, it is crucial for organizations to balance technological advancements with ethical considerations. Implementing robust data protection measures and regularly auditing the algorithms for bias can help mitigate potential risks associated with face-scanning software. Furthermore, providing candidates with access to their data and the rationale behind hiring decisions can foster a sense of accountability and transparency in the recruitment process.

In summary, face-scanning software such as HireVue represents a significant shift in how companies approach hiring, offering potential benefits in efficiency and candidate assessment. As this technology continues to evolve, it is essential for organizations to navigate the ethical implications thoughtfully, ensuring that the hiring process remains fair, transparent, and respectful of candidates' rights. Balancing innovation with ethical practices will be vital in building a more inclusive and trustworthy hiring landscape.

Amazon's Flex Program Algorithm

The firing of Stephen Normandin, a Phoenix-based Amazon Flex driver in 2021, highlights the complex role of algorithmic decision-making in modern labor management. Normandin, who had reliably delivered for Amazon over nearly four years, was let go based on performance metrics tracked by an automated system. Amazon's Flex program, which manages drivers through algorithms, evaluates various performance indicators, including timeliness and customer feedback. In Normandin's case, the algorithm flagged his account as underperforming due to delivery delays—many of which were beyond his control, such as access restrictions and traffic issues. Amazon's automated system terminated him without human input, demonstrating how data-driven decision-making, though efficient, can lack flexibility and consideration for situational context.

Amazon's system assesses drivers by assigning performance rankings such as "Fantastic," "Great," or "At Risk." These ranks heavily influence drivers' job security, and the reliance on algorithms to generate these assessments allows Amazon to oversee a vast workforce systematically. It also means drivers can face penalties for factors they cannot mitigate. Normandin's case exemplifies how, in place of human managers who might consider real-world variables, the system applied strict metrics without room for appeals. This lack of oversight, combined with an automated dispute process, further underscored Amazon's approach to minimizing human involvement in labor management.

The case has generated discussions on the ethical and practical implications of automated "algorithmic bosses," which offer companies scalable oversight but often at the expense of fair and context-sensitive decision-making. Without the capacity to understand complex situational factors, these systems risk disadvantaging workers based on rigid standards that may not reflect actual performance capabilities. This approach, while intended to streamline operations, can marginalize the human elements of work, such as adaptability and contextual understanding, which are critical for roles such as driving where variables are frequently unpredictable.

Normandin's situation spotlights a broader need for a balance between efficiency and fairness in AI-driven workplaces. Experts argue for a hybrid approach, blending algorithmic analysis with human oversight to ensure workers have recourse in cases of potential algorithmic errors. By combining human judgment with data, companies could create fairer and just outcomes, especially in cases involving employment termination.

Finally, this case emphasizes the importance of transparency and accountability in AI-driven management systems. While algorithms are designed to operate impartially, they can reflect bias embedded into data or programming. The push for regulatory oversight in algorithmic labor management underscores the necessity for systems that support not only corporate efficiency but also worker well-being, providing them with equitable treatment and opportunities to appeal decisions that impact their livelihoods.

HEALTHCARE AND MEDICAL APPLICATIONS

Google Health's AI in Breast Cancer Detection

In 2020, Google's AI division made headlines with its AI system designed to improve breast cancer detection through mammograms. Early studies showed that the system could outperform radiologists in certain aspects of cancer detection, particularly in reducing false negatives, meaning fewer missed cases of cancer. As with many AI systems in healthcare, however, the model exhibited performance discrepancies when applied to diverse populations.

The AI system had been trained primarily on datasets from patients in the United States and the United Kingdom, which lacked sufficient representation from minority groups and patients with less common medical histories. When tested on different demographic groups, the AI struggled to maintain the same high level of accuracy, raising concerns about health disparity. For example, the system showed lower accuracy in detecting cancer in women from minority backgrounds, which could exacerbate existing healthcare inequality.

While the technology represented a significant advancement in medical diagnostics, it also highlighted the crucial role of dataset diversity in AI healthcare applications. Medical AI systems must be trained on data that reflects the diversity of the population they are intended to serve to ensure equitable outcomes. Google acknowledged these limitations and continues to refine the AI system to address its shortcomings.

The case demonstrates both the potential and the risks of AI in healthcare. While AI can enhance diagnostic accuracy and efficiency, it can also introduce new bias and disparity if not carefully designed and tested across diverse populations.

Healthcare Algorithm Racial Bias

A widely used algorithm that predicts patients' need for additional medical care underestimates the health needs of the sickest black patients, exacerbating existing racial disparity in medicine, researchers have found. In 2019, researchers uncovered a significant racial bias in a healthcare algorithm developed by Optum, utilized by major health systems across the United States to prioritize patients for enrollment in care management programs. This algorithm aimed to allocate healthcare resources by identifying patients with the greatest need based on their health status and projected healthcare costs, but it systematically underestimated the risk scores of black patients, making them less likely to be identified for additional care compared to white patients with similar health conditions.

The bias in Optum's algorithm stemmed from its reliance on health-care costs as a proxy for health needs, neglecting the systemic barriers that black patients face, such as limited access to healthcare services and economic disparities. Historically, black patients incur lower healthcare costs on average, not due to fewer health needs but because of structural inequity. Consequently, the algorithm misinterpreted lower spending as a sign of better health, leading to a misallocation of resources that perpetuated healthcare disparity instead of alleviating it.

The revelation of this bias led to widespread scrutiny and raised ethical concerns about AI's role in healthcare, particularly regarding its potential to reinforce existing inequality. Critics emphasized the necessity for algorithms, especially in life-critical sectors, to incorporate equitable metrics that genuinely reflect diverse populations' health needs. The study's authors recommended more representative datasets and cautioned against using cost-based metrics as proxies for need, as they can obscure the health realities of marginalized populations. Following this discovery, Optum and the healthcare providers using the algorithm began revising or replacing it to address its shortcomings.

This case exemplifies how even well-meaning AI systems can perpetuate or worsen existing social inequality when built on biased or incomplete data. It highlights the need for ongoing monitoring, auditing, and ethical consideration in the development and deployment of AI systems, particularly in sensitive areas such as healthcare, where missteps can have life-altering consequences.

Stanford Vaccine Algorithm

In late 2020, as COVID-19 vaccines became available, healthcare institutions across the United States developed strategies for distributing their limited supply of doses to those at highest risk. Stanford Medical Center was among them, and it implemented an AI-driven algorithm to prioritize recipients. Frontline medical residents, who were treating COVID-19 patients directly, were shocked to learn that only 7 of the 1,300 resident physicians had been prioritized for the first 5,000 doses. The remainder of the prioritized individuals included administrators and senior doctors who were either working remotely or had limited exposure to COVID-19 patients. This glaring oversight raised questions about the reliability and fairness of the algorithm in accurately assessing priority for critical resources.

The problem stemmed from the algorithm's design, which relied heavily on factors such as age, job title, and institutional seniority rather than specific levels of exposure to COVID-19 patients. Consequently, more senior faculty members—regardless of their role in patient care—were moved to the top of the vaccination list. The residents, who often had the most frequent, close contact with COVID-19 patients, were largely overlooked due to their lower institutional standing, even though their role placed them at much greater risk of contracting and spreading the virus. This oversight was not only frustrating for the residents but also revealed a critical flaw in the way AI-driven systems can deprioritize those with the most pressing needs.

Public backlash followed swiftly, with residents and healthcare advocates highlighting how the algorithm had failed to account for the specific circumstances and risks faced by frontline workers. In response, Stanford Medical Center issued an apology and quickly revised its prioritization system to include more frontline workers in the initial rounds of vaccination. The damage had been done, however, and the incident sparked a broader conversation about the potential pitfalls of AI algorithms in high-stakes decision-making. Critics pointed out that the algorithm's rigid criteria overlooked critical contextual information, raising concerns about whether similar systems were being deployed across other healthcare facilities.

The Stanford vaccine algorithm case has since become a cautionary tale about the limitations of using automated systems to allocate scarce resources. It highlights the necessity of combining AI decision-making tools with human oversight, especially in healthcare settings, where ethical and situational nuances are essential. The incident underscores the importance of carefully designing AI systems to align with the specific goals and values of their intended applications. As a result, this case has contributed to ongoing discussions about the ethical and operational standards needed to ensure that AI is used responsibly, particularly in life-or-death situations such as pandemic response.

SOCIAL MEDIA AND ALGORITHMIC INFLUENCE

Facebook's Ad Targeting

In 2018, Facebook's ad targeting algorithm came under scrutiny for allowing advertisers to exclude certain groups of people from seeing ads related to housing, employment, and credit opportunities. Investigations revealed that advertisers could exclude users based on characteristics such as race, gender, age, or ethnicity, violating anti-discrimination laws. This practice created a system in which marginalized groups could be denied access to critical services, further entrenching societal inequality.

Civil rights organizations, such as the American Civil Liberties Union (ACLU), brought lawsuits against Facebook, accusing the company of facilitating discrimination. While Facebook's ad algorithm was not explicitly programmed to promote bias, its design allowed advertisers to make discriminatory decisions. This highlighted the broader issue of how AI systems can unintentionally reinforce existing bias in society by allowing users to filter or exclude groups based on sensitive characteristics.

In response to the backlash, Facebook agreed to make changes to its ad platform. The company introduced new policies prohibiting advertisers from excluding people based on race, gender, or age in areas such as housing, employment, and credit. Facebook also worked with civil rights organizations to create a more transparent and fair advertising system, though concerns about the effectiveness of these changes remain.

The case demonstrated the risks of giving AI systems too much control over critical societal functions, such as access to housing or employment. It also emphasized the need for strong oversight and ethical guidelines when developing algorithms that can impact vulnerable populations.

YouTube's Algorithm Promoting Extremism

YouTube's recommendation algorithm, designed to maximize user engagement by suggesting videos based on viewing history, has been criticized for promoting increasingly extreme and polarizing content. Investigations revealed that the algorithm often pushed users toward conspiracy theories, misinformation, and radical political content. The system, optimized for keeping users on the platform for as long as possible, inadvertently promoted videos that elicited strong emotional responses, even if they were misleading or harmful.

As users engaged more with extreme content, YouTube's algorithm would continue to recommend similar videos, creating a feedback loop that radicalized some viewers. This phenomenon has been particularly concerning in the context of political polarization, public health misinformation (such as anti-vaccine content), and extremist ideologies.

Critics argue that YouTube's prioritization of engagement metrics over content quality has had severe societal consequences, contributing to the spread of misinformation and extremist views.

In response, YouTube has taken steps to reduce the visibility of harmful content by tweaking its algorithm and implementing stricter content moderation policies. Many argue, though, that these changes have not gone far enough, as harmful content continues to circulate on the platform. The tension between free speech, content moderation, and AI-driven recommendations remains a contentious issue for YouTube and other social media platforms.

The case exemplifies the ethical challenges that arise when AI systems prioritize business objectives—such as engagement and profitability—over societal well-being. It highlights the need for careful consideration of the broader implications of AI algorithms in influencing public opinion and behavior.

Microsoft Tay Chatbot

Microsoft's AI-powered chatbot, Tay, was designed as a fun experiment in conversational AI. The bot was programmed to learn from its interactions with users on Twitter/X and other social media platforms, adapting its language and responses over time. Within hours of its release, however, Tay became a public relations disaster. Users quickly realized that they could manipulate the bot into making inflammatory statements, including racist, sexist, and hate-filled messages. As a result, Tay began posting highly offensive content, embarrassing Microsoft and showcasing the dangers of deploying AI without proper safeguards.

The root of the problem lay in Tay's unfiltered learning process. The bot was designed to mimic the language it encountered, which made it vulnerable to manipulation by users with malicious intent. Trolls and pranksters bombarded Tay with inappropriate content, exploiting the lack of oversight to turn it into a platform for spreading hate speech. Within 16 hours of its launch, Microsoft took Tay offline and issued an apology for the bot's behavior.

The incident highlighted a key challenge in AI: creating systems that can learn and interact with humans while maintaining ethical boundaries. Microsoft had not anticipated the possibility that Tay would be exploited in such a way, exposing a flaw in how the bot's learning algorithms were structured. While the company later reintroduced a safer and more controlled version of the bot, Tay's failure remains one of the most infamous examples of AI gone wrong.

This case underscores the importance of implementing safety mechanisms in AI systems that interact with the public. It also serves as a reminder that AI, when trained on real-world data without supervision, can easily be led astray by the worst aspects of human behavior.

Twitter's Image-Cropping Algorithm

In 2020, Twitter (now known as X) users discovered racial bias in the platform's image-cropping algorithm, which consistently preferred white faces over black faces in preview images. The issue gained widespread attention after users conducted tests by posting photos of black and white individuals together, only to find that the algorithm often cropped out black individuals, even when they were the focus of the image.

Twitter's image-cropping algorithm was designed to automatically crop images to fit within limited space, focusing on what it determined to be the most important parts of the image, but the algorithm's prioritization was biased toward lighter-skin tones. Twitter initially defended the algorithm, stating that no bias had been detected in internal tests, but after further public pressure and analysis, the company acknowledged the issue.

In response, Twitter disabled the automatic cropping feature, allowing users to control how their images were displayed in tweets. This case prompted a broader conversation about bias in AI, particularly in algorithms that handle visual data. It also highlighted the importance of transparency and user feedback in identifying and addressing bias that may not be evident in internal testing alone.

The incident serves as a reminder that AI systems can inherit and amplify societal bias if they are not properly vetted and tested. It also emphasizes the need for diverse datasets and inclusive development practices in the creation of AI technologies.

Google Photos Misclassification

In 2015, Google Photos, an AI-powered photo recognition tool, sparked outrage when it misclassified images of black individuals as "gorillas." The tool, designed to automatically categorize and tag uploaded images, failed in a way that was not only embarrassing for the company but also deeply offensive. This incident quickly gained media attention, raising alarm about racial bias in AI image recognition systems. It was a stark reminder of the unintended consequences that can arise when AI algorithms are not carefully designed and tested, especially in sensitive areas such as facial recognition.

The root of the issue lay in the training data used to develop the algorithm. AI systems rely heavily on large datasets to learn how to recognize and classify images and, in this case, the dataset was not sufficiently diverse or representative of different skin tones and facial features. Algorithms trained predominantly on images of light-skinned individuals can struggle to accurately identify people with darker skin, leading to biased and often harmful outcomes. The Google Photos error underscored this systemic problem in AI development, where insufficient attention to diversity in training data can lead to significant racial bias.

In response to the controversy, Google immediately issued an apology and removed the ability to tag images as "gorillas" from its platform. Despite this swift action, the incident provoked a much-needed broader discussion about the racial bias that can emerge in AI technologies, particularly in image and facial recognition systems. The implications of such bias go beyond misclassification; they reflect deeper societal inequality and the potential for AI to reinforce it if not properly addressed. This specific case highlighted how easily AI systems can replicate existing prejudice when they are not designed with inclusivity in mind.

The Google Photos misclassification incident has since become a landmark example of the need for fairness and accountability in AI development. It illustrated the crucial importance of diverse, well-represented datasets and rigorous testing for bias before deploying AI technologies to the public. As AI systems become increasingly integrated into everyday life, this case continues to serve as a reminder that companies have to ensure that their technologies do not perpetuate harm or inequality. Google's failure with its photo recognition tool remains a critical lesson for the tech industry on the importance of prioritizing fairness and inclusivity in AI systems.

Addiction by Design Using Adaptive Algorithms

Adaptive algorithms on social media are designed to keep users engaged by continuously learning from their behavior, refining what they see to match their interests more closely. These algorithms track everything—from the posts users like and share to the amount of time spent watching specific videos or interacting with particular accounts. By analyzing this data, platforms such as Facebook, Instagram, and TikTok can tailor content to match each user's preferences, creating a highly personalized experience that encourages prolonged usage.

This continuous refinement is what makes these algorithms adaptive. The longer a user engages with the platform, the more accurately it can predict what will hold their attention next, optimizing content to capture their interest more effectively over time. While this technology enables users to connect with topics and communities they care about, it also plays a role in making the platform more addictive. Research has shown that these adaptive algorithms can contribute to compulsive behavior, as users find themselves scrolling through an endless feed curated precisely for them. This cycle, often referred to as *the dopamine loop*, exploits psychological triggers by providing intermittent rewards that make it harder for users to disengage.

The ethical implications of adaptive algorithms are increasingly a point of concern. As these platforms become more skilled at predicting and influencing user preferences, they also expose users to potential risks, including mental health issues linked to excessive screen time and feelings of inadequacy fueled by curated, idealized content. Many social media companies have faced scrutiny for prioritizing engagement metrics and profits over the well-being of their users, sparking debate about regulation and the responsibility of tech companies in managing the social impact of their technologies.

FACIAL RECOGNITION AND ETHICAL CONCERNS

Clearview AI Facial Recognition

Clearview AI, an FRT company, came under fire in 2020 after it was revealed that it had scraped billions of images from social media and other Web sites without users' consent. The company built a massive database of facial images that law enforcement agencies and private companies could use to identify individuals. This technology raised significant concerns regarding privacy violations, data security, and the potential misuse of AI-powered facial recognition.

Clearview AI's tool allowed users to upload a photo of an individual, and the system would then match the image with others from its vast database, often providing links to the individual's online presence. Law enforcement agencies, in particular, found the technology useful for identifying suspects and solving crimes, but the lack of transparency and consent from the individuals whose images were used ignited a fierce debate about the ethics of scraping public data for private profit and surveillance purposes.

The concerns surrounding Clearview AI were not limited to privacy violations. Critics pointed out that FRT has been shown to be biased, particularly against people of color and women. Studies have indicated that AI systems trained on biased or unrepresentative datasets often struggle to accurately identify non-white faces, leading to higher rates of false positives and misidentification. This is especially troubling when law enforcement agencies use such technology, as it can disproportionately affect marginalized communities, leading to wrongful arrests and other injustices.

In response to the backlash, several social media platforms, including Twitter/X, Facebook, and LinkedIn, sent cease-and-desist letters to Clearview AI, demanding that the company stop scraping their users' data. Moreover, privacy advocates and civil rights organizations called for stronger regulations governing the use of FRT, particularly in law enforcement. Several United States cities, including San Francisco, went as far as banning the use of facial recognition by government agencies, citing concerns over privacy and potential abuse.

Legal challenges against Clearview AI also began to mount, with lawsuits being filed in various jurisdictions, accusing the company of violating privacy laws such as the Illinois Biometric Information Privacy Act (BIPA). This law requires companies to obtain explicit consent before collecting or using biometric data, and Clearview AI's practices were seen as a clear violation. Amid growing public outcry, some law enforcement agencies halted their use of the tool, and regulators started to scrutinize the broader implications of FRT more closely.

The Clearview AI controversy underscores the broader ethical issues surrounding the use of AI in surveillance and the need for clear guidelines to protect individuals' privacy and civil liberties. The case serves as a reminder of how AI technologies, when used without proper oversight, can infringe on basic human rights and contribute to an environment of unchecked surveillance. It also highlights the importance of developing AI systems that are both transparent and accountable, especially when they have the potential to affect individuals' lives in such a profound way.

PimEyes: Navigating the Ethics of Facial Recognition

PimEyes is a facial recognition search engine that allows users to upload a photo and find matches of that face across publicly accessible Web sites. It is designed to identify where someone's image appears online, pulling results from an extensive range of sources, including news sites, blogs, social media, and other online platforms. Originally created for benign uses, such as finding unauthorized uses of one's own photos, the service has gained notoriety for its potential to violate privacy, often uncovering images people didn't realize were publicly accessible. This capability has drawn both privacy advocates and the general public to question the ethics of such powerful facial recognition tools.

PimEyes uses advanced algorithms to generate a highly accurate search that relies on facial features, distinguishing it from standard image searches by platforms such as Google. It doesn't simply match images but uses detailed analysis to detect similarities across angles, lighting, and changes in appearance, creating a highly precise mapping of facial characteristics. As a result, individuals can find every instance of their face that has been uploaded to publicly accessible sites, regardless of when it was posted or if their name is associated with it. While this can be useful for people wanting to manage their online image or prevent misuse, it also presents serious ethical concerns.

One of the most troubling aspects of PimEyes is its potential for misuse by stalkers, harassers, and other malicious actors. With just a single photo, an individual can locate images of someone across multiple Web sites, often without that person's consent or knowledge. This has allowed stalkers to track their targets, finding not only recent photos but potentially older ones that are linked to various aspects of their online presence, sometimes leading to severe safety risks and harassment. The ability to track someone's photos in this way has opened discussions around the need for regulatory oversight, as the technology can be exploited for dangerous and invasive purposes.

In response to such privacy concerns, PimEyes allows users to opt out and have their images removed from its database. This is not the default setting, though, and many users are unaware that their photos could appear in search results on the platform. While PimEyes maintains that it operates within the legal boundaries of publicly available data, critics argue that its technology facilitates privacy violations and could enable stalking, harassment, and the exploitation of vulnerable individuals.

The PimEyes case highlights a broader issue in FRT—the balance between privacy and technological advancement. As facial recognition becomes increasingly sophisticated and accessible, the ethical implications for individual privacy and safety grow more pronounced. PimEyes exemplifies how unrestricted facial recognition access could lead to unintended consequences, emphasizing the need for greater controls and ethical guidelines for similar tools in the future.

ALGORITHMIC DECISION-MAKING IN EDUCATION

Navigate Risk: Predictive Analytics and Educational Steering

Navigate Risk is an algorithm developed to assess and predict students' academic performance and risk factors in higher education settings. It utilizes a variety of data points, including academic history, demographic information, and engagement metrics, to create a comprehensive profile of each student. Universities employ this software to identify students who may need additional support, enabling targeted intervention aimed at improving retention and graduation rates.

By analyzing patterns and trends within the data, Navigate Risk can highlight students at risk of falling behind or dropping out. This proactive approach allows institutions to allocate resources more efficiently, ensuring that academic advisors, counselors, and support staff can focus on those who may benefit most from intervention. Such targeted support systems are intended to enhance student success and promote a more inclusive educational environment.

The use of Navigate Risk raises concerns about the potential downsides of algorithmic assessments. For instance, students identified as at-risk may feel stigmatized or pressured to change their academic trajectories, potentially leading to a push into different majors that might not align with their interests or strengths. This redirection can diminish students' agency in making educational choices and may ultimately impact their long-term career satisfaction.

Moreover, reliance on algorithms can inadvertently reinforce existing bias if the underlying data reflects systemic inequality. For example, if a university's data predominantly reflects challenges faced by certain demographic groups, the algorithm may unfairly target those students for additional scrutiny or intervention. This situation highlights the need for universities to ensure that their data practices are equitable and inclusive, taking into account the diverse backgrounds and experiences of their student populations.

In summary, while the Navigate Risk algorithm has the potential to enhance student support services by identifying those in need of help, it also presents challenges that require careful consideration. Institutions must balance the benefits of data-driven insights with the ethical implications of algorithmic decision-making, ensuring that all students are treated fairly and equitably throughout their educational journeys.

UK A-Level Grading Algorithm

In 2020, the COVID-19 pandemic forced the cancellation of A-level exams in the UK, which left the government with the challenge of determining students' final grades. To address this, an algorithm was introduced to calculate grades based on a combination of a student's past performance, teacher predictions, and the historical performance of their school. The intent was to create a fair and objective way to assign grades, but the results sparked widespread outrage.

The algorithm disproportionately downgraded the grades of students from disadvantaged backgrounds, especially those attending underperforming schools. In contrast, students from higher-achieving schools saw their grades either maintained or inflated. The algorithm's reliance on historical school performance meant that individual student efforts were often overlooked in favor of broader statistical trends. As a result, many hardworking students, particularly from poorer areas, received lower-than-expected grades, threatening their university prospects.

Mass protests erupted across the country, with students, parents, and educators calling for the algorithm to be scrapped. The public backlash forced the UK government to abandon the algorithm just days after the results were released. In the end, students were allowed to receive their teacher-predicted grades instead. The case highlighted the dangers of relying on AI in high-stakes situations without considering the social implications and potential for unfair outcomes.

This case study underscores the importance of transparency and fairness in algorithmic decision-making, particularly in education, where the consequences of AI errors can be profound and long-lasting for students.

Secret Teacher Evaluation System

The secret teacher evaluation system in Houston was a controversial initiative by the Houston Independent School District (HISD) designed to assess teacher performance through a proprietary, data-driven system developed by the SAS Institute, known as the Educational Value-Added Assessment System (EVAAS). Launched around 2012, EVAAS used students' standardized testing data, in addition to other factors, to gauge teacher effectiveness, comparing them against statewide averages to evaluate each teacher's impact on student learning. Besides evaluating teachers, the algorithm was used to fire teachers and give bonuses.

The system's algorithms, however, were kept confidential, which meant teachers were unable to fully understand or challenge the evaluations impacting their careers. Concerns quickly grew that the system's opacity infringed teachers' due process rights, as they had no access to the specific calculations affecting their employment status.

In 2014, the Houston Federation of Teachers and individual teachers filed a lawsuit, arguing that this lack of transparency violated due process and unfairly jeopardized teachers' livelihoods. They claimed the system's reliance on test scores pressured teachers to narrow their curricula toward test preparation, hindering broader educational goals such as critical thinking and individualized instruction. In response to these issues, a federal judge sided partially with the teachers, noting that the system's secretive nature and reliance on algorithmic decision-making could unfairly harm teachers without giving them an adequate chance to dispute potentially erroneous evaluations.

The backlash against EVAAS ultimately led HISD to terminate its contract with SAS in 2016. While the system was not replaced, there remains debate over the use of similar value-added models in teacher evaluations across various districts, as many argue that these models unfairly focus on test scores rather than a comprehensive assessment of teaching quality. The case underscores ongoing concerns about the use of opaque algorithms in high-stakes decisions in education, echoing broader national debates on fairness and accountability in AI-driven evaluations in the public sector.

PRIVACY AND ETHICS

AcurianHealth-Walgreens Privacy Controversy

AcurianHealth, Walgreens, and NaviStone have partnered in a way that raises significant concerns about consumer privacy within the healthcare sector. AcurianHealth is known for its expertise in recruiting patients for clinical trials, using extensive health data to pinpoint suitable candidates. This information often comes from pharmacies such as Walgreens, which monitor consumer purchases and medication histories. By collaborating with AcurianHealth, Walgreens contributes valuable insights into patient demographics and health-related behavior, which help shape marketing strategies and recruitment efforts for clinical trials.

NaviStone enhances this collaboration by offering advanced online tracking capabilities. This company specializes in analyzing visitor behavior on Web sites, allowing AcurianHealth and Walgreens to create targeted marketing campaigns. By examining how consumers interact with their digital platforms, NaviStone enables these organizations to deliver tailored advertisements based on specific user behaviors. This integration of health data analytics with online tracking raises substantial privacy concerns, as patients may not be aware that their health information and browsing habits are being used to inform targeted marketing efforts.

The partnership between these companies highlights serious ethical dilemmas surrounding consumer privacy and the transparency of data usage. While AcurianHealth and Walgreens argue that their approaches can enhance patient engagement in clinical research and improve healthcare outcomes, the techniques employed often lack clear consent from individuals. Many consumers may be unaware of how their health data and online activities are being monitored and utilized, leading to concerns about the exploitation of sensitive health information for corporate gain.

This scenario is indicative of a larger trend in the healthcare industry, where marketing strategies increasingly rely on data-driven approaches that may infringe upon patient privacy rights. The reliance on personal data can result in aggressive marketing tactics that prioritize company interests over individual rights and confidentiality. As fears surrounding data security and misuse continue to rise, there are growing calls for stricter regulations governing the collection and use of health information. Advocates stress the need for patients to have greater control over their personal data, promoting ethical practices in data usage over profit-driven motives. The activities of AcurianHealth, Walgreens, and NaviStone serve as a significant case study in the necessity for robust privacy protections in an era where data plays a critical role in healthcare.

Ethics in AI: The Case of Dr. Timnit Gebru

The responsibility for the ethics of AI spans several levels: from corporate leaders and policymakers to researchers and engineers who design, develop, and deploy AI systems. This question of responsibility became highly visible in 2020 when Google controversially dismissed Dr. Timnit Gebru, a leading AI ethicist, following her research that highlighted ethical concerns in large language models, specifically those related to bias, environmental impact, and opacity.

Dr. Gebru's work underscored the responsibility of tech companies to address ethical risks in AI models that could perpetuate discrimination or produce socially harmful effects. Her research team at Google's Ethical AI department was dedicated to identifying and mitigating such risks, including how AI systems could unintentionally enforce stereotypes, create environmental strain due to high computational requirements, and perpetuate inequality through biased data.

When Dr. Gebru's paper on these topics faced resistance from Google's leadership, it ignited a public debate about the role of ethics teams within corporations and how they can operate independently to ensure that AI technologies serve the public good rather than solely corporate interests.

Dr. Gebru's firing raised awareness of how corporate interests can conflict with ethical oversight, especially when such research might impact revenue or reputation. This incident has since led to calls for stronger external regulatory frameworks and greater accountability within corporations developing AI. It also amplified the conversation about the importance of diversity and inclusivity in AI ethics teams, given that Dr. Gebru was one of the few black women leaders in AI, and her dismissal highlighted issues of power dynamics and representation in tech.

The case demonstrates that, while companies are responsible for fostering ethical AI practices, this responsibility is often at odds with profit motives. External oversight, transparent research practices, and ethical guidelines that operate independently of commercial objectives are crucial to ensure AI is developed in a way that aligns with societal values and human rights. Dr. Gebru's experience emphasizes the need for companies to provide ethicists with the autonomy needed to critique and reshape corporate practices and for broader systemic policies to ensure ethical AI development at a large scale.

INDEX

www.ingramcontent.com/pod-product-compliance
Lightning Source LLC
Chambersburg PA
CBHW071405050326
40689CB00010B/1765